RISE ABOVE

POSITION YOURSELF FOR SUCCESS

CEDRIC M. KENNY

Rise Above: Position Yourself for Success

First published in 2012

by
Bennett, Coleman & Co., Ltd.
7, Bahadur Shah Zafar Marg
New Delhi-110002

Published, Design & Distributed by

Times Group Books

Times Annexe, 9-10, Bahadur Shah Zafar Marg,
New Delhi-110002

Printed at: Azure Press Pvt. Ltd.

ISBN - 93-8229-919-X
Price: ₹250

Cedric's latest publication takes a path-breaking approach to personal development. In the corporate world, which has a plethora of talent, developing a USP which is tied to one's core values is essential for success. Just as corporations concentrate upon their core competence, this book helps individuals first define their core values and then takes them through a comprehensive method of building upon those values to emerge as successful professionals.

The author goes beyond professional development and defines a clear method of developing an inward-out approach to reaching a new level of self-awareness. Professional success is bound to be a natural outcome of this balance of motivation, determination, ethics and self-awareness.

ASHOK BAJPAI
CEO, Essar Hypermart, Essar Steel Pvt. Ltd

In today's competitive marketplace, soft skills and professionalism of employees are key factors for organizations to succeed and win.

Cedric Kenny's timely and eloquently penned book provides practical nuggets on how to develop an organization's brand identity through its employees, each of whom is its brand ambassador. Also, for self-exploration and self-improvement, **Rise Above** *is an excellent read!*

RAJIV KAUL
President, The Leela Palaces, Hotels and Resorts, Sahar, Mumbai

Rise Above *is full of practical, time-tested tips on living a more productive, happier life.*

If everyone followed Cedric Kenny's guidelines, how much better business organizations, the world over, would work!

GEORGE W MOE, PhD
Chief Engineer, Vista Research, Inc.
Arlington, VA, USA

If my memory serves me right, Cedric M Kenny has been associated with training workshops at FICCI Ladies Organization (FLO) since its inception in 1983. We, at FLO, hold him in high esteem as consultant, trainer and life coach.

Rise Above *adds to Cedric Kenny's already impressive body of work. If you want to know, and then act on what truly motivates employees, this book is a must-read. Each chapter offers you no-nonsense, down-to-earth advice on behaviour and attitude which employers expect from their employees.*

Rise Above *is the modern-day Bible for employers, employees and students in search of answers. This is not a book to be read at one go. Read a chapter, digest it and allow its principles to change your personality as you turn to the next chapter.*

I recommend this book as a read-to-follow handbook for all those who want to achieve success. Best of all, the book is actionable and doable!

NEENA MALHOTRA
President, FICCI Ladies Organization, New Delhi

Who better than Cedric M Kenny to write a book on **Rise Above***?*

Cedric has been a brand ambassador and a living testimony on this most crucial subject, ever since my family and I have known him. He has epitomized this subject by letting his passion shine through in everything he has done. His book will help unleash the potential we all possess, because consumers love brands whose owners are as passionate as they are.

Going by the success of his previous books, you can expect the best from Cedric. That "never rest on your laurels" attitude successfully translates into exciting and superior products that continue to wow and delight readers.

Thank you, Cedric, for creating such a valuable blueprint for success.

RONNIE LOBO
Vice President, Operations — South Asia, Carlson Hotels, Asia Pacific

Rise Above *is an essential handbook for all employees. Cedric M Kenny's unique and compelling vision of the corporate world excites young minds to think beyond the obvious. The author has significant experience in virtually every capacity of corporate grooming, be it as corporate trainer, management consultant, or academician. And above all, his greatest strength is as* Life Coach*!*

Rise Above *articulates a profound awareness of the struggle between being just another 'executive' and evolving into a 'successful leader'. Each chapter is sensitively crafted to help individuals aspire to climb higher and achieve success. Creating one's own personal brand is different from developing individual personality, but he has made this journey interesting and rewarding.*

Cedric M Kenny is a man of great integrity. He is extremely dedicated to his work and he is ranked among the unique corporate trainers who can empathize with employees and touch their souls, enabling them to reach higher goals. **Rise Above** *is easy to read and easy to grasp because the author uses common idiom and ordinary examples to explain the most intimate and personal struggles employees experience. I am confident this book will help thousands of young minds achieve greater success in their professional and personal life.*

AMIT KUMAR
(Tata Administrative Service)
Senior Manager, Corus Group UK, Tata Steel Europe — London

"A prisoner cannot free himself from his prison. He needs first to bond with the one who is already free." This in essence is what **Rise Above** *can do for you. You can free yourself from the shackles of your own self-imposed limitations.*

I strongly recommend that you read this extraordinary self-help guide over and over again. You will be amazed at the great power of inspirational words which offer insights into everyday life. Cedric M Kenny is an inspirational writer and an excellent corporate trainer and I am proud to know him.

ROBIN TREGER
CEO & MD, Treger Sports Inc., South Africa

As the sphere of the professional world continues to grow and expand, so do the obstacles and challenges for professionals. **Rise Above** *helps in dealing with such challenges and queries — answers to which are usually not easily accessible or readily available.*

Cedric M Kenny has appositely addressed very pertinent issues plaguing us today and given us a deep understanding of professional etiquettes, customs and norms existing across the globe. With the shrinking of the professional global village and rapid intersecting of common professional paths, several questions remain unanswered about the manner or way in approaching or dealing with such issues; the book gives a deep insight into this.

Rise Above *helps us in harnessing deeper qualities amongst us, in honing our personal and professional skills further and using them to the utmost to achieve our goals. Indeed, professionals from all walks of life will applaud the author for sharing valuable knowledge and information which is an essential requirement in today's world.*

TANYA MOHAN
Security Analyst
United Nations Department of Safety and Security (UNDSS)
United Nations Development Programme (UNDP) Philippines

CONTENTS

Acknowledgement *15*
Author's Note *16*
Foreword *17*
Prologue: Where Eagles Soar *21*

SECTION 1
Map Your Career Path 23

Chapter 1
BUILD YOUR BRAND IDENTITY: *Know Yourself* 25
- Build on the Strengths You Possess 27
- Your Attitude Determines Your Altitude 27
- Keys to Self-improvement 28
- 10 Ways to Develop Your Brand Identity 29
  - + You Set Goals 30
  - + You Are Disciplined 30
  - + You Are a Person of Integrity 30
  - + You Keep Your Promises 31
  - + You Are Eager to Learn 31
  - + You Are a Positive Person 31
  - + You Are a Good Speaker 32
  - + You Are a Good Listener 32
  - + You Enjoy Meeting People 32
  - + You Welcome Feedback/Criticism 33
- Personality Development – A Lifelong Brand Investment 33
- Why Changing Bad Habits Is Tough 34
- New Motivational Techniques 34
- Powered by Positive Energy 35
- Determination Leads to Success 37

Chapter 2
SUPERCHARGE YOUR BRAND VALUE: *Know Your Mind* 39
- You Can Re-set the 'Wiring' in Your Brain 40
- Improving Behaviour Made Easy 41
- Mindset or Mind Games 41
  - + Hamster-on-the-Wheel Syndrome 42
  - + Mind Games Workaholics Play 42
  - + Mindset of Bad Employees 43

Know Your Brain Structure 44
Two Brains Working in Tandem 45
Right Brain and Left Brain Functions 46
Stimulate Your Brain to Function Positively 49
Make Your Birthday Resolutions Meaningful 50
Ambition – Your Success Trigger 50

Chapter 3
GIVE YOUR BRAND THE MORAL SEAL: *Workplace Ethics* *53*
- We Live in a Fishbowl 54
- Deliver What You Promise 55
- Cause of Breakdown in Ethics 56
- Ethical Values Are Etched in the Soul 57
- Corporate Responsibility and Compliance 58
- Employees' Success Strategies 59
- Core Values Employers Expect 60
  - + Strong Work Ethics 60
  - + Moral Conscience 61
  - + Honesty and Integrity 61
  - + Work with Sincerity 61
  - + Manage Time Efficiently 62
  - + Professional Attitude 62
  - + Dependability and Reliability 62
- Use Ethics for Profit 63

Chapter 4
MARKET YOUR BRAND EQUITY: *Get the Job You Want* 65
- You Can Get That Job 66
- Eye-catching Online Résumés 67
- Tips to Prepare Powerful Online Résumés 68
  - + Show a Positive Mindset 68
  - + List Your Technical Knowledge 68
  - + Use Keywords Wisely 68
  - + Mention Qualifications and Experience 69
  - + Avoid Lengthy Résumés 69
  - + Don't Sell Yourself Short 69
  - + Keep Your Résumé Error-free 69
- Why People Fail Interviews 70
- What the Company Wants – Ideally 70
- Tips to Get Shortlisted and Get the Job 71

+ Command over Spoken and Written English 71
+ Be the Right Candidate 72
+ Display Your Accomplishments 72
+ Research the Company 72
+ The Day Before the Interview 73
+ Feel and Look Energized 73
+ Dress Professional 73
+ Be Punctual 74
+ Release Stress Before You Take the Elevator 74
+ Face-to-face at the Interview 75
Interaction Without Contradictions 76
Use the Art of Persuasion to Get the Job 76
+ Get 'Yes' Responses 77
+ Use the Mirror Effect 77
+ Strike the Right Emotional Chords 78
Negotiate Your Salary 78
Know Your Worth 79
Be Courteous 80

SECTION II
Develop Your Professional Personality 81

Chapter 5
EMBELLISH YOUR BRAND IMAGE: *Executive Grooming* 83
How to Dress Rich 84
Invest in Proper Corporate Attire 85
Mismatched Clothes Pull Your Image Down 86
Wardrobe Tips for Men in Search of Success 86
+ Formal Shirts 87
+ Formal Trousers 88
+ Undergarments 88
+ Socks 89
+ Shoes 90
+ Ties 90
+ Belts 92
Power Dressing for Women Who Desire Success 93
+ You are Judged by What You Wear 93
+ Clothes and Accessories to Avoid 94
+ Clothes and Accessories to Consider 95
+ Shoes 95

Informal Corporate Attire – Men and Women 96
Your Success Mantra: Always Dress Well 96

Chapter 6
ADD POLISH TO YOUR PERSONAL BRAND: *Corporate Hygiene* 99
Hygiene Habits Affect Business 100
Corporate Hygiene Lessons 101
+ Polish Your Brand with Cleanliness 101
+ Oral Hygiene to Stop Bad Breath 102
+ Hand Hygiene to Arrest Infections 103
+ Clean Fingernails 103
+ Bathe to Scrub Off Bacteria 104
+ Improve Your Body Odour 104
+ Get Rid of Smelly Feet 105
+ Keep Your Bed Fresh and Clean 105
+ Tips to Groom Your Hair 106
+ Smell Fresh in Hot and Humid Weather 107
+ Care for Healthy Skin 107
How to Use Corporate Washrooms 108
Implementing Corporate Hygiene Policies 108
How to Handle Errant Employees 109
Don't Slip – Watch Your Step 109

Chapter 7
PRUNE YOUR BRAND IMAGE: *Powerful First Impressions* 111
First Impressions Last Forever 113
Turn On Your Charm 113
Good First Impressions Generate Business 114
Origin of First Impressions 114
You Can Get People to Respect You 115
Take a Lesson from Gatecrashers 116
Basic Pruning Tips 117
+ Have a Positive Attitude 117
+ Dress to Impress 117
+ Shine Your Shoes Every Day 117
+ Walk Briskly 117
+ Good Manners always Impress 118
+ Listen More; Talk Less 118
+ Speak with Clarity 118
+ Your Handshake Is Important 119

+ Maintain Your Carriage and Poise 119
+ Be on Time 119
+ Keep Business Cards Handy 119
+ Never Lie 120
Your Company's Moral Image Counts 120
First Impressions on Workplace Conditions 121

Chapter 8
EMPOWER YOUR BRAND VALUE: *Business Etiquette* 123
Lubricant for Raise and Rise 124
Master the Essentials of Business Etiquette 125
A. Office Customs and Practices 125
+ Equality Among Colleagues 125
+ Ranks are Supreme 125
+ Tips to Treat a Lady 125
Annoying and Offensive Office Habits 126
+ Loud Laughter 126
+ Irritable Noises 126
+ Boorish Mannerisms 127
+ Eating and Preening at the Desk 127
+ Respect the Privacy of Others 127
+ Do Not Be Curious or Intrusive 127
+ Do Not Spread Gossip 128
+ Mind Your Language 128
+ Stop Complaining and Whining 128
+ Antisocial Habits to Avoid 129
+ Don't Be Physically Intimate with Colleagues 129
Quick Tips on Office Etiquette 129
B. Business Communications 130
+ E-mail Etiquette 130
+ Telephone Etiquette 132
+ Stop Improper Mobile Phone Usage 134
C. Business Introductions 134
+ When You Are Introduced – *Quick Tips* 136
Business Etiquette – Your Brand Ambassador 136

Chapter 9
GARNISH YOUR CORPORATE BRAND: *Table Manners* 139
Polished Table Manners Is Butter for Business 140
+ Sitting at Table 141

+ Use of Napkins 141
+ Be Considerate Towards Others 142
Formal Business Meals 143
+ Setting the Table Right 143
+ Drink from the Right Glass 144
Fine-tune Your Business Meal Manners 145
+ Hold Forks and Knives Properly 145
+ How to Serve Yourself 145
+ Passing the Dishes 146
+ Eating with Grace 146
Add a Touch of Corporate Class 147
+ Breaking Bread 147
+ Cutting Fruit 148
+ Finger Foods 148
+ Scooping Soup 148
+ Drinking Beverages 149
+ Sipping Tea and Coffee 149
Eating with Fingers 149
Two General Remarks 150

SECTION III
Master Business Communication Skills 151

Chapter 10
INTERACTIVE SOCIAL NETWORKING: *Art of Conversation* 153
Don't Be 'Victimized' by Social Anxiety 154
Talk and Be Noticed 154
Be a People's Person 156
You Can Conquer Inhibitions 157
Use Humour in Conversation 158
Conversation Killers – the *Don'ts* 158
+ Don't Be Silent 158
+ Don't Fidget with Your Phone 159
+ Don't Smell Foul 159
+ Don't Eat and Talk at the Same Time 159
+ Don't Monopolize the Conversation 159
+ Don't Interrupt Others 160
+ Don't Interrupt Interruptions 160
+ Don't Be Pretentious 160

+ Don't Cut Anyone Off 161
+ Don't Be Piggish 161
Art of Conversation Can Be Learnt 161
Mellowed Voices Charm Listeners 162
Make Your Voice Sexy and Attractive 163
Tips to Improve Your Voice Quality 164
Exercises for a Sexy Voice 164
Converse with Poise and Confidence 166

Chapter 11
EFFECTIVE BRAND POSTURING: *Get Fluent in* Bodytalk 169
Use *Bodytalk* to Leap-start Your Career 170
Develop the 'Street Smart' Instinct 171
Analyse Text with Sub-text 171
Every Twitch Tells a Tale 172
Watch How People Behave Outdoors 172
Power Walk You Can Imitate 172
Props Promote Powerbase 173
Tips to Improve Body Language 173
+ Be Aware of Your Body Expressions 174
+ Practise in Front of a Mirror 174
+ Use Your Inner Eye 174
+ Fake It till You Make It 174
Caution: Body Language Can Be Misread 175
Body Language Has Many Layers 175
Observe How the Body Speaks 176
+ Our Eyes 176
+ Our Face 177
+ Our Hands 178
+ Our Feet 178
+ Our Voice and Tone 179
+ Our Space 179
Use Body Language to Influence Customers 180
Understand Global Clients Better 181
Effective Cross-Cultural Negotiations 182
+ Business of Relationships 182
+ Negotiation Styles 182
+ Be Culturally Correct 182

Chapter 12
BLOW YOUR BRAND TRUMPET: *Speak like Steve Jobs* 185
Steve Jobs' Speaking Techniques 186
+ Capture Audience Attention 186
+ The Rule of Three 186
+ Focus on the Benefits 187
+ Rehearse, Rehearse and Rehearse Again 187
Effective Speakers Exude Leadership Qualities 188
Nervous Tension Can Paralyse You 189
Make Nervous Tension Work for You 189
+ Treat It as a Mind Game 189
+ Fill Your Mind with Positive Thoughts 189
+ Use *Quick-fire–Stealth* Ammunition 190
Tips on *Quick-Fire–Stealth* Preparation .190
+ How to *Plan* a Speech 190
+ How to *Write* a Speech 191
+ How to *Rehearse* a Speech 192
+ How to *Deliver* a Speech 193
+ How a *Speech* is evaluated 195
+ How a *Speaker* is evaluated 196
PowerPoint – Its Use and Abuse 196
Powerless With PowerPoint 197
Stay Hungry. Stay Foolish. 198

Epilogue: Paradise Lost and Regained 200
Appendix I: Face-to-face 205
Appendix II: Test Your Comprehension 224
Check Your Answers 239

Acknowledgement

This book would never have seen the light of day without the support of several people I am indebted to. I offer them my profound gratitude for the encouragement I received.

I thank Robin Treger, who encouraged me to write again after a hiatus of three years. Robin pushed and pushed till I finally gave in and the chapters began to quickly take shape. His advice still rings in my ears, "What you got from the planet, give it back to the planet. Don't take it with you." Thank you, dearest friend, for literally pushing me into writing this book and for the testimonial.

I am indeed grateful to Shobha Arora, who graciously allowed me the space and time and patiently put up with 'author moods' while I was single-mindedly focused on completing this book. I thank Varun Arora (one of the most creative and brilliant minds in advertising) for giving me so many valuable inputs in organizing the content, structure and title of the book. Both, mother and son, join me in the hope and prayer that all my readers will touch the peaks of success through the pages of this book.

The content of this book is the contents of my workshop notes and summaries that span for over thirty years. Many ideas came from the teachings of the Jesuits and from the research and writings of social psychologists, modern thinkers, and management gurus whose names remain anonymous through the passage of time. I am indebted to all of them and this tribute is in recognition of my gratitude to them.

I thank an old friend who I cherish dearly. Mathukutty M Monippally readily consented to write the *Foreword* to my book and I am truly indebted to him for doing so in spite of his busy calendar. For the glowing testimonials, I thank Neena Malhotra, Rajiv Kaul, Ronnie Lobo, Ashok Bajpai, George W Moe, Tanya Mohan and Amit Kumar.

Rise Above is my fourth book — my first with Times Group Books (TGB). What a refreshing experience it is to work with a young team of publishers! Madhulita Mohanty is the National Editor of Times Group Books, and she is so much more! Sincerity, transparency, charm and determination are some of the qualities that won me over instantly. And, there are others so dedicated at TGB, like Chetananand Singh, who did an excellent job in editing my manuscript, and Subhasish Munshi for his creative inputs. To the ones I met and those I didn't at TGB — to all who had a hand in giving shape to ***Rise Above*** — thank you.

Author's Note

No one can claim ownership for the teachings on *Life Skills*. The wisdom is handed down from generation to generation; authors simply repackage old wine in new bottles. The lessons in this book have come from the reservoir of teachings handed down by the great masters from ancient times to the modern era. In the "Psalm of Life", the English poet Henry Wadsworth Longfellow aptly wrote, "*Lives of great men all remind us / We can make our lives sublime, / And, departing, leave behind us / Footprints on the sands of time*".

If this book helps to bring out the best in you — in whatever measure — I would consider my efforts well rewarded. After all, we profess to walk on the footprints of inspirational people, even though we dilute the truth to suit our conveniences.

There are many stories in this book about people I have counselled, advised, motivated and mentored as corporate trainer, consultant and life coach. The facts I relate are accurate, but some of the details have been changed and the names of individuals, too, in an effort to keep their identities private and confidential.

FOREWORD

During the Kurukshetra war of the Mahabharata, Duryodhana, the leader of the Kauravas, approaches his mother Gandhari every morning and seeks her blessings. She loves him deeply and is proud of his prowess, but does not wish him victory. She says, "May Dharma win!" On the 18th day of the war, Bheema kills Duryodhana, the strongest of Gandhari's hundred sons and the last one remaining, and brings the war to a close.

Gandhari is furious. Sage Vyasa, her father-in-law, tries to reason with her. How can she get angry with the Pandavas after they have won the war? Didn't she want Dharma to win?

She agrees that the righteous side has indeed won the war, which was provoked by the evil doings of her sons, especially Duryodhana, and her brother Shakuni. But she is a mother and the elimination of all her children at the hands of the Pandavas fills her heart with grief and anger. A fair-minded woman, she is willing to forgive all the Pandavas except Bheema, because he broke the rules of engagement and killed Duryodhana by hitting him below the navel during the final mace fight. How could he cheat?

Bheema hears this question as he approaches her along with his brothers. He can of course confront her with a long litany of Duryodhana's unjust and treacherous deeds that led to the dreadful war which has cost everyone heavily. What right does she have to accuse Bheema of using unfair tactics?

But that is not what the victorious Bheema does. Such a response from him, however articulate, truthful and forceful, would certainly have inflamed Gandhari further and invited a terrible curse from her. Instead, Bheema humbly asks her for forgiveness and adds, "What I did was unfair, disgraceful. But I did it to save my life. Mother, no one could have killed your son in a fair battle."

Bheema doesn't stop there. He mentions several instances of foul methods Duryodhana adopted to humiliate and even eliminate the Pandavas and their wife, Draupadi. Then he stuns Gandhari with a question: "If you did nothing to stop your sons from doing *adharma* against us all these years, how can you accuse me of *adharma* now?"

Bheema says everything he wants to and justifies his action, but first he wins Gandhari over by admitting his wrongdoing, seeking her forgiveness for what he did in self-defence, and giving her son the highest praise a Kshatriya warrior could hope for.

Bheema's initial words soften Gandhari so much that she is ready to admit her own role in bringing about death and destruction in the Kuru family and in the kingdom. With the tongue she raised to curse Bheema, she calls him 'my child.' Bheema achieves a fair degree of reconciliation.

You may wonder why I talk about an ancient epic and Bheema in Cedric Kenny's book, ***Rise Above***, in the modern world. Well, Bheema is a model for those who want to refine their soft skills. He not only escapes the angry, grieving Gandhari's curse but also wins her affection and blessings in spite of being the main destroyer of her sons. He doesn't mince words when he points out that Gandhari is also responsible for the death of her sons. She agrees.

What is Bheema's secret? Obviously he knew what to say when and how to say it in a volatile situation. Is it something that we can learn? How do we learn it? Who do we learn it from? Where do we start? How do we proceed?

We don't know who taught Bheema this smart communication strategy. Perhaps it came naturally to him just as writing came naturally to Rabindranath Tagore and painting to Michelangelo. But most of us have to invest time and effort to refine our soft skills and communication strategies to survive and thrive in the complex personal, social, and professional contexts we find ourselves in.

Technical or the so-called hard skills are essential, but they can't take us very far. They make up the platform; but it is soft skills that help us build our personal brands. Technical skills can quickly become obsolete. Soft skills belong to a different order. We don't lose them once we acquire them. But we have to refine them by understanding ourselves and others more and more deeply. This is where Cedric Kenny's book offers us invaluable help.

There are many self-help books in the market. They promise to transform us overnight. Quite a few of them are in the 'for dummies' mould. ***Rise Above*** differs from them in many respects.

First of all, it has been written for a wide range of readers: young and old, employed and unemployed, experienced and inexperienced, teachers and students, trainers and trainees. And everyone finds relevant insights into building up their personal brands. This is one of the major strengths of the book.

Second, the style of writing is conversational. It is full of lively examples, catchy metaphors and memorable phrases that capture the insights very crisply. Take for example, the statement, "Your Attitude Determines Your Altitude."

Third, the book is a systematic exploration of the process of building oneself as a brand. It aptly starts with self-knowledge, goes on to what it means to develop a professional personality, and finally to the essence of business communication skills. It also emphasizes the need for integrity and values because the brand is being built from within, not applied like a coat of polish.

And finally, the author. This is the greatest strength of the book. He has earned the right to advise us on how to build our personal brands, because he has helped thousands of people develop personal effectiveness. He has been donning several caps successfully: corporate trainer, management consultant, mentor, life coach, family counsellor, psychologist, and academician. He is as comfortable with adolescents as with widely travelled senior executives.

I hope thousands of people of all descriptions pick up and benefit from ***Rise Above*** as they have from his earlier books.

MATHUKUTTY MONIPPALLY
Professor of Communication
Indian Institute of Management
Vastrapur, Ahmedabad - 380 015

Prologue

WHERE EAGLES SOAR

This book is for you — with a degree in one hand and a fistful of dreams in another you want to be rich and successful. You want to be a millionaire. Who doesn't? Millionaire dreams come free. Nightmares, depression and frustration feed on millionaire dreams. According to Harvey Mackay, "A dream is just a dream. A goal is a dream with a plan and a deadline." To have a goal-oriented dream with a plan and a deadline requires grit, guts and the will to do it. And it is not wrong to want to be a millionaire before you hit 30, or is it 40? India is in its youthful prime. You have fire in your belly and money is a commodity to die for. What holds you back?

Those with jobs or jobless, graduates or graduating, new applicants or new recruits, teachers, professors and corporate trainers who prepare and inspire millions of job-ready aspirants each year — this book is for you. Whether you are in training or trained, experienced or inexperienced, you must be thoroughly prepared and battle-ready for conquest in the corporate jungle. Getting a job and keeping it have become more complex and more demanding. Technical skills alone are not enough to take on the corporate world. You must be armed with the latest multi-dimensional arsenal of social skills in order to survive and succeed. ***Rise Above*** is your handbook for survival and triumph. Get your personal copy today!

You are the product of the age of gizmos and geeks — the age of social media, websites, Facebook, LinkedIn, Google, Twitter, blogs and branding. Everything about you and your work is about branding. You are the brand. The way you project yourself is the way you are perceived by people — as a brand. Your personality, attitude, business etiquette, grooming, manners and behaviour become your personality package. Your brand identity is linked with your reputation. People live and die by the reputation they form. How do you want to see yourself? Are you dependable? Are you dispensable? What will satisfy you — ultimately? Do you have it in you to give what the organization wants? Your reputation depends on it.

Rise Above will show you how to mould an effective new personality to project your brand new image. You will learn to position yourself to be noticed, to be appreciated and rewarded. It is time to rise above your shortcomings and overhaul your image. Think for a moment and rise like the eagle. Close your eyes and, in your mind, become an eagle. With eyes shut, imagine you are the eagle flying high as you rise above everything else. Feel the wind in your face, feel the rush of exhilaration as you soar higher and higher — into the clouds. The eagle symbolizes speed and power and fearless determination — qualities which add excitement, zip and fun to your personality. Make the 'eagle' the symbol of your brand identity to soar high in the corporate skies.

India has evolved. India is the land of opportunities. India is techno-savvy. To meet India's evolving demands, ***Rise Above*** will teach you new cutting-edge social skills which will add value to your personal brand image, and help you grab whatever opportunities come your way as you fly to the top of the corporate hill.

Rise Above is your road map with an in-built navigational aid divided into three sections. Each section offers many skills, insights and inputs to touch your core strengths — and sharpen your appetite for more. In *Section I*, you will know yourself and know your mind and find simple, practical and ethical ways to imbibe skills to get the job you want, and grow in the job. In *Section II*, your personality will shine out as you groom yourself in so many ways to put your best foot forward so that you are admired as a valued asset of the organization. In *Section III*, you will master complex styles of communication beginning with the art of conversation and body language so that you do not offend people across continents and cultures. You will also learn effective techniques to make presentations with confidence. The *Epilogue* sums up your life's purpose: you were born to work — oh boy, and how!

Those of you who want more out of this book, turn to the *Appendix*. The *Appendix* section is your personal workbook in two parts. *Appendix I* holds a psychological mirror to your personality. Follow the instructions carefully and you will sculpt your personality as you want it to be. *Appendix II* deals with comprehension and retention — two indispensable assets for those who desire to rise where eagles soar in the business world. How good are you at comprehension and retention? ***Rise Above*** your complacency to find out. Take the test and check for yourself whether you really have it in you to reach your perch, like the eagle, on the corporate hilltop.

SECTION I

MAP YOUR CAREER PATH

Chapter 1
BUILD YOUR BRAND IDENTITY
Know Yourself

Chapter 2
SUPERCHARGE YOUR BRAND VALUE
Know Your Mind

Chapter 3
GIVE YOUR BRAND THE MORAL SEAL
Workplace Ethics

Chapter 4
MARKET YOUR BRAND EQUITY
Get the Job You Want

KNOW YOURSELF
Personality=
Brand Identity
Positive attitude
Set goals
Discipline
Integrity
Keep promises
Eager to learn
Efficient
Team player
Enjoy meeting people

chapter 1

BUILD YOUR BRAND IDENTITY

KNOW YOURSELF

Smashing glass ceilings requires more than fists of steel. You need corporate character — the personality for success. To develop corporate character, you need self-knowledge and strong determination. You must have not only the knowledge to identify the success skills you possess but also the determination to chip away the rough edges of your personality traits that pull you down. Glass ceilings are mostly of our own making.

Sangita is ambitious. She wants to make it big in the corporate world. She is restless, impatient and impulsive. In nine years, she has switched five jobs — from personnel to HR, and from sales and marketing to accounts. She is lured by the money. From BPO to hotels and from airlines to pharmaceuticals, she has criss-crossed her career trajectory. She has begun to drift but she doesn't know it. Jumping jobs is like boarding different ships, and in many cases it means drifting in the corporate sea.

Occupation, by nature, is dynamic, but it can also be static. Sangita has been busy working her way inside corporate mazes, but is getting nowhere. Most employees get lulled by the salary they earn and never know they are drifting. For course correction, Sangita must equip herself with a road map and a compass. She cannot rely on instinct and feelings alone to succeed in the corporate world. She must have a focus and a plan. The road map and compass will point to the direction she must navigate in to reach her career goals.

Sangita has many qualities and talents, but she is confused; she does not know how to use her talents effectively. Just as quality-conscious masons use the best of well-baked bricks to lay the foundation of a house, employees must wisely apply the best talents they possess to build a powerful brand identity. To rise above, an accurate road map and the compass are essential corporate tools for career navigation. Without self-awareness, employees are unable to harness their talents to build a career. Self-awareness is the compass to self-improvement. Self-improvement is the road map that guides you on the road to success.

According to the 2011 Asia-Pacific Wealth Report by Merrill Lynch and Capgemini, in 2010, eight of the 20 fastest-growing high net-worth individual (HNWI) populations were in Asia-Pacific markets. India is one of these eight countries. Indians, by nature, are hardworking Asians — a powerful brand identity. If you want to be considered a serious contender to join this elite millionaire club, you will have to restructure your thinking, your attitude, your learning, your habits and your actions — brick by brick — to build yourself into a new personality.

Before you start rebuilding and restructuring your personality, you must be able to identify the shortcomings you have in order to overcome them. To know the difference between the obstacles (which must be eliminated) and the stepping stones (which you need to polish), you must know yourself — very well.

You probably think you know yourself very well. If that is so, ask yourself, "What am I *really* good at?" Do you know what you are *really* good at? If you do so, then write it down. Most probably, that question will make you think about your assets. Self-awareness is important to build on your assets. As you count your assets, you will notice that some of your habits are offensive to people and compromise your good qualities.

Many smart executives suffer disappointments because they never knew the difference between what they liked doing and where their strengths lay — and they made wrong decisions. Do you also suffer from doubts? Are you in the wrong job, or is the job not right for you? Employees who doubt their abilities develop stress, lose their cool and find fault with co-workers for not finding their 'groove' in the company. You must realize that people are not working there to help you find your 'groove'. You have to do it on your own.

> *You are your greatest asset. Put your time, effort and money into training, grooming and encouraging your greatest asset.*
>
> Tom Hopkins

It is like getting into a crowded train. Don't expect fellow passengers to make you comfortable on the train. Passengers look out for themselves. If you don't want to get pushed around, don't stand by the exit doors. If you want a seat, wait in the corridors where people are seated. Knowing what you want will make the journey less stressful. Or else, commuting in crowded trains will always be a traumatic experience. Similarly, lack of self-knowledge affects your work and your attitude, and you will go from one job to another like a rolling stone that is kicked downhill.

BUILD ON THE STRENGTHS YOU POSSESS

To know yourself, you must know what you are competent at — your core strength. Achievements and capabilities highlight core competency. Core competency is made of two parts. One part of core competency makes you job-capable. Job capability is linked to academic qualifications which are essential to get hired. Technical knowledge is also called hard skills. The second part of core competency makes you excel at the job. Excelling at the job depends on your attitude, behaviour, manners, grooming and common courtesies, which together are called soft skills, also known as EQ skills or social skills.

You could be the most qualified person in the room, but if you lack soft skills, you will never get the job. Such deficiency often destroys career trajectories of many aspiring young workers and they usually end up thinking they were in the wrong job or the job wasn't right for them. Lack of this basic self-knowledge will rob you of job stability. Without soft skills you will face difficulties in performing the job well.

Self-knowledge is absolutely essential for anyone seriously intent on choosing the right career path leading to success. Some get stuck in a job, while others jump jobs as though they were riding different horses at the circus. Philosophers and religious gurus hammer out one basic teaching: *know yourself*. Blame it on the pressures of modern lifestyles; where is the time to reflect, you will ask? The daily routine consumes you — day after day. The truth is, when you don't have time to analyse your strengths and weaknesses, you will make wrong choices, which ultimately confine you to a life of whining mediocrity.

YOUR ATTITUDE DETERMINES YOUR ALTITUDE

Some people fail and some people succeed. What divides success from failure? Remember, it is always choices. The choices you make determine whether you will succeed or whether you will *struggle* to succeed. For some, 'struggle' becomes the all-consuming career path they will walk all their lives. "Success or failure," says Walter D Scott, "is caused more by mental attitudes than by mental capacities." Choices borne out of conviction and purpose may lead to positive results. But choices borne out of compromise and convenience always lead to average or negative results. Some wake up to a new day of opportunities; others wake up to another day of grind. Those in the former category wake up full of zip and jump out of bed, while those in the latter wake up lazily and prefer to stay in bed — a little bit longer. Gird yourself with a positive attitude and you will touch new altitudes of self-awareness.

It would be wrong to suggest that self-knowledge by itself is the key to success. Along with it, you will need to master a range of skills to which you must be willing to dedicate a few minutes every day — about the time you spend on a tea break. You will also need to observe others around you and practise some of their skills that make them stand out. You may think you are pretty good at what you do, so why copy others? To be counted among the best, it is important to not only work on the skills you have and sharpen them, but also add new ones. You may have to check out other sources to pick up new skills that have worked well for others. You can practise new skills from this book as well as learn new ones by observing your relatives, friends, colleagues and people at large.

You may have a high opinion of yourself and become complacent. Or, you may have a low opinion of yourself and destroy your confidence. You must be balanced in your self-evaluation. Check how you function at home, at office, and socially. Write on a piece of paper what you are best at and worst at, and you will know a great deal about yourself. Start on a positive note and identify your strengths which make you a likeable person. Thereafter, note the areas which put people off you. Rarely do people want to be honest with themselves and accept responsibility; they prefer to blame others, believing it is their problem. Rather than accepting the way you are, you can choose to roll up your sleeves and work on personal improvement. Self-knowledge reinforced by self-improvement is the master key to opening the doors which lead to success.

On his maiden visit to India, Warren Buffett, chairman of Berkshire Hathaway, told the media what an asset Ajit Jain (head of Reinsurance Division) was to his organization. Can you imagine the heady feeling you get when the boss tells the world you are a great asset to the organization — that your organization is willing to hire many more people with *your* brand of skills? In the world of cut-throat competition, a sharp business mind alone does not make Ajit Jain an indispensable asset. Soft skills are what has given him a sharp edge over his closest competitors. Corporate houses are constantly reinventing themselves to keep up with market demands. To keep pace with your company's image, you have to reinvent yourself like Ajit Jain.

KEYS TO SELF-IMPROVEMENT

To be acclaimed the Ajit Jain of your organization, you must be committed to polishing the skills you already have and developing new ones. You don't have to spend days attending classes or listening to lectures on self-improvement. Just be with yourself, say for 10 minutes, without distractions. When you are alone and by yourself, look inward. Be your own critic and coach. Be your own student and teacher. When you allow yourself to move on from the path of self-knowledge to the path of self-improvement, you will be charged with dynamism. This dynamism will ignite in you a burning zeal which keeps you excited and passionate — wanting and desiring self-improvement.

Those who exercise daily at the gym know the first month is the hardest for beginners. And those who pass the period of trial begin to gradually enjoy the gym. Working out at the gym makes them feel good about themselves. They feel relaxed, energized and rejuvenated after every workout, and they never stop going to the gym, no matter how busy or tired they are. Some people suffer guilt pangs on the days they are unable to go to the gym.

Initiating changes in your behaviour is as tedious for you as it is for first-time gym-goers. It does not happen automatically. Ideas are like seeds which need to take root. You need to plant the idea in your head that you must improve your skills. After you have planted the idea, you will water it by reminding yourself again and again to fit it into your schedule in order to enable you to act upon it. The idea will gradually germinate into action. As you become determined to develop your personality and begin to modify your behaviour, the first three months will have gone by without a break. This is your trial period. By the end of the three months, you will have achieved a great deal of transformation in your behaviour and mannerisms, which will be noticed by people around you. A kind word or a compliment when reciprocated will make you feel worth the effort you put in to become a better person. From then on, you will never want to stop the process of change.

> *Ideas are like rabbits. You get a couple, learn how to look after them, and pretty soon you have a dozen.*
>
> John Steinbeck

10 WAYS TO DEVELOP YOUR BRAND IDENTITY

Press a button on the machine and you get ready-to-serve instant coffee. For a polished personality which will bring you recognition, however, pressing a single button is not enough. You will have to press a number of buttons for a long period of time. Developing your personal brand identity is not a one-month activity. It takes time and is a daily process. It depends entirely on your attitude and dedication to improve your brand image.

When you walk the path of *10 Ways to Develop Your Brand Identity*, you will recognise the attributes that draw people to you and the personality flaws that drive people away. Your commitment to improving your social skills and converting flaws into attributes will make you a much-sought-after people's person.

1. You Set Goals

Like all top-level competitive athletes, professionals and achievers, you set goals. Setting goals gives you a 'track' to run on and a 'path' to walk, so you know where you want to go in life. Goal setting puts your plans in sharp focus and motivates you to transform your vision of the future into reality within a time span. It enables you to set priorities and avoid distractions which can easily derail your vision. By knowing exactly what you want to achieve, you know where you have to concentrate your efforts to achieve optimum results. Your confidence grows as you recognise your own ability and competence in achieving the goals you set.

2. You Are Disciplined

You set a *timetable* in your head by reminding yourself to stop daydreaming and get on with the job. The timetable helps you set a daily routine to keep you organized. Following a timetable makes it easy to achieve a lot more in a short period of time. As a beginner in time management, you must be patient as it takes time for habits of discipline to set. External factors will hinder you from being disciplined, hence you must be resolute. (You cannot wake up bright-eyed at the crack of dawn when you went to bed at two in the morning.) Being constantly late for work, for meetings or in submitting reports and other tasks not only affects the company's efficiency, but also shows that you are not fit for the job. To show that you are executive material and an asset to the company, you must value time. Don't treat the timetable as a burden. Those who are not time-conscious consciously impede the company's growth as well as their own.

3. You Are a Person of Integrity

Integrity is about doing what is right and not what is convenient. A person of integrity is made of high moral fibre. To be acknowledged as a person of integrity is one of the highest praises you can achieve. Knowledge, honesty, dignity, loyalty, dependability, and respect for people are some of the finer qualities of a person of integrity. It conveys your ability of being trustworthy, accountable and principled. Self-respect is all about your individualism and about how you control your emotions to act in a way that is principled and morally correct. Sachin Tendulkar is loved because he is the master blaster at the crease, and he is worshipped as the god of cricket because of his integrity.

4. You Keep Your Promises

You must never make promises which you cannot fulfil. To keep the promises you made is to stand by your commitment which people expect you to honour. The downside is the temptation to make every single person in your department happy, which is often misguided as it usually produces opposite results. Burdening yourself with excessive commitments will only lead to unnecessary stress and tension. You have to learn to prioritize your tasks and plan accordingly. This helps you organize what is to be done on an immediate basis and what can wait. Also, it enables you to arrange time to enjoy yourself with people and things that are closer and more important to you and your family.

5. You Are Eager to Learn

You keep your brand fresh and up to date. If you were an 'expert' two years ago but stopped learning and challenging yourself, you are not an expert anymore. All brands have a shelf life and come with an expiry date. No matter how good you are at your work, without upgrading your knowledge and skills you run the risk of becoming stale. You cannot ride one idea forever. If you don't continue adding new ideas to what you know, you will end up making way for new 'experts' to take the company forward. Set aside a fixed time for learning and use each day to upgrade your knowledge and skills. However busy you are, be sure to schedule self-study into your timetable, and don't miss that appointment.

6. You Are a Positive Person

It is so refreshing to be in the company of people who have a positive attitude and outlook in life. Contrarily, it is boring to suffer the company of people who only complain, whine and speak badly of other people. It is wise to keep a safe distance from this depressive lot of people. As a positive person, you entertain positive thoughts and release positive energy around yourself. People enjoy your company because your

> *Every day think, as you wake up, today I am fortunate to be alive; I have a precious human life. I am not going to waste it. I am going to use all my energies to develop myself.*
>
> Dalai Lama XIV

positive energy is infectious. Your enthusiasm brings out the best in you, and you get over stressful situations because you plant positive thoughts in your mind. You accept whatever work is assigned to you wholeheartedly with the belief that the task at hand may be difficult but not impossible. You treat all tough assignments as a challenge and will do them to the best of your ability, never mind the extra hours.

7. You Are a Good Speaker

The importance of being a good conversationalist and an effective speaker can never be undermined. The more you read and cultivate new interests, the more interesting you are to others — provided you speak up. Read about new ideas with an intention to share them with your colleagues. When you speak out new ideas you not only test their validity but also reinforce them in your memory. Pay attention to details and learn new skills with the intention to express yourself without sounding pompous, boring or nervous. Meeting new people gives you the opportunity to share what you know and to exchange views with them. A good speaker invests many hours of hard work to master the English language — pronunciation, diction, intonation, enunciation and inflection — to sound polished and cultured.

8. You Are a Good Listener

To be an excellent conversationalist, you must be a good listener. As an effective communicator, you *learn to listen* and *listen to learn*. You pay close attention and ask questions to get more information. Practise listening with all your senses — this is called active listening or empathetic listening. The habit will grow on you gradually. Haven't you felt it that whenever someone listened to you intently, it made you feel very special to that person? Being a good listener will add to your brand identity and make you a more charming person, an effective manager and a better negotiator.

9. You Enjoy Meeting People

You already know the importance of social networking in promoting your brand identity. And meeting people is the physical aspect of social networking. To train yourself to enjoy the company of people, you begin by planting friendly thoughts in your mind. You cannot be afraid of people or shy of meeting or conversing with new people. Be bold and take the initiative to greet and introduce yourself to people and groups you've never met earlier. Make it a habit to remember their names and repeat these in conversation so that they will be drawn to you. Listen closely to what they say so that you find something to like about them and their work and to compliment them instantly. The qualities you admire in them and compliment them for are the ones you make a mental note of to practise when you are by yourself. You will find meeting new people and groups very stimulating because you can use those opportunities to spread your dynamic charm.

10. You Welcome Feedback/Criticism

No one is perfect and people have rough edges which rub others the wrong way. Feedback/criticism does not make you look small; instead, it helps you fine-tune your skills to gain an edge over your competitors. The service industry relies heavily on feedback and on the opinion of the people they serve. Organizations put in place elaborate feedback formats, which are scrutinized by departments of personnel, HR and training so that mistakes don't reoccur and the employees learn to put their best foot forward. Strange as it may sound, try and ask colleagues, friends and family to give you frank feedback on your performance and behaviour. Their honest feedback should not hurt or offend you. Instead, welcome people's criticism so that you can modify and improve your behaviour and develop new skills.

PERSONALITY DEVELOPMENT – A LIFELONG BRAND INVESTMENT

It is commonly said, you've got to have the "*personality*" for success. Success is attained by people who have charming personalities. Your brand identity becomes your personal asset when you add multi-dimensional skills to your personality. You must always think of personality development as a long-term investment. You may not have realized that your personal brand identity has the potential to last longer than the job you hold. Some companies close down, others merge, or you may change jobs from time to time, but while all that happens, your personal brand identity continues to live on. When you switch jobs, your personal brand identity stands by you as a guarantee and you never have to start from scratch. Indeed, a good personal brand identity is a lifelong invaluable investment.

> *If you wish to achieve worthwhile things in your personal and career life, you must become a worthwhile person in your own self-development.*
>
> Brian Tracy

People try to improve their personalities a number of times. After all, who doesn't want to look attractive and good to others? The word *attractive* has to do with dress and grooming. *Good* has to do with manners, habits and behaviour. Your attempt to improve your image may include minor external changes such as buying new hi-fashion clothes, getting a new hairstyle, colouring your hair, shaving your head or sporting a moustache. Rarely do people attempt more serious internal changes such as improving communication skills, attitude, and business etiquette, and quitting bad habits. Obviously, bringing about internal changes is more challenging than, say, buying new clothes.

WHY CHANGING BAD HABITS IS TOUGH

We are creatures of habit. Many of our habits are acts of convenience. We have different habits for different situations and occasions. Some habits build relationships while some destroy them. Domestic violence, verbal abuse and physical abuse are destructive habits. And there are people who are habituated to smoking, alcohol, drugs, gluttony, smut and sleaze, and lots of *other stuff* that compromise your work and professional image.

People make resolutions to quit their bad habits, believing that they will succeed. They keep flogging the habit horse without getting off the nag. Take, for instance, the habit of smoking. When you made the resolution to quit smoking, you were high on motivation and were determined never to smoke. You reminded yourself, time and again, that you would never smoke. Handling cravings — 'cravings for a nicotine fix' — is the biggest problem when trying to quit an old habit. Some people who pray and meditate for inner strength to quit smoking feel an increased urge or craving for a puff. When cravings gnawed at you, and they kept gnawing at you for days and weeks on end, you told yourself, "I'm not going to smoke. I've quit smoking. I'll not smoke. No smoking for me…" Do you get the picture? You are sitting on the 'smoking horse' and flogging it. Since you are already in the saddle, it won't be long before you light up again and ride off with the habit. In the same vein, imagine telling a person who is passionate about burgers and wants to go on a diet, "Don't *think* of a big, fat, juicy burger." The first thought that hits them is the picture of a big, fat juicy burger!

NEW MOTIVATIONAL TECHNIQUES

Most people at some point in their lives want to quit an old habit because it affects a relationship or their professional image or whatever. While a few succeed, most people give up on themselves. There is an easier way to quit a bad habit than flogging the habit horse. When you want to quit something, it means you want to get it out of you — to discard it. It is like putting your hand inside your pocket and trying to pull out the thing you want to throw away, but your hand is stuck in the pocket and it will not come out. So, you are stuck with the habit that is stuck inside you. Soon you will be frustrated and you will stop pulling at it and gradually give in to the old habit.

Let us attempt another route. Let us try 'putting in' instead of 'pulling out.' After all, putting in is easier than pulling out. Ask yourself, "If I'm going to get this 'thing' out of my pocket, what am I going to put in its place?" This is an entirely new dimension to the technique of quitting a bad habit. Instead of opening a 'debit account' (to pull out the bad habit), you must open a 'credit account' (to put in a new habit). "*Putting In*" is your trump card and not "*Pulling Out*". 'Cravings' will stop as soon as the putting-in activity begins. When you begin to operate the 'credit account' you will not have the time or the inclination to spare even a thought for the old bad habit. You literally ignore the old nag.

You start to focus on the new habit you decided upon and not only absorb your mind with the thought of acquiring the new habit, but also entertain thoughts on how you will put it into operation, on which occasions and circumstances you will use it, the good it will do to your image, the joy it will bring to others, the wealth of goodwill it will bring to your organization, and a zillion other positive possibilities. Each possibility is a thought and an idea bursting with positive energy. As you occupy your mind and body, intellect and will, passion and emotion to make the new habit operational, your pocket will be so stuffed with positive dreams and positive ambition that the old habit will die — forgotten, neglected and buried under a heap of new exciting ideas. When you have used this technique successfully, you will join the chorus and ask, "Who said, *old habits die hard*?"

POWERED BY POSITIVE ENERGY

And there is yet another way! This is a mind game. You can call this mind game *self-indoctrination*. You will fill your mind and body with positive energy. You start with a positive question. How do rock stars, athletes and sportspersons perform in front of thousands of people, especially when the stakes are so high? What gives them the courage and the drive to push themselves to extreme limits of performance? After all, they are ordinary people. The secret lies in their extraordinary zeal. Obviously, they have very strong faith in themselves. Their extraordinary faith activates an internal drive that tells them that they can and will succeed, and that they will overcome any and every obstacle that comes in their path. Is this quality unique only to them? Or can this quality be acquired by you and others — ordinary people?

> *... because you have so little faith. I tell you the truth, if you have faith as small as a mustard seed, you can say to this mountain, 'Move from here to there' and it will move. Nothing will be impossible for you.*
>
> New Testament, Matthew 17:20

The expression *self-fulfilling prophecies* was coined by the sociologist Robert K Murton to describe a particular behavioural outcome that dates back to Indian and Greek mythology. Murton pointed out that a prediction about the outcome of a situation could develop a new behaviour which led to the prediction coming true. For example, if you believed that you were going to be late for a business meeting, the belief would lead you to alter the strategies you use to get ready for the meeting. You would, for example, turn back from the parking lot and rush to the apartment to look for the misplaced mobile phone. In the end, you would reach late for the meeting. Had your belief not altered your preparation for the meeting (and had you not lost valuable time looking for the mobile phone), you might have had a good chance to be there on time, if not ahead of time.

Now, you may consider a positive prediction. The astrologer says, "You will marry a doctor..." At the conscious or subconscious level, you rearrange your priorities and 'look for a doctor' and you may either marry one or wait for one to come along. Literally, you restructure your behaviour to make this belief become a reality. Psychological research shows that *self-fulfilling prophecies* work for both negative and positive predictions, indicating, again, that the beliefs you hold have an impact on what happens to you.

It has also been proved scientifically that feelings and actions are mutually interdependent. One can change the other. Actually, your mind is conditioned to respond to your feelings. So, when you feel negative, you act and talk negative. And if you consciously act and talk positive, you will start feeling positive. And that exactly is the underlying principle of these techniques.

Armed with these new techniques, you can start building your confidence right now by telling yourself that whatever it takes, you have it in you to change your habits. The more you believe you are capable, the more you will become so. Get into the routine of telling yourself that you can learn new skills and make a habit of them, and you will be successful in all aspects of your life. In doing so, you will find that you can handle many more challenges life throws at you and that you always had the potential for it.

DETERMINATION LEADS TO SUCCESS

Rise Above will help you deal with internal and external changes in your personality and also coach and guide you to overcome your shortcomings and manage yourself. To do that you will need to cultivate a deep understanding of yourself, not only of your strengths and weaknesses, but more importantly of how you learn, how you work with others and what your values are. The quicker you come in contact with the real you, the faster you will progress. It's only when you learn to manage your habits and behaviour with determination that you will achieve true success.

Recession is for whiners. These are not hard times. These are challenging times. These are times of unprecedented opportunities. You need passion, ambition and the will to invest in skills to rise to the top, regardless of where you started out. Get yourself an action plan and hitch it to a goal. When you put your plan into action and reach your goal, you will come to be identified by those qualities you worked at, and you will contribute to your own happiness as well as to others'. You will feel proud and honoured to be identified and remembered by the positive brand image your personality is attached to.

KNOW YOUR MIND

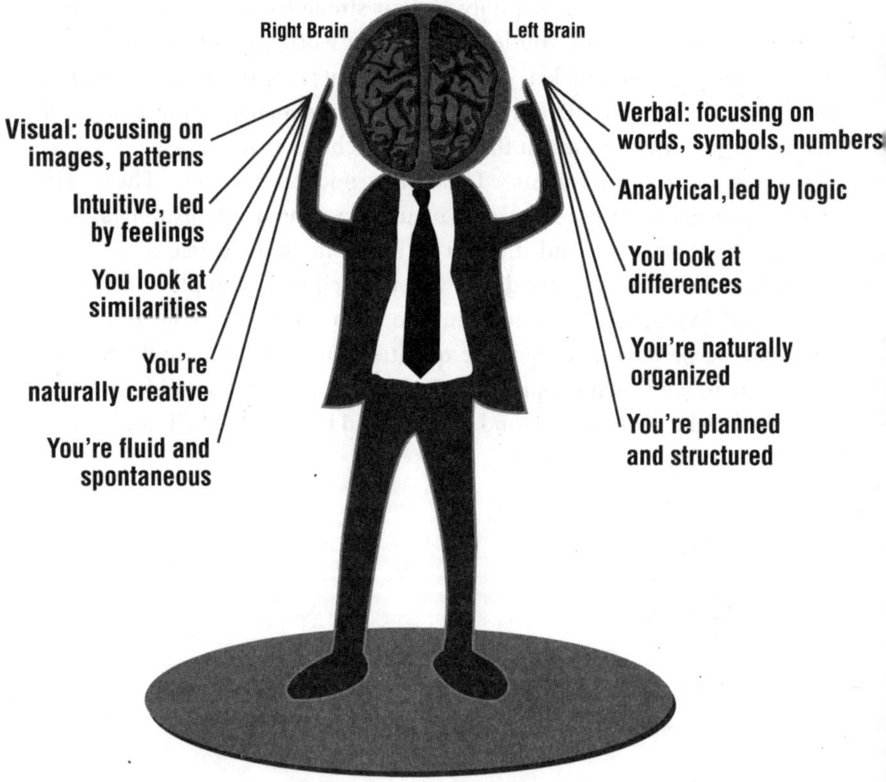

Chapter 2

SUPERCHARGE YOUR BRAND VALUE

KNOW YOUR MIND

Year-end appraisals were on. The HR manager glanced at Ashutosh's personal file. It said, he was enthusiastic but made excuses for lapses. He was quick to commit but low on keeping promises. He was friendly but lacked team spirit. He was loyal but uninspiring. The manager closed the file. He noted, Ashutosh had potential but never used it.

Ashutosh wore rings with gems for protection. The gems protected him from stress and office hostilities. He wore rings for migraine and indigestion, and a gold chain with a moonstone protected him from heart disease. He even skipped dinner on Thursdays as penance to appease a deity. The astrologer advised Ashutosh to be patient; the bad-luck phase would last for two more years.

The fault... is not in our stars, but in ourselves, that we are underlings, *said Shakespeare. Our weaknesses and failings are rooted in our brains and not in our stars. Ashutosh put his faith in astrologers and in the power of gems — but not in himself. He had the potential to better his career growth provided he improved his behaviour and mindset. Ashutosh had the power for self-improvement: He had to apply his mind to use it.*

Supercharge Your Brand Value *explores the roots of your behaviour and attitude. For instance, being forgetful is a character flaw which can be set right. Are you dominated by the right brain or the left? This chapter helps you demystify the functions of your mind and use your full potential to rise above. You can avail yourself of the cutting-edge techniques to develop a strong character and a corporate personality. Recent research on how the brain controls your moods and behaviour will open your mind to accepting new ideas with minimum effort. The revelation will bring you greater success in your job and satisfying relationships in your social life.*

People judge you by what they see: your actions, habits and attitude. You are judged to be a likeable person with an attractive personality when you project positive behaviour. On the other hand, you are not liked when you project negative behaviour. There are good people and there are bad people. What makes a person caring? And what makes another one selfish? Do you know that you are a product of *pre-wiring*? Your behaviour springs into action as though on *autopilot mode*, depending on the signals your motor muscles receive from the neurons in your brain. Your brain controls your actions, characteristics, habits and attitude fully. All your actions — the good, the bad and the ugly — are controlled by your brain, which receives impulses from its left and right side. To bring about a change in your personality, you will first have to know how your mind works. The key to improving behaviour lies in your brain and not in the resolutions you made.

Do you want to know why you behave the way you do? Recent research shows that it all boils down to which side of the brain dominates your actions — the left brain or the right brain. When one side of the brain becomes more dominant, it could be because the other side is not stimulated. Your goal is to have both sides of the brain — the left brain and the right brain — stimulated so that they function in tandem and do not allow one to dominate the other, especially in areas which are crucial to your personal, social and career growth.

YOU CAN RE-SET THE 'WIRING' IN YOUR BRAIN

Know your mind and empower yourself to improve your negative habits. If you are slothful, it is not because you chose to be lazy. Your brain was 'wired' to be slothful. This knowledge is dynamite in your hands because now you know what causes negative and positive habits. This knowledge will help you change your course of behaviour. It will motivate you to stay focused on your personal development. It will strengthen your resolve to work hard to '*un*-wire' the '*pre*-wired' brain and '*re*-wire' it so that you can re-programme your behaviour (actions) as you want to.

Imagine yourself in the role of an 'electrician' who has to fix faulty wiring at an apartment. You will open the fuse box and study the situation to identify the fault points. Having identified the problem, you will un-wire the fault points in the pre-wired fuse box and re-wire it correctly. Similarly, in the case of your personality, you are the electrician who has to re-set the wiring in your brain so that you can improve your skills without frustration. This is a personal challenge you set yourself to as you are determined to overcome your quirky behaviour and remind yourself to polish those skills which are absolutely essential to climbing the ladder of success.

Dr Glen Johnson, a clinical neuropsychologist, compares the brain not to a computer but to an orchestra. "In an orchestra, you have different musical sections. There is a percussion section, a string section, a woodwind section, and so on. Each has its own job to do and must work closely with the other sections. When playing music, each section waits for the conductor. The conductor raises a baton and all the members of the orchestra begin playing at the same time playing on the same note. If the drum section hasn't been practising, they don't play as well as the rest of the orchestra. The overall sound of the music seems 'off' or plays poorly at certain times. This is a better model of how the brain works. We used to think of the brain as a big computer, but it's really like millions of little computers all working together."

IMPROVING BEHAVIOUR MADE EASY

Like the orchestra conductor, the symphony of your actions must not be discordant. You must ensure that your behaviour is primed to please people. Let us say that there are certain behaviour traits you have identified which are not in tune with the company's policy and which will obstruct your career growth. In the past, you made several attempts to improve yourself but you did not succeed. People said you were not motivated enough or you were not strong-willed to change your behaviour. None of that is true. Your behaviour traits depend on how your brain was 'wired'. Now you know that the right brain dominates your left brain or vice versa, which compromised your career growth and made you look clumsy, incompetent or antisocial. You can use that knowledge to overcome your shortcomings and offensive behaviour. This does not call for brain surgery, and you don't need surgical instruments to work that change. You need firm determination to apply yourself to changing your habits.

MINDSET OR MIND GAMES

Business houses draw people from different backgrounds — cultural, educational, socio-economic, religious, regional, the rich, the poor and the middle class. Each individual comes packaged with a unique mindset — some are 'wired' to do good and some are 'wired' to do bad. As you interact and intermingle with the workers every day, how do you know who to trust and who to avoid? It is better to be safe than sorry. How do you know if you are in bad company? How do you know who to befriend? How do you spot character flaws in smooth operators and glib talkers? Is it possible to be a wise judge of people? Or, are you the problem?

1. Hamster-on-the-Wheel Syndrome

Have you watched hamsters — small furry rodents that look like guinea pigs — in a pet shop? The hamster rides on the wheel fitted inside the enclosure. It keeps itself busy, very busy — its little legs moving quickly, the wheel turning, but the hamster going nowhere. Indeed, that is a lot of activity for the little hamster, but no progress.

Do you suffer from the hamster-on-the-wheel syndrome? Look at yourself. Even after years of slogging, you are still slogging at the same job, doing the same things you did last year or perhaps working on another similar product. Or did you change the job? Yes, you did. But nothing changed. It's the same routine again. A sales job is a sales job — all companies work the same way, you tell yourself. You are still doing the same stuff you did last year in your last job. In fact, you have been so busy working month after month that you did not notice that, like the hamster, you are peddling the wheel in the corporate cage and going nowhere. While you keep peddling, more work piles up. "I have to do this… I have to complete that… and if I don't do this, the boss will be angry… and I missed yesterday's deadline… I still have last week's emails to read… and…"

Eventually, the hamster's stamina and concentration fade and it falls out of the wheel. If your motivation, productivity, energy and concentration levels have dropped, that is the first phase of your fall. Gradually, you will soon get stressed and burn out — that is the final phase of the hamster-on-the-wheel syndrome. Before that happens, commit yourself to 're-wiring' your mind and change your habits.

2. Mind Games Workaholics Play

> *One of the symptoms of an approaching nervous breakdown is the belief that one's work is terribly important.*
>
> Bertrand Russell

Does any of the following sound familiar? Pressure from your boss to bring in results, pressure from yourself to deliver, meeting deadlines — the more unrealistic the deadlines, the more challenging it is — working 12 to 16 hours daily, constantly thinking about work, being impatient with those who don't share your work priorities, taking work home, and little or no personal life from which you derive pleasure. If you are 'wired' for work, you better watch out. You are on the road to becoming a workaholic, if you are not already one.

Chances are you are a workaholic if you feel compelled to work for the sake of working, and you feel panic, anxiety or a sense of loss when you are not working. The stress that goes along with working too much leads to substance abuse, sleep disorders, anxiety, erectile dysfunction and ultimately to physical problems like heart disease. Most workaholics are either perfectionists or those who have a need for control — or a combination of both traits.

Workaholics can harm company efficiency as well as co-workers' morale. If the workaholic is a manager or a top executive, they may expect long hours from subordinates, may force them to try to meet impossible standards, and then rush in to save the day when the work is deemed substandard since the staff is full of nincompoops. The workaholic may look like a hero coming in to solve crisis after crisis. Sometimes, the workaholic may have unwittingly created the problems to get the endless thrill of more work.

Workaholic-ism is nurtured by addiction-cum-obsession. Workaholics usually bury themselves in work to escape from a bad relationship or to make up for an absence in one's personal life. The quickest way for workaholics to cure themselves is to *manage time effectively* — inside office and outside it. After office hours, disconnect yourself from work; mobile phones and laptops are not an extension of the human body. For the workaholic to overcome their obsession to work, they need to turn off and put away those devices and take time out to relax, exercise, and spend time with family and friends. If you are unable to do it on your own, consult a doctor and get professional help before it is too late.

3. Mindset of Bad Employees

For the employers, bad employees are their worst nightmare. Now, all organizations have a fair share of good and bad employees, though degrees vary. In some organizations, the split is wide open; in others, it is an undercurrent. It is easy to spot bad employees when their actions and activities are overt. It is difficult to do so when their actions and activities are covert. Bad employees ruin the reputation of the company, destroy employee morale, stall production, decrease sales and keep the work environment tense.

To grow in any organization and rise to the top, you must not only steer away from trouble but also not be seen to befriend bad characters. There are many types of bad employees with inclinations for wrongdoing, and it is essential to know their characteristics so that you could detect them from afar and stay away from them.

Some examples of bad employees with negative tendencies are those who

- **Always talk badly.** They make themselves look good by making others look bad. They are disrespectful, abusive and vulgar, and use rude language towards their co-workers, managers, the opposite gender, clients and customers.
- **Gossip and fight.** They either start rumours in the office or chat with their co-workers to collect gossip about others. They tattle around and then pretend to be shocked that everything is out in the open. They promote a negative work environment so that employees fight with each other.
- **Act religious.** With religious ringtones on their mobile phones, they begin their sentences with reference to the gods and flaunt external symbols of religious rituals. But their deeds are shockingly corrupt and evil.
- **Lack initiative to work well.** They are lazy and always make excuses for their poor performance. They procrastinate and never meet deadlines, always asking for extensions. They are incompetent but act as if they were the hardest working employees in the office. They are on the rosters only for the pay.
- **Act authoritarian.** They think they are always right and argue over everything, even if they are new to the job. They put themselves in charge and order the co-workers around.
- **Are mentally or emotionally unstable.** They lose their emotional balance easily and break down over small issues. Their unpredictable mood swings and violent temper tantrums can endanger co-workers and customers.
- **May have a history of criminal offences.** They may have been involved in cases of fraud, violence, sexual abuse, stealing or other serious offences which may damage the name and reputation of the organization.

KNOW YOUR BRAIN STRUCTURE

Psychology journals have documented that good behaviour goes unnoticed, but bad behaviour gets noticed. At times, people behave badly to draw attention to themselves, never mind the harm it causes to others. Breaking the law gives some people a 'high'. Are you among them? Do you attract bad company? Do you take risks? Do you bend rules? Do you take the law in your

> *If someone is going down the wrong road, he doesn't need motivation to speed him up. What he needs is education to turn him around.*
>
> Jim Rohn

hands? Are you a bully? Do you flirt with danger? It is all in the mind. Your behaviour is 'wired' to your brain. The 'wiring' in the brain stimulates you to act the way you do.

Let us look at the brain. The frontal lobe of the human brain is divided down the middle into two halves, known as the left brain and the right brain. There's a big cord-like fold dividing the brain into two distinct and separate parts. The two parts are connected to each other by a thick cable of nerves at the base of each part and are linked to the spinal cord.

How does information come into the brain? A lot of information comes in through the spinal cord at the base of the brain. If the spinal cord is severely damaged, you won't be able to move or feel anything in your body. Information goes out from the brain to make body parts such as arms and legs do their job. There is also a great deal of incoming information such as hot, cold, pain and joint sensations. Vision and hearing do not go through the spinal cord but go directly into the brain. That is why a person can be completely paralysed, unable to move their arms and legs, but still see and hear with no problems.

Different parts of the brain control different bodily and mental functions. The left side of our body is 'wired' to the right side of our brain and vice versa. For whatever reason nature did this cross-over, it applies even to our eyes, which process a majority of their sensory data on the opposite sides of the brain. Research tells us that the right brain and the left brain are responsible for different thought patterns and behaviour traits and that the way in which a person thinks and acts depends on which side of the brain is dominant. But this does not mean that a person who is left- or right-brain-dominated does not use the other part of the brain at all. For instance, a lefty doesn't keep his right arm hanging uselessly. It is just that one side of the brain is *more* dominant than the other. In most cases, the two parts of the brain work in tandem to enable people to function as well-rounded personalities.

TWO BRAINS WORKING IN TANDEM

Has this happened to you? You met an old acquaintance. You recognised her instantly but couldn't remember her name. Or, your colleague talked about a common friend. You remembered the name but couldn't put a face to it. In the first instance, when you met an old acquaintance, your right brain instantly recognised her while the left brain dozed off. Since the left brain 'napped', you couldn't put a name to that face. In the second instance, the left brain immediately recalled the name of the common friend spoken about while the right brain dozed off. The right brain failed to put a face to that name, so you had no visual to associate with the name. When you are in the company of people, this can be quite annoying or irritating: inability to put a name to the face, or a face to the name, can bring you embarrassment. In normal circumstances, you are expected to remember the name of the person who was known to you. You are expected to recall the face of the person who you knew and whose name was mentioned in conversation. The coordination happens only when the left and the right brain work in tandem.

> *What is the recipe for successful achievement? To my mind there are just four essential ingredients: Choose the career you love, give it the best there is in you, seize your opportunities, and be a member of the team.*
>
> Benjamin F Fairless

While we have a natural tendency to lean towards one way of thinking, the two sides of our brain usually work together in our everyday lives. Since the right brain absorbs new information in chunks, it is the job of the left to sift and sort it in an organized fashion. The right brain focuses on the visual and processes information in an intuitive and simultaneous way, looking *first* at the whole picture and then at the details. The focus of the left brain is on verbal, processing information in an analytical and sequential way, looking *first* at the pieces and then putting them together to get the whole. In the normal course, both sides of the brain work in consonance, mixing and matching each side's abilities as a fully functional human brain. However, there is no clear-cut definition of the functions of the two parts of the brain. Each can do the work of the other effectively, though not efficiently.

RIGHT BRAIN AND LEFT BRAIN FUNCTIONS

Working on improving your manners, behaviour and habits was never made easier than this. No one ever pointed out to us that our actions were the result of mis-wiring in the brain and not that of our being delighted in causing disappointment or hurt to others. New research on behaviour has proved that the origin of our actions lies in the brain. Not knowing what actions originate from

> *Don't limit yourself. Many people limit themselves to what they think they can do. You can go as far as your mind lets you. What you believe, you can achieve.*
>
> Mary Kay Ash

which side of the brain will lead to confusion and frustration. On the other hand, knowing the functions of the right and the left brain will strengthen your resolve to apply your mind to improving your personality. By identifying the characteristics, capabilities and functions of the left and the right brain and by knowing how both sides process information, you will

(i) easily reinforce the skills which come to you naturally;
(ii) quickly sharpen those skills which are 'rusty' and 'forgotten'; and
(iii) eagerly learn new skills to present yourself as a polished, cultured and multi-faceted personality.

RIGHT BRAIN	LEFT BRAIN
• **Visual:** focusing on images, patterns	• **Verbal:** focusing on words, symbols, numbers
• Intuitive, led by feelings	• Analytical, led by logic
• Processes ideas simultaneously	• Processes ideas sequentially, step by step
• 'Mind photos' used to remember things; writing things down or illustrating them helps you remember	• Words used to remember things; you remember names rather than faces
• Makes lateral connections from information	• Makes logical deductions from information
• You see the whole first, then the details.	• You work up to the whole step by step, focusing on details.
• Organization skills lacking	• Highly organized
• Free association	• Likes making lists and planning
• Likes to know why you're doing something or why rules exist (reasons)	• Likely to follow rules without questioning them
• No sense of time	• Good at keeping track of time
• You may have trouble with spelling and finding words to express yourself.	• Spelling and mathematical formula are easily memorized

• You enjoy touching and feeling actual objects (sensory input).	• You enjoy observing.
• Trouble prioritizing, so often late, impulsive	• You plan ahead.
• Unlikely to read instruction manual before trying	• Likely to read an instruction manual before trying
• You listen to how something is being said.	• You listen to what is being said.
• You talk with your hands.	• Rarely use gestures when talking
• You're naturally creative.	• You're naturally organized.
• You think better lying down.	• You think better sitting up.
• You prefer visual instructions with examples.	• You prefer verbal instructions.
• You love cats.	• You love dogs.
• Good at sports, philosophy and religion	• Good at maths and science
• You look at similarities.	• You look at differences.
• You prefer summarizing to outlining.	• You prefer well-structured assignments instead of open-ended ones.
• You know object function.	• You know object name.
• You are restless during long verbal explanations.	• You can remember verbal material.
• You absorb ideas in chunks.	• You're skilled at sequencing ideas.
• You're a lumper: connectedness is important for you.	• You're a splitter: distinction is important for you.
• You are intuitive.	• You are rational.
• You respond to demonstrated instructions.	• You respond to verbal instructions.

• You solve problems with hunches, look for patterns and configurations.	• You solve problems by looking at the parts of things logically and sequentially.
• You're fluid and spontaneous.	• You're planned and structured.
• You prefer elusive, uncertain information.	• You prefer established, certain information.
• You prefer drawing and manipulating objects.	• You prefer talking and writing.
• You like open-ended questions.	• You like multiple-choice tests.
• You're free with feelings.	• You control your feelings.
• You prefer collegial authority structures.	• You prefer ranked authority structures.

STIMULATE YOUR BRAIN TO FUNCTION POSITIVELY

The information given in the two columns above throws light on which side of your brain stimulates and controls which behaviour of yours. To improve your behaviour, look at your positive and negative traits. Identify them one by one, make a note of where they stem from, and think of ways to either change them or polish them. To fine-tune your personality, first study your strengths and weaknesses, its pros and cons, and then begin to 'readjust' your behaviour traits. With the precision of a lab technician, study and understand the functions of the right and the left brain to improve your personality.

> *The highest reward for a person's toil is not what they get for it, but what they become by it.*
>
> John Ruskin

For instance, if you want to control distractions, you must first find out which side of your brain stimulates restlessness. On the other hand, you may have trouble being creative because you are overly analytical. Like a skilled lab technician, tell yourself you will not fight your natural instinct of order. Instead, you will explore new methods to nurture creativity and practise new techniques which blend with the part of your brain that is analytical and organized. To further explain this idea, suppose you are structured in your habits and you take pride in being organized, then don't look for ways to become *more* creative at the cost of dismantling your old habits of 'structure'. The downside of creative people is they tend to be disorganized, lack time management, and are unable to prioritize well.

MAKE YOUR BIRTHDAY RESOLUTIONS MEANINGFUL

No matter how old you are, or how set you are in your ways, with this knowledge at your command you have in your hand the master key to effect whatever changes you want in your personality and behaviour. The more you understand how your mind works, the more you will be in control of your behaviour. Many people renew pledges to improve themselves on the New Year's Eve only to fall back on old habits after the New Year's Day celebrations. A good time to take stock of your 'Purpose of Life and Living' is your birthday. On your birthday, make a firm resolution to rid yourself of mental sloth and lazy habits and transform your personality. As you cherish your family, relatives and close friends on your birthday, so will you cherish the gift of life and your resolution to live a more meaningful life as a better human being.

AMBITION – YOUR SUCCESS TRIGGER

The Gfk Roper Youth Report pointed out that Indian youth are more ambitious than their counterparts throughout the world. It was also observed that compared to their global counterparts, Indians readily walked the extra mile and worked extra hours, even on holidays, to meet company deadlines. But, what went unmentioned was the fact that in most cases, those who kept slogging and putting in extra hours hardly received anything extra in return. You may be a hard worker, but working without a goal and a plan is to work without ambition.

> *Keep away from people who try to belittle your ambitions. Small people always do that, but the really great make you feel that you, too, can become great.*
>
> Mark Twain

Ambition has many definitions — from the bad to the good. It can be termed as the inner drive that pushes you to achieve your aims through whatever means. Too much ambition can result in being ruthless and having negative social character traits. Overly ambitious people are greedy. Greed is a strong driving force. Competitiveness, jealousy and vainglory are offshoots of greed that compel people to take high risks. Risk-taking is 'wired' in the brain; so also the proclivity to be law-abiding or to bend rules is controlled by the brain. One way or the other, the brain controls all your actions.

John Baldoni writes in an article for *Fast Company*, "Ambition by itself is neither positive nor negative. What you do with the drive, like all human drives, is what matters… If ambition causes you to cut corners ethics-wise so much so that you sacrifice integrity and values, then ambition can be destructive. Conversely, if you channel your ambition into fulfilling organizational goals that build a stronger and better company and do it in ways that help employees and customers, then ambition is a positive." Employers like ambitious workers.

Ambition is the strong power drive for success and is a positive personal character trait. A person with ambition dreams of moving up the corporate ladder. An ambitious person is hardworking in striving to achieve goals. If you are ambitious, you will make extra effort to learn new skills to add more value to your brand so that you will quickly make a mark for yourself in your job and get the promotion you worked hard at.

WORKPLACE ETHICS

Chapter 3

GIVE YOUR BRAND THE MORAL SEAL

WORKPLACE ETHICS

After working for 14 years, Parvathi was fired as senior housekeeper in a hotel in Mumbai. To be employed in an iconic five-star deluxe hotel which enjoyed international recognition was indeed prestigious. Parvathi spoke English, Marathi, Hindi and German fluently. She was good at her job. The weekly tips in pounds, euros and dollars, when added, amounted to more than the month's salary she earned. In addition, she used her handbag to carry items of exotic caviar, dairy, meat and seafood products, liquor and cutlery. Occasionally, she brought home silk neckties and scarves, undergarments, jewellery, wallets, mobile phones and laptops. With the passage of time, she became reckless and greedy.

Parvathi's husband was an electrician. He was a casual employee in the state government establishment. After every few months, he would be 'rested' and then re-employed. Her husband helped her sell off her 'earnings' in the grey market. It took the company some years to zero in on Parvathi because she was its model employee. Indeed, she was a trusted employee. Her superiors were shaken by the betrayal of trust by one of its star employees. The GM summoned her to his office and in quiet dignity asked for her resignation. The company allowed her a quick and quiet exit.

Unethical behaviour in the workplace, like Parvathi's, is rampant in many companies. The continued presence of unethical workers bleeds the company, and when they are caught the exposure gives the company a bloody nose. They know that globally recognised companies with high reputation will not risk their reputation to make a public display of employees caught in unethical practices. This emboldens employees to dare companies to take the legal course. The law is weak on corruption and the cases drag on for decades.

Weak laws are no excuse for employees to behave unethically. To rise above, employees must hold themselves responsible and accountable for their behaviour in the workplace.

Like Narayana Murthy and Anna Hazare in India and Howard Gardner in the US, many voices are raised by leading business houses, educational institutions, NGOs and social activists on the urgent need for tough legislations on ethics. The human species is the worst predator on the planet. Without a strict code of ethics, humans usurp its wealth of natural resources to fuel their greed and exploit fellow humans for personal aggrandizement. Plundering, cheating, bribing, stealing, extortion, coercion, nepotism, and misuse and abuse of position, rank and authority, backed by toothless laws, are symptoms of a society afflicted by the cancer of corruption. The cause of corruption is the lack of morals and ethics in public life. Corruption has no boundaries and it is not the preserve of any creed, caste, colour or nation. In fact, the political machinery could be held responsible for the collapse of ethics in public life. Wherever corruption and bribery are rampant, you will notice that dishonest bureaucrats and corrupt politicians have cocked a snook at ethics by weaving a web of ineffective laws to protect and obscure the sources of slush money. Weak laws offer loopholes for murky transactions. Like maggots on festered wounds, unscrupulous businessmen feed on weak laws left open by their political benefactors. When strict regulations supported by harsher penalties are enforced, ethics will perhaps have a chance.

WE LIVE IN A FISHBOWL

People say the world has shrunk to the size of a global village, and we live in a global village. That is not true. The world has shrunk further — to the size of a fishbowl. Believe it or not, we live in a fishbowl. There is no place to hide. Just when you think you have created foolproof smokescreens to mislead people, strong winds of transparency blow them away to reveal the misdeeds, leaving you embarrassingly naked. The words you have weaved to cover your misdeeds are on public display. You tell tall tales, burp, belch, snort, sneeze, skid or fall — it is all there for public consumption on www, Facebook, sms and Twitter. No matter how deep you have buried the contentious bone of ethics, some reporter with the nose of a bloodhound will dig it out and wag it under your nose and bay for your blood. Never before was private life so ruthlessly questioned in the public domain, and never before had personal greed and 'vaulting ambition' so brazenly defied the logic of good sense, fair play, morals and ethics. Murky tales on dark deals of deceit which were secretly sealed in private chambers of intrigue, are exposed to the public in sordid stories with immoral endings.

Human beings love to listen to stories — and get taken in. Conversations, presentations, and sales pitch are about stories. Human chatter is about stories. Everyone has a story to tell — of good deeds and bad deeds, of selling and buying, of hopes and dupes. Some have compelling stories to tell and some make up stories. Political leaders tell high-minded stories at election time and fail to live up to them. Some corporate leaders do the same to their employees and shareholders and have fallen flat on their faces embroiled in scams and scandals. Fishbowl transparency demands ethically transparent lifestyles. The time has come for leaders to walk the talk in public view. It is important for leaders to tell compelling and morally enriched stories since the audience craves for them; but it is also more compelling for ethical leaders to live the stories they tell. 'Walk the Talk' is about ethical action, not about platitudes.

DELIVER WHAT YOU PROMISE

The client had a foolproof case. The lawyer studied the case file and assured the client of 100 per cent success in the case. The client gave the lawyer the case file and a fat cheque as retainer fee. As soon as the client turned his back, the crooked lawyer brokered a deal with his counterpart in the opposite party in exchange for the file. In another example, a sales executive promised the customer a one-year replacement guarantee on the product with six after-sales free service plan for three years. But the company's warranty card did not cover this. In yet another instance, a company salesman boasted about the product he was selling. It supposedly was capable of doing many things because it had superior features, which actually it did not. Or, recently you did business with a company representative who introduced himself a notch higher in the organization's rank, giving you the impression that you were dealing with the company's VP. Why did they do what they did, you will ask. And they would shamelessly answer that to do business nowadays, one has to be pliable. Is that true, or is truth 'pliable'? Could they deliver what they promised to clients and customers?

You have heard of students graduating in business, medicine, engineering, accounts, aviation, law, etc., who cheated and passed the exams. Or, you have heard of teachers and professors who wrote 'guide books' on the subjects they taught

> *To give real service you must add something which cannot be bought or measured with money, and that is sincerity and integrity.*
>
> Douglas Adams

and the students who bought the books passed the exams with very high marks. The air you breathe is polluted. The milk you drink or offer at the temple and the sweet *prasad* you devoutly consume is mostly adulterated; and, to top it all, to get a birth or death certificate, you have to bribe the *babu*. The municipal sweepers who clean the roads and pavements near your residence demand *baksheesh*. On a larger scale, politicians and businessmen have siphoned off billions in shady deals — a few got caught and went to jail.

CAUSE OF BREAKDOWN IN ETHICS

People lament that the youth of today have no moral conscience and ethical values. Why blame the youth for it? When you look at the moral fibre of people who head the ministries and departments of education, the truth will reveal itself. A century ago, honest people with high ethical and moral values wanted to pass those values to future generations, so they introduced catechism and moral-science classes in the school curriculum. A century later, very clever people with no ethical values wanted to ensure that future generations were never reminded about ethics and morality, so they deleted catechism and moral-science classes from the school curriculum on frivolous grounds of caste and creed. That was the beginning of the downfall of ethics and morals in public life.

Today's youth worship the power of money. And rightly so, because that is what they were taught during their impressionable years. If today's youth are unable to touch their conscience, it is because they were never taught how to do so. Those clever people, the guardians of education who deleted catechism and moral-science classes from the curriculum, introduced in their place subjects on money matters — how to make money and how to hoard money — never mind the means to the end. And that is the way business conducts itself today; the means are compromised to achieve the end. "*More* profit" is the business mantra.

In the bygone generation, when students learned catechism and moral science, they were taught about compassion and conscience. Children were taught how to get in touch with their conscience through stories, parables and anecdotes with moral endings, which also included prayer, reflection, meditation and contemplation. Catechism and moral-science classes taught students, during those impressionable years, very important life skills related to morality, ethics and social behaviour. The youth of the past had a moral conscience and their business decisions were governed by a sharp business mind as well as ethics. They, too, worked for profit; but the means were not compromised to justify the end.

ETHICAL VALUES ARE ETCHED IN THE SOUL

In the absence of the 'inner voice of conscience' which governs an individual's ethical behaviour as well as that of strict laws to govern societal ethical behaviour, corruption seems to have had a stranglehold on the moral life of society and goes unchecked. Despite the ethical vacuum, people are still morally aware of right from wrong, and good from bad. The distinction between good and bad, between right and wrong is intrinsically etched in the soul of every individual, and they inherently know in the recesses of their subconscious level the difference between good deeds and bad deeds. To know the difference between right and wrong is called discernment. When you exercise the knowledge that processes moral values, you keep discernment awake in your conscience. Discernment is asleep when you do something bad or wrong which negatively impacts others and you justify your wrong deeds. Also, there are people who intentionally commit wrong deeds so that others get blamed for it and are made to suffer. They consider themselves smarter than others because they were not caught. This chapter is an attempt to ignite your soul and awaken the power of discernment in your conscience. When you become aware of right from wrong and good from bad, your inner voice of conscience, which governs your attitude and behaviour, will give you an ethical edge to succeed in the workplace.

> *Ethics is knowing the difference between what you have a right to do and what is right to do.*
>
> Potter Stewart

It was reported that some educational institutions across the country were trying to find the best way to impart ethics to the youth. Some were employing ethics courses tied to specific disciplines such as business or law. Others were toying with generic ethics courses. Some were teaching basic ethical principles. Others preferred case studies. All that may sound good until you realized that very little, if any, of it had anything to do with discernment — teaching students to understand the difference between right and wrong will help them make ethical choices.

The study of ethics must be integrated into disciplines such as Business Ethics, Commerce Ethics, Law Ethics, Medicine Ethics and Hospitality Ethics, as opposed to Business and Ethics, Commerce and Ethics, etc., as is currently taught. Classes on Ethics must not be offered as optional subjects. Rather, the study of ethics should be integral to the study of all disciplines so that the practice of ethics will govern every sphere of human interaction.

When disciplines of art, commerce and science are intertwined with principles of ethics, people will not shy away from making ethical choices.

A systematic failure in teaching, promoting and upholding ethics does not mean a complete breakdown in the practice of ethics. Thankfully, the study of ethics is not similar to that of maths. If you never studied trigonometry, you could be a trigonometry dud for the rest of your life, and that will not make you unethical. Unlike the subject of maths, the seeds of morality and ethics are planted in the souls of people. Like all human beings, you too possess intrinsic knowledge of good and bad. Whether you have the discernment to use that knowledge depends on your perceived conduct and behaviour. Your employers, superiors and co-workers also are gifted with the intrinsic knowledge of good and bad and instinctively know what is morally right and wrong. That is why most corporate houses expect their employees to conduct themselves as morally good human beings whose behaviour reflects good ethics.

CORPORATE RESPONSIBILITY AND COMPLIANCE

In the absence of a strict code of ethics, business enterprise in India remains severely bruised by major scams, though not dented. That is because there are many institutions, corporate houses, entrepreneurs and professionals who support and uphold high ethical values and practices. Such companies are at pains to consciously project an ethical image, and ensure that their employees' work culture supports and enhances it. While some corporate houses make a conscious effort to teach basic work ethics to their employees, most institutions ignore the issue, presuming that employees already possess good ethics and are expected to work in an ethical manner. They presumably equate the employees' qualifications, work experience and competency to good ethics.

> *We need timeless principles to steer by in running our organizations and building our personal careers. We need high standards. . . the ethics of excellence.*
>
> Price Pritchett

More and more employees rely entirely on their college background and qualifications to find or hold a job. Your academic background trains you to master the hard skills which are essential to apply for the job. But 'workplace readiness' demands more than just hard-skills training. Employers expect workers to have soft skills before they are hired for the job. These include diligence, positive attitude, regular attendance, good character and business etiquette — in other words, employers look for workers with strong work ethics. To get the job and hold on to it and then grow in it, you need to acquire the whole gamut of values-based skills which form your core personality. From making a good first impression to knowing what interpersonal skills are required, you also need to be aware of what the employers look for, look at, and measure when they hire and promote employees. Employees who are unaware of the company's expected standards on corporate behaviour risk promotions or even their jobs.

Ethical employees are critical to the success of any business. As an executive of the company, you must be able to recognise and filter out the good from the bad. Employees who consistently demonstrate good work ethics are invaluable assets to the company. Honest officers who perform their duties with high ethical standards must be rewarded and must not be sidelined or persecuted as is the practice in some public and private sector companies.

EMPLOYEES' SUCCESS STRATEGIES

Don't mess with your brand value if you want that job, raise or promotion — or simply want to be recognised as a person of honesty and integrity. Don't ever feel that you are stuck in a monotonous job. If you feel that your job is monotonous, don't blame the job; blame it on your negative attitude. Remember the old saying that an idle mind is the devil's workshop? Do you work for the devil? The devil runs a workshop called monotony, which breeds negative attitude and sustains itself with negative thoughts. You must convert monotony into success. Don't be lazy and you will be able to kill monotony and put a shine to your brand value. You will automatically enhance the value of your brand when you embrace ethical values of self-discipline.

Put yourself in your employer's shoes and you will know exactly what your boss expects of you — an employee of value. In addition to your job qualifications and work experience, your superior looks for personal values, characteristics and personality traits that project good ethics. As soon as you join the company, you must show that you have the right personality traits which the company values. Do not make the mistake of missing the opportunity to show your supervisors that you have what it takes to be successful on the job, and that you possess all the personal characteristics the company's promoters value. Being sensitive to what the company and your superiors value will bring you long-term recognition and rewards. Take every opportunity that is available to learn to adopt new behaviour skills along with new working methods that are required for success in the workplace.

CORE VALUES EMPLOYERS EXPECT

When employees are hired they are expected to bring to the workplace three ethical values or personal qualities that cannot be taught on the job. The three core values expected of you are:

- i) good attitude;
- ii) good work ethics; and
- iii) good morals.

If employers bypass these virtues when making the selection, it will be difficult for the company to build a good team of workers. Employees without positive core character traits are bad choices since attitude, good behaviour and morals cannot be taught on the job. Employers must properly screen the candidates and make sound hiring decisions to weed out those prospective employees, especially in leadership or supervisory positions, who do not have these three core characteristics.

Employees, on their part, must learn to broadcast their moral and ethical values alongside their technical skills. Go ahead and make a fresh start. Show your boss and your co-workers the *really* real stuff you are made of. You are the embodiment of the three core ethical values which employers look for in employees. You can demonstrate the three core values of your character through strong work ethics and a sharp moral conscience. You work with honesty, integrity and sincerity. You manage time efficiently. You maintain a professional attitude. And, most important of all, you are a dependable and reliable worker. The following tips will help you reinforce and master core ethical skills in the workplace:

> *In law a man is guilty when he violates the rights of others. In ethics he is guilty when he thinks of doing so.*
>
> Immanuel Kant

1. Strong Work Ethics

Show good work ethics at the workplace. Employers value employees who are willing to work hard. In addition, it is important to work smart, for which you have to learn new and efficient ways to complete tasks and save time while completing daily assignments. Doing more than what is expected on the job is a good way to show the management that you utilize good time management skills and don't waste valuable company time attending to personal issues not related to the job.

2. Moral Conscience

Good parenting is at the root of developing a moral conscience. Having good morals comes from being raised to understand what is fundamentally right and wrong. More than likely, your moral conscience was probably set by the time you were 10. People learn about moral values as they grow up at home under the influence of their parents. By the time you enter the working age, it's probably too late to learn good morals. As a child, you were also influenced by the attitudes of others towards work. If a parent demonstrates a dislike for a job or a fear of unemployment, children will tend to assimilate the same parental attitudes. Parents who demonstrate a strong work ethic tend to impart a strong work ethic to their children.

> *Even the most rational approach to ethics is defenceless if there isn't the will to do what is right.*
> Alexander Solzhenitsyn

3. Honesty and Integrity

Employers value employees who maintain a sense of honesty and integrity above all else. Good relationships are built on trust. When you were hired for the job, the employer made the first move by reposing trust in you. Thereafter, it is payback time; it is your responsibility to prove to the company that you will discharge your duties with honesty and integrity. You may think you are smart when, on the sly, you visit social network sites, download games, surf the net, text messages or send emails to friends on company time. But that is not being honest. Employers want to know that you are trustworthy and that they can trust what you say and what you do, especially when you are not being supervised.

4. Work with Sincerity

Reporting late to the office and leaving early or loitering at colleagues' desks, lingering over breaks and having extended lunch hours can keep insincere and lazy employees busy at the workstations throughout their careers. Who cares if very little gets done — or nothing at all? They do all they can in their power and make every effort to pack in a full month of dishonest work, for which they will claim full salary. People who are work-conscious feed the mind with disciplined thoughts. Employees who work with sincerity don't procrastinate, or shirk from work. They are systematic in their approach to the day's work; they identify the jobs that have to be done and make sure they do it well in time.

5. Manage Time Efficiently

To show your superiors that you are a good worker, you must learn to manage your time effectively and efficiently. If you lack time management skills, you will be perceived as a lazy or confused worker because no matter how hard you work, you will never be able to accomplish your task in time. Sincere employees who can manage their work and time efficiently are invaluable assets to the company. Time-conscious employees understand their responsibilities and execute their jobs without any prodding from superiors.

6. Professional Attitude

Employees who whine, complain and find faults with co-workers are not projecting a professional attitude in the workplace. Similarly, employees who share their private lives with their colleagues or speak badly about co-workers and superiors do not project a professional attitude. If you need advice on emotional issues it is best you seek professional advice but not in the workplace and definitely not during office hours. Employers value employees who demonstrate professional behaviour at all times during office hours. Employees who work their careers with a professional attitude, look, speak and dress to maintain a polished corporate image.

7. Dependability and Reliability

Dependability and reliability are very essential qualities in employees. You will find that dependable and reliable employees are regular and punctual to work. Employers value employees who come to work on time, are at the desk when they are supposed to be, and can be relied upon for their actions and behaviour. When employees consistently arrive late at work and routinely fail to complete their projects, the company loses time,

> *The glue that holds all relationships together, including the relationship between the leader and the led, is trust, and trust is based on integrity.*
>
> Brian Tracy

money and business. Employees who sneak in and out of the office or make lame excuses for their absence or delay in completing their tasks are neither dependable nor reliable.

USE ETHICS FOR PROFIT

Being honest to one's job is a challenge many ethical employees face at the workplace. In today's turbulent world, employees of integrity and honesty are hard to come by. It is a known fact that a mere five per cent of the workforce carries the organization to success. The remaining 95 per cent of the workers are hangers-on (parasites) who earn their salaries from the efforts of the five per cent hardworking employees. When so many companies are helplessly stuck with lazy and incompetent workers, the promoters and top executives of those companies must ensure that ethical workers are respected, encouraged and rewarded. Unfortunately, the opposite is true. In companies where the atmosphere is vitiated with sloth and corruption, it is common practice to obstruct, ridicule and persecute hardworking and competent employees who execute their duties efficiently and ethically.

> *Our lives improve only when we take chances – and the first and most difficult risk we can take is to be honest with ourselves.*
>
> Walter Anderson

In some organizations, the moral compass never points north, towards ethics; it usually points in the direction of profits. Top executives encourage workers who are astutely shrewd at circumventing rules to balance their books. In other organizations, the code on morals and ethics is weak and toothless. The workplace could be seething with hostility and negativity because of bad vibes, leading to bad decisions. The top management will have to pull up its socks and address issues on workplace ethics and morality sooner than later. Respect for ethical practices will eliminate workplace hostility and cut-throat competition, and promote employee trust, which will have a positive impact on work productivity and profits.

GET THE JOB YOU WANT

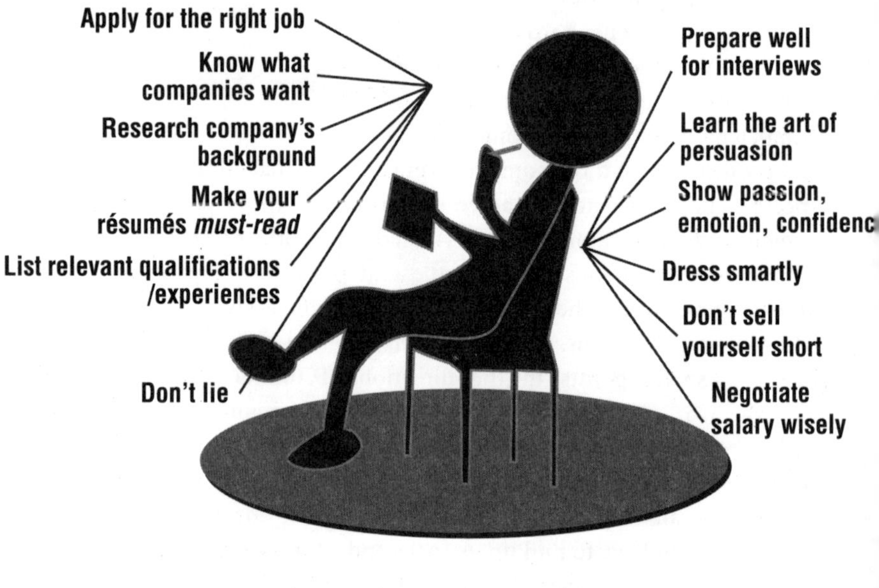

Chapter 4

MARKET YOUR BRAND EQUITY

GET THE JOB YOU WANT

Priyamvada was jobless, desperate and depressed. Seven months had gone by since she did her MBA. On an average she sent out four to six applications a week. Her applications went unanswered.

Nobody spoke English in the outskirts of the town where Priyamvada lived. In school and college, she studied through 'guide books' which were written in the vernacular. English was also taught in the vernacular. She spoke a little English in grammatically fractured sentences and with hesitation. To speak a sentence in English, Priyamvada first thought of the idea in vernacular and then translated it into English.

Some clever instructors at the MBA course showed the students how to solve the English language problem. They downloaded sample résumés from the net and used the cut-and-paste technique. One good résumé will do the trick. It was so simple to master English, they assured the students.

Each year, colleges churn out over three million job-ready youth. In spite of so many companies wanting to hire employees, there is a high rate of unemployment. The youth lack critical skills to make the grade. Ironically, the colleges that certify the youth as 'job-ready' are not in sync with what companies actually want. Priyamvada and the students in her class were misled by their teachers.

You may not realize that you are marketing your personal brand with each résumé you send. With this realization comes the responsibility to rise above mediocrity and seriously prepare for the interview. The chapter on Marketing Your Brand Equity *offers you proper guidance and professional help on the skills and the mindset you need to research the company and the job advertised. You will also learn to write impressive résumés, prepare for the interview, face the interview confidently and get the job you want.*

Every job interview is stressful. Changing jobs, switching them or being jobless is inviting an old friend, *Stress*, to live with you. Old buddy Stress is a very persuasive guest. Once in, he takes over your peace of mind. He dictates your moods. He influences your behaviour. He controls your life, your sleep, everything. And when you go to a job interview, you take with you not only a file folder filled with hopes and aspirations, but also Stress. "Get rid of stress" is easier said than done. But there are ways to tame stress, provided you have a will to do so. You must be ready to dedicate a large amount of time to prepare for each interview. Preparation and practice to improve your social skills will help you take charge of stress and harness its negative influence over you.

From the time you submit your résumé and till the time you are called for the interview, you must be ready and eager to improve your knowledge base and polish your skills. At times you may have felt that, having gone through a few interviews, you have learnt the A to Z of job interviews. If you did not introspect, you learnt nothing. Every job interview should be a learning process. Learn from your mistakes so that you don't repeat them. Carry out a post-interview analysis immediately after the interview is over while it is still fresh in your mind. Review tough questions and make notes for your next interview on areas where you might have handled difficult questions better. Use the experience gained at every interview to improve your technique and overall presentation. To be selected, you need thorough preparation matched with a positive mindset.

YOU CAN GET THAT JOB

> *There are no menial jobs, only menial attitudes.*
>
> William John Bennett

In the book *Put Your Mindset to Work: The One Asset You Really Need to Win and Keep the Job You Love*, Harvard lecturer Paul Stoltz and co-author James Reed revealed that employers are most interested in candidates who have a certain mindset — regardless of skill set. According to Stoltz and Reed, "a resounding ninety-six per cent of employers say they would prefer to 'hire, promote, pay and retain' people with a particular mindset over a desired skill set. And ninety-eight per cent of employers thought it more likely that a person with the right mindset could easily develop the right skill set if they had to, rather than the other way around." When employers hire you for the job, they want to see that you are passionate with fire raging in your belly as well as sensitive.

To package yourself in a manner that you are spotted in a crowd and then chosen for the job, you must know what the interviewer wants. To be short-listed, the interviewee must connect with the interviewer on three levels: (i) intellectual, (ii) experiential and (iii) emotional. Consider this: Out of the many résumés, what was so special about your application that it was set aside by the interviewer and shortlisted? Out of the shortlisted candidates, what was so special about the skills and experiences you had which impressed the interviewer? In the final round, what was so unique about your personality that would benefit the company if they hired you? On the first level of intellectual connection, your academic package coupled with technical skills gave you the edge over others. On the second level of experiential connection, your social skills coupled with job experience which fitted the company's profile, gave you the added edge. On the third level of emotional connection, your passion quotient won you the job. You were able to connect emotionally with the interviewer, who *felt* you could be 'trusted' with the job. In the human equation, passion is the glue that binds trust. A company hires an employee in whom it can repose trust.

EYE-CATCHING ONLINE RÉSUMÉS

Times have changed — and how! Gone are the days of simply mailing your résumés and waiting to receive a call for an interview. The Internet has taken over the recruiting landscape and you are required to submit résumés online. More and more recruiters use the web as a place to search for talent and conduct employment background checks. Your online presence should at least contain social network profiles on Facebook, LinkedIn and Twitter.

Unfortunately, most people have one version of their résumé and concentrate primarily on how it looks on paper, without paying much attention to its electronic version. In fact, most job seekers post and share exactly the same document online without customizing it for the e-world.

While an online résumé brings greater efficiency to the process for recruiters, it can be awfully maddening for job seekers. But it doesn't have to be that way if you know how to navigate the system. In today's world of websites, and electronic applicant-tracking systems, your electronic résumé should be properly prepared

> *Success in the knowledge economy comes to those who know themselves – their strengths, their values and how they best perform.*
>
> Peter F Drucker

for being stored, distributed, tracked and searched electronically through the software tools recruiters use these days.

Posting résumés in outdated or unsupported file formats is the biggest mistake you could make. Never post your résumé in word-processor formats such as Microsoft Word, WordPerfect and Lotus. These formats are less portable and some applicant-tracking systems are bad with handling some of the older and newer formats. The best format for uploading and sharing your résumé electronically is Adobe PDF. It is the most popular and widely supported format for sharing documents and will work virtually everywhere, regardless of the computer brand or the operating system. This format allows you to retain all the font styles and formatting in your résumé so it will look attractive and presentable.

TIPS TO PREPARE POWERFUL ONLINE RÉSUMÉS

Show a Positive Mindset

The résumé is an introduction of yours. It is your first opportunity to make the first great impression on your employers. Presentation matters. Pay heed to your language skills. Never lie on your résumé. Check your internet slate from time to time and keep it clean. Never make yourself out to be what you are not. No matter how smart you think you are, you'll get trapped in your own lies and cut a sorry figure.

List Your Technical Knowledge

List your technical knowledge first, in an organized way. Your technical strengths must stand out clearly at the beginning of your résumé. You should list the relevant buzzwords which reflect your knowledge and experience. List all the operating systems you know. List all the programming languages and platforms you are experienced with. List all the software you are skilled in. Let the interviewer know at a glance where your strengths lie.

Use Keywords Wisely

Your résumé must contain important keywords and you must know how to use them wisely. Think of novel ways to optimize them. For instance, use a highlighter to mark the keywords used to describe the requirements and responsibilities of each position. When responding to a specific job posting, use the technical words from the job description as keywords in your résumé. Figure out how and where to add the most relevant keywords, assuming you have the specific knowledge, skills and experience for the job. Applicant-tracking systems will search for keyword matches — the more the matches, the better, for these often determine if a recruiter opts to view your résumé. Never submit a general résumé or cover letter for all job openings.

Mention Qualifications and Experience

List all your certifications, languages, skills, workshops attended, or anything that could work as a keyword. List your qualifications in order of relevance, from the highest to the lowest. List your degree and educational qualifications first only if they are truly relevant to the job for which you are applying. If you have already done what you want to do in a new job, you may list this first, even if it was not your most recent job.

Avoid Lengthy Résumés

As a rule of thumb, résumés reflecting experience of five years or less should fit on one page. More extensive experience can justify the usage of a second page. Consider three pages as the absolute limit for experiences that run into 15 years and more. Avoid lengthy descriptions of whole projects, of which you were only a part.

Don't Sell Yourself Short

This is by far the biggest mistake of all résumés — technical and otherwise. In trying to be brief, you sell yourself short. Your experiences are worthy for review by recruiters. Treat your résumé as an advertisement for you. "Sell" yourself by highlighting all of your strengths, especially your ethical and moral ones. Employers prefer workers who have honesty and integrity. You should communicate what you are truly and genuinely passionate about. There is far too much competition, and employers like to see people who are enjoying their work because such employees will be more productive and help foster a positive corporate culture.

Keep Your Résumé Error-free

Before you press the 'submit' button, proofread your résumé a number of times for a couple of days to ensure that there are no hidden mistakes. Be sure to catch all spelling mistakes, grammatical errors, unusual punctuations, inconsistent capital words and redundancy of articles (*a*, *an* and *the*). Ask a friend who is attentive to details to review your résumé and to give an honest and objective opinion. Get a third and fourth opinion if you can, just to be absolutely certain that your résumé is without silly mistakes.

WHY PEOPLE FAIL INTERVIEWS

This is not to prophesy your failure at the interview. Instead, this is to give you a peek into the company's recruitment files so that you can prepare yourself in such a manner that you are better prepared to sidestep the pitfalls placed in the path to the job. Get to know in advance what your adversary's game plan will be. When you know the adversary's game plan, you can beat them to their game. It is to your advantage to know what the opposite camp is thinking so that you can prepare yourself by knowing the worst in order to give your best at the interview.

Even a small slip is held against you because the interviewer is on the lookout to catch you on the wrong foot — to fail you. Your faults can range from physical to metaphysical. Any one of the following slips is good enough to fail you. Your command over spoken English is poor. Your English pronunciation, grammar and diction is so bad that it appeared you spoke with marbles in your mouth. You gave irrelevant answers. You sat in the chair before you were told to sit. You squeezed the interviewer's hand hard and shook it vigorously. You were too excited to listen to questions and interrupted the interviewer. Your voice was high-pitched. You spoke with a pretentious accent, sounded pompous and made negative comments about your former employers and co-workers. Your preparation was of poor quality, your presentation was poor, and overall you projected poor communication skills. You were nervous, high-strung and kept pumping your legs. You made bad first impressions. Your mobile phone suddenly shrieked out some crazy ringtone. Your attire was not smart. Your tie was too loud; or was it stained? Your shirt cuffs and collar looked frayed. You pulled out a crushed, bunched-up kerchief to mop the sweat off your nervous face. Your shoes lacked shine while your socks rested over the rim of your shoe line limply. Your cologne gave the interviewer a sneezing fit.

> *When defeat comes, accept it as a signal that your plans are not sound, rebuild those plans, and set sail once more toward your coveted goal.*
>
> Napoleon Hill

WHAT THE COMPANY WANTS – IDEALLY

Ideally, the company is on a search for an employee who is an embodiment of qualities that are superhuman. The potential employee must speak

English flawlessly in a well-modulated voice with a cultured diction and possess persuasive skills good enough to sell air conditioners to Eskimos. They call it 'strong communication skills'. The person must be a computer geek, team player, analytical thinker and problem solver, have polished business etiquette and excellent grooming with high energy levels, be eager to take initiative, work beyond the hours of duty and travel to the ends of the earth at a short notice. The ideal candidate must be honest, loyal, reliable, dedicated, passionate, emotive, gifted with leadership skills and oozing with confidence. Is that realistic? Does such a person exist? This is your challenge to become the person the company wants. When the company is on the lookout for apples, bring them the apples they want, not bananas. If you package yourself exactly as the company wants, the job is yours! The bottom line is: Fit your profile and your portfolio to suit the job requirement and the company's image.

> *People often become what they believe themselves to be. If I believe that I cannot do something, it makes me incapable of doing it. But when I believe I can, then I acquire the ability to do it even if I didn't have it in the beginning.*
>
> Mahatma Gandhi

TIPS TO GET SHORTLISTED AND GET THE JOB

When getting the job you want is your topmost priority, you must prepare yourself for the job interview thoroughly. Your aim is to beat the competition hands down. To be noticed and picked up in the sea full of thousands of candidates is an extraordinary feat that calls for extraordinary skills. You need to know not only what skills are required but also how to acquire them so that you are marked 'extraordinary'. ***Rise Above*** will guide you to brush up and polish the skills you require to get the job you want.

Command over Spoken and Written English

Learn how to speak English because the world does business in English. If your résumé is written in poor English with spelling and grammatical errors, you will never be shortlisted for interviews. To get shortlisted and get the job you want, command over spoken and written English is absolutely essential.

Be the Right Candidate

Your résumé will be shortlisted only if you are able to match your skills, capabilities and achievements to the job requirements. To achieve your goal, you will have to prepare a few draft copies of your résumé before the final copy emerges. Begin by studying the job advertisement very carefully. Write the key job requirements including technical skills, qualifications, age, experience and skills that are considered essential and desirable by the company. Next, write the job description and the qualities required to fill the vacancy. In another column, match them point by point with a statement of what you have to offer. This exercise will give you confidence to make an effective presentation when called upon.

Display Your Accomplishments

Like jewellers who show off the facets of the prized VVS diamond and show how the diamond will enhance the beauty of the person who will wear it, you must display your talents — your polished skills and accomplishments — and show how they will benefit the company. You must convince the interviewer that you would be the best investment for the company if they hired you for the job. The company is a vertical. You, with your accomplishments as an entity, are another vertical. There is no gain for the company or you when two verticals stand parallel to each other. Like the jeweller, you must show how you and your accomplishments will enhance the gains of the company. Match your career accomplishments to what the company is looking for. When answering questions, always link your achievements and qualities to what you know about the company from the homework you did. This is not the time to be modest. Impress upon the interviewer the fantastic asset you will be to the company — the jewel in the crown!

Research the Company

"What do you know about our company?" is an age-old question that still does the rounds. It is vital that you get information about the ownership of the company, its country of origin, products, services, markets, staffing, turnover, everything. Do your homework and be aggressive about it. Visit the company's website and study its vision, mission, product line, financial position, net worth, stock prices, departments, competitive advantages, its five-year growth strategy and future direction. Know who the competitors are. Know everything — find out everything you can about the company. Whatever you discover about the company, discuss it during the interview. This impresses the interviewer. On the other hand, don't rely on advertisements and literature put out by the company as they tend to glorify the company's image. Before you submit your résumé, find out about the company's reputation. Is there a history of good or bad industrial relations? Are there any criminal lawsuits? Are employees happy? Is the company in an expansion mode, or is it the reverse?

The Day Before the Interview

Read the job interview letter once again to verify the day, date, time and venue of the interview. Do you know the venue? Get directions if you are not sure and allow yourself enough time to reach there early. To be very sure, you may visit the place a day or two before to know the shortest possible route. Check your file folder and review the résumé and all documents, reference letters, awards, testimonials and notes which you will carry with you. Though you have sent the résumé online, always carry its two copies laser-printed on plain white bond paper. Hand over one copy to the interviewer and keep the other with you for ready reference. (Avoid back-packs to the interview.) If you carry a briefcase or file folder, it should look new, not shabby. Rehearse your notes and your presentation, especially the short speech on "tell us about yourself." The best way to rehearse is to ask a friend or relative to sit through the mock interviews and field tough questions.

Feel and Look Energized

Get a good night's sleep the night before your interview. You need to be alert, refreshed and cheerful when you meet your interviewers. Don't expect to look your best if you slept past midnight. If you had a late or restless night, you will look tired at the interview and your brain will function sluggishly. You need a sharp mind and good stamina to endure the day. Even though stress will make food taste unpalatable, it is essential that you eat a healthy breakfast or meal before the interview. You don't want to hear the growls of an empty stomach when your mind is focused on the interview. Sound sleep and healthy food will recharge your batteries and you will feel fully energized.

Dress Professional

What will you wear to the interview? Remember to dress simply but elegantly. It is advisable to lay out the clothes you will wear, including the kerchief, and see that they are clean and pressed the night before. Also, put out a clean pair of socks that match the colour of your trousers and polish your shoes the night before. When you are confused about the choice of clothes, choose to dress conservatively. Dress professionally in order to be taken seriously. Employers reject candidates who are dressed inappropriately. They hire candidates whose ensemble fits the image of their company. It's true you won't be offered a job for dressing appropriately. But dressing inappropriately will surely not get you the job. Always dress to make the impression you want: successful, competent and businesslike.

> *Never continue in a job you don't enjoy. If you're happy in what you are doing, you'll like yourself, you'll have inner peace. And, if you have that, along with physical health, you will have had more success than you could possibly have imagined.*
>
> Johnny Carson

Be Punctual

Why do most Indians report late? The reason could be climate. Research shows that in farming countries like India, people are climate-dependent for a good harvest. Life is laid-back there and folks don't feel the pressure of time. Reporting late is a way of life. On the other hand, in industrial countries, where activities are regulated by the clock, people are time-conscious. Reporting in time is a way of life. Problems of punctuality arise when the two cultures blend. A farmer would never fire a worker who often reports an hour late; your company will. A farmer appreciates the worker who lingers on after work hours; your company won't. If you did not apply for a job on the farm, be sure you are punctual for the job interview. Be there 15 minutes early. Never commit to two interviews in the same span, say that of the morning hours. You are bound to be stressed at the first and late for the other.

Release Stress Before You Take the Elevator

You are in front of the office building. Keep your head clear and focused on the purpose of your visit. Don't let negative thoughts overwhelm you. This is not the time to be distracted with stress and tension. The stomach stores not only food but also stress. Some feel nauseous when stressed. Why puke out the food when you can breathe out the stress? When you feel stressed, tense and intimidated, breathe slowly and let the air go right down to the pit of your belly by allowing the belly to balloon. Then breathe out s-l-o-w-l-y as you squeeze your belly in, like deflating a balloon. After letting off the accumulated toxic air, you will feel energized. As you repeat this exercise a few times, give yourself a dose of positive thoughts. Pull your shoulders up, stick your chin out, plant a smile on your face and put that dazzle in your eyes — after all, you are here to dazzle them with your personality and charm them into making you the job offer. Use the power of positivity at your disposal to outshine the competition and get the job.

Face-to-face at the Interview

Your first direct contact with the company is the reception desk or the secretary. If the person is preoccupied, don't lose your patience; you are not at the ticket counter. And why start on a negative note? In some companies, the secretarial staff is told to give feedback on first impressions and behaviour traits of the assembled recruits. On arrival, first put your mobile phone on silent mode and then give the receptionist or secretary your name and the time of your appointment, and at the same time assure the person that you have reached ahead of time and do not mind waiting for your turn. Also, find out if you have to mark your attendance.

When you enter the office, greet the interviewer and wait to be told to sit down. Sit up with your back straight; do not slouch or slump your shoulders. Since interviewers usually sit behind broad desks, do not spill over the desk to reach out to shake hands unless the interviewer reaches out first. When you shake hands, your hand must be firm, not hard, and definitely not limp. It is courteous to ask permission to place the slim file folder — not the briefcase — on the table. Never fold the résumé or other sheets of paper in the folder. Include a pen and writing paper in the folder for taking notes. When requested, provide a typed list of names, addresses, phone numbers and letters of personal and professional references. If you don't want them to think you are ADHD-challenged, don't fidget with your mobile phone, pen, paper, hair, buttons, bows or tie. Don't rearrange objects on the table. Don't sit stiff either. Be enthusiastic. Use your eyes, hands and voice to show your passion and intensity.

During the interview, stay calm and at the same time maintain high energy levels without getting excited. Enthusiasm is an asset while excitement is a liability. Smile to hide the nervous tension whenever you feel it build inside you. Maintain eye contact with the interviewer. You need time to think and come up with bright answers, so listen closely to the interviewer. Listen to the entire question before you answer; be alert and pay attention; or else you will be embarrassed if you forgot what the question was! At times when you are faced with a difficult question and you need a few seconds to think of a smart answer, quickly rephrase the interviewer's question, making it appear that you were listening carefully to what was asked. The seconds you spent rephrasing the question and the milliseconds spent by the interviewer in affirming what you said was ample time for you to come up with a quick smart answer.

INTERACTION WITHOUT CONTRADICTIONS

At the interview, you are the brand, the seller as well as the product. Your time has come to put your brand image on display and sell yourself as a must-buy-now product of high value. In a casual tone the interviewer will say to you, "Tell us about yourself." Don't be fooled by the tone. The tone may be casual but the overtones are serious. As you unwind, the interviewer will study you like some alien bacteria under a microscope. Since you have limited time to paint your self-portrait in the best brushstrokes possible, write down all your accomplishments and rehearse in advance for this moment. You have two or three fleeting minutes to impress the interviewer to put you on the 'must-employ' list. Enumerate your strengths and tell the interviewer in concrete terms the things you are currently working on towards your professional growth which will benefit the company. If you have changed trajectories, talk positively about any career changes you may have had and the experiences you gained which will benefit the new job. No matter how intense the grilling, you must avoid arguments and contradictions.

> *The will to win, the desire to succeed, the urge to reach your full potential, these are the keys that will unlock the door to personal excellence.*
>
> Eddie Robinson

USE THE ART OF PERSUASION TO GET THE JOB

To get the interviewer to agree with you, you must be gentle and sweet and walk the emotional route. *Persuasion* is a Latin word which means 'through sweetness'. You take the emotional route because you quickly want a number of 'yes' responses from the interviewer. A 'no' response is dangerous to the interview. When the interviewer or the client shakes the head in disagreement, it is a signal to quickly apply emergency brakes to your train of thoughts and change tracks immediately. To continue mindlessly on this track is to invite resistance and rejection. Disagreements, arguments and contradictions put out negative auras. From a simple head-shake, you stimulate the glandular, muscular and nervous system of the interviewer into rejecting your ideas and you. The simple head-shake gradually builds resistance in the body to what you said, and the interviewer concludes the interview with an emphatic 'no.' Thereafter, the more you argue and insist on making your point, the more firmly the interviewer affirms you are wrong.

1. Get 'Yes' Responses

To get 'yes' responses, you must enter, figuratively speaking, from the interviewer's door and later come out through *your* door. The key to open the doors of persuasion is already in your hand. The meeting is the common ground of interest to both parties. So use the common-ground advantage. Admire the company and enumerate its many achievements, and you have entered their 'door'. And, now that you are in, understand the situation from their point of view. If you were them, what would you do? What would your opinions and options be? What action would you take that would be beneficial to them? Observe and appreciate how they act, how they speak, how they think and how they function, and begin to reflect their mood and postures. The more you reflect their mood and postures, the more 'yes' responses you will get. You succeeded in entering through their 'door' with 'yes' responses. Your next move is to come out through your door. Which means that you convince them that you are the best person for the job.

2. Use the Mirror Effect

When your gestures, postures and speech characteristics, especially pace, pitch and tone, match those of your interviewer, you are mirroring their body language. We do it all the time when we converse with people we like. When the interviewers are pleased with you, mirror their mood with your body language. It helps create a feeling of empathy, understanding and trust.

On the other hand, when two persons disagree and argue, you will notice that both sides display combative and threatening postures, gestures, voices and tones. When two persons' body language signals are not synchronized (you lean forward to make a point with intensity but the other person pulls back on the seat to create 'distance' between you and what you said), there is disagreement. Conflict arises when mismatched signals translate into unconscious feelings of discomfort, leading to discord or even rejection.

Mirroring is not simply copying, mimicking or imitating. It becomes effective when movements and gestures are reflected in a similar way as the interviewer's so that the effect remains unconscious and subtle. Copying to imitate or mimic your interviewer would be considered as ludicrous and insulting.

3. Strike the Right Emotional Chords

To come out through your 'door' depends on your mastery of the art of persuasion. It entirely depends on how skilfully you have learnt to copy the interviewers' postures, gestures, tone of voice and words. With subtle ease, you must copy their style and their approach as you wax eloquent about your experiences, accomplishments, achievements vis-à-vis the company's future growth. For instance, when an interviewer leans forward to make a point, you cannot pull yourself back; cross your arms and sit smugly. You also draw yourself forward to reflect the intensity of the moment, establishing an emotional bond. This is your moment to assure the interviewers with all the zeal you can command that your competence, your style, your passion and fervour match their company's goals. Speak with gusto and enthusiasm and let your eyes show the depth of your emotion.

Present your ideas with words that convey your depth of feeling and warmth so that you touch emotions rather than intellect. Simultaneously, you must create imagery with words when you appeal to the intellect through feelings rather than exchanging cold ideas, using cold words. To arouse feelings, you must be intensely earnest; your words and gestures must reinforce your message. Your intensity, your sincerity, your enthusiasm must be infectious. Your spirited ideas, shining through your eyes, radiating through your voice and proclaiming through your body language, will appeal to the intellect and emotions of the interviewer. You must keep the 'yes' responses flowing through the head and heart of the interviewer. This will block contradicting and opposing ideas from being voiced. Only when you are able to change the head-shake into head nods, will you have mastered the art of persuasion.

> *The fastest way to succeed is to look as if you're playing by somebody else's rules, while quietly playing by your own.*
>
> Unknown

NEGOTIATE YOUR SALARY

The only reason you worked hard preparing for the interview was to earn a good salary. Unfortunately, most people feel awkward or uncomfortable

> *The man who does not work for the love of work but only for money is not likely to make money nor find much fun in life.*
>
> Charles Schwab

to discuss salaries at the interview because they do not know how to handle the salary negotiation. Take the example of Anthony. He, like many other employees, felt inadequately prepared to negotiate a salary. After he got the job, he realized he was grossly underpaid because the company hired him at less than the market price. Many employees believe that the management pays a pittance for the blood they suck. That could be one of the reasons why employees like Anthony deliberately under-work. To spite the company, they put in less than half their potential at the workplace and spend the rest of the time in inventing novel ways of pretending to work hard without actually working.

When the management sees low morale and bad attitude, they feel justified in paying low salaries to incompetent and inefficient workers. It is a vicious cycle of stimuli and responses. The workers respond to the management's stimuli (low pay), and the management responds to the workers' stimuli (incompetence). The madness should stop because it is a no-win situation for both parties. The company bleeds to give employees like Anthony a bloody nose, while Anthony takes a salary for holding his bloody nose.

KNOW YOUR WORTH

Do your homework well. At the time you research the company where you have applied for the job, you must also find out the salaries the company pays its employees. Are the pay scales on par with other companies? Do they pay on time or is it a payable-when-able policy? Does the company pay additional benefits like commissions, bonus, amenities, annual raise and other perks? Also, find out from friends or relatives what their companies would pay for the job you applied. New jobs are hard to find, but you must also keep your dignity. Before you go for the interview, you must decide on the minimum salary you will accept. When you negotiate a salary, start with a top figure (the market trend) before you settle for the minimum.

If you are desperate to get the job you may want to be flexible and agree to accept the salary they offer. Don't show your excitement to seal the offer so quickly. Wait. Be patient. A low salary comes with an additional offer of allowances, bonuses, incentives and performance-related raise. It is important to keep your cool in spite of the excitement raging inside you when you negotiate the fine print of your salary. In a calm and quiet voice ask the company to specify the benefit package, which includes perks, incentives, allowances, etc. And get this in writing. As with any negotiation, your goal is to have a win-win situation.

BE COURTEOUS

With a pleasing smile, warmly thank your interviewers individually before leaving. Do the same with the secretarial or reception desk. As soon as you reach home, write 'thank you' letters to each person who interviewed you, and send it by post, fax or e-mail. The letter should be very brief. Recap any major assets you would like to remind them of. Correct any issues that you felt might have been misunderstood. If the note is not sent out on the day of the interview itself, it would be a wasted exercise. 'Thank you' letters are surprisingly rare and incredibly effective. Treat your interviewer as you would treat a kind and gracious host.

SECTION II

DEVELOP YOUR PROFESSIONAL PERSONALITY

Chapter 5
EMBELLISH YOUR BRAND IMAGE
Executive Grooming

Chapter 6
ADD POLISH TO YOUR PERSONAL BRAND
Corporate Hygiene

Chapter 7
PRUNE YOUR BRAND IMAGE
Powerful First Impressions

Chapter 8
EMPOWER YOUR BRAND VALUE
Business Etiquette

CHAPTER 9
GARNISH YOUR CORPORATE BRAND
Table Manners

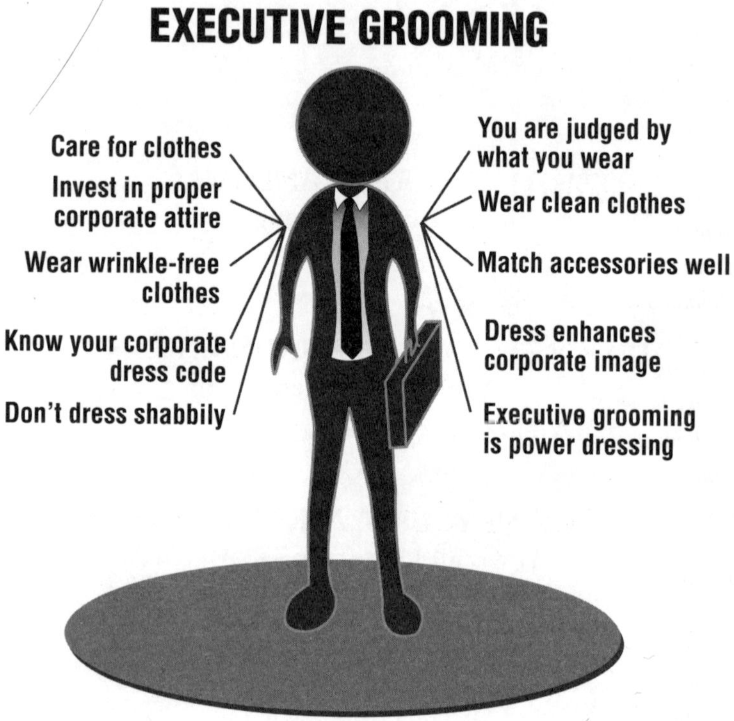
EXECUTIVE GROOMING
Care for clothes
Invest in proper corporate attire
Wear wrinkle-free clothes
Know your corporate dress code
Don't dress shabbily
You are judged by what you wear
Wear clean clothes
Match accessories well
Dress enhances corporate image
Executive grooming is power dressing

Chapter 5

EMBELLISH YOUR BRAND IMAGE

EXECUTIVE GROOMING

Irfaan was a sincere worker — but disappointed. He worked hard because he wanted a promotion and a raise. But nothing of that sort happened. The department he worked in was clannish, he grumbled. The co-workers were not friendly to him. Some of them made fun of him. It was so obvious to him that the HoD was lenient to people of his caste — why else would they put Irfaan down?

Irfaan's focus was on the job and not on grooming. He liked to wear bright-coloured clothes. He was fond of broad stripes and checked shirts and wore them to the office. He also wore T-shirts. On days when employees wore casuals to work, he wore shirts with large flowery prints and faded jeans. He did not know how to wear a necktie so he never bothered to wear one. He walked in slip-on shoes without socks. He usually kicked off his shoes under the desk and worked barefoot, giving his feet 'air to breathe'.

Like Irfaan, many employees develop complexes because they dress shabbily to the office. They may unintentionally dress inappropriately or have a casual attitude towards corporate dress code. They may not know the difference between home wear, casual wear and office wear simply because nobody ever told them about it.

Embellish Your Brand Image *gives you the lever to lift your head in pride and climb the corporate ladder — appropriately groomed. You will learn to dress for the job you want and not for the job you have. Put away your personal complexes and low self-esteem and put on the right dress to rise above, and you will experience total confidence every day you report to work.*

The clothes you wear to the office shout out loud that you either 'belong' to the company or are in the wrong company. To grow in your organization, your office dress must find acceptance by the establishment and not the other way round — that the company must accept the way you dress. To build your professional brand image, you must dress to look competent and as professional as the organization you represent. You are the company's brand ambassador. Even the scent of your cologne must have the soft, subtle power to draw people to you, not drive them away. Quality clothing speaks of money, recognition, dominance and power. It also represents better treatment, service and appreciation. People like to be associated with the leader, especially when such leadership is presented with polish and good taste.

Clothes are expensive to buy. New clothes look shabby and worn out very soon on some people, while others wear their clothes for many years without looking shabby. Some people know how to look after clothes and some do not. Those who look after their clothes get a lot more mileage out of them than people who do not.

HOW TO DRESS RICH

Money saved is money gained, they say. And how true! Before we go into the details of how to invest in clothes, let us first deal with the problem of caring for clothes. When you care for clothes, it will not only save you money but also give you that rich feeling and a confident personality.

You dress according to seasons. When winter is over, you carefully put away your warm clothes and bring out another set of clothes for the summer. For each season you must have at least three separate sets of clothes: (1) for home, (2) for office and (3) for social functions. Clothes you wear at home must never be worn to the office or to a party. Clothes you wear at home during the day are not the same you sleep in. (When you wake up in the mornings in your office or party clothes, it's obvious you have completely lost the compass on good grooming habits. You simply don't care about clothes. If you look around, you will notice that some of the company's chauffeurs dress better than you.) Your office attire must have two sets of clothes: one for daily wear and the other for special occasions. And there are social functions to attend. Social functions also have two sets of clothes — informal and formal. And what you wear at social functions during the daytime is different from what you wear at the evening party.

When you undress, never throw your clothes on the chair, bed or elsewhere. Instead, spread them carefully on a clothes hanger. Clothes hung on pegs soon get shapeless. Clothes that have to be washed must be put away in the clothes bin and not thrown on the floor or hung inside the cupboard. Clothes that are stained must be washed quickly or else the stains cling to the fabric and never come off. When you don't care for clothes and wear clothes that are stained, shapeless and creased, you not only look shabby but also begin to feel worthless.

Crocs and slippers are worn at home, poolside or the beach; never to the office or to formal parties. Sneakers and sports shoes must be worn at casual functions and for sports activities and never as formal wear. Dress shoes made of leather or look-like leather should always have laces for office wear and cut below the ankle — not above the ankle. To ensure that your shoes don't look shabby within a month or two of daily use, invest in two pairs of formal shoes and rotate them every day. Before you wear your shoes, make it a habit to brush and polish them till they shine. Your party shoes should not be your daily office shoes. They could be fancy and fashionable.

INVEST IN PROPER CORPORATE ATTIRE

Buying clothes is a very expensive proposition and you don't go out and buy the whole lot of clothes at one go. You do it gradually over a period of time. Invest in clothes that are contemporary, in-style and attractive, and that at the same time enhance your professional image. In hot and humid weather, you will want to wear cotton garments. The problem with cotton fabric is that it crumples easily and gives you a 'crushed' look even before you have reached office. So, it is wise to invest in cotton-blend shirts and trousers to look fresh throughout the day. Don't buy clothes that are a size too tight with the hope that you will soon jog in the park, work your abdomen at the gym, or go on a diet and shed weight. Always buy clothes that are a little loose than a little tight. A tight outfit makes you look bloated.

When buying clothes as office attire, first look around the office and get to know the company's style and its business character. Take a cue from how the executives are dressed. People in top positions closely watch how their colleagues are dressed. To be perceived by the top executives that you are ready and able to fill a vacancy at the top slot, you must dress for the job you want and not for the job you are in. To get maximum mileage from the clothes you buy, invest in clothes that are in fashion but conservative in style.

MISMATCHED CLOTHES PULL YOUR IMAGE DOWN

More men than women wear mismatched and ill-fitted clothes. Or is it that women can carry it off better than men? More men than women are found to be dressed shabbily. Also, more men than women are untidy in their personal habits. It is observed that among urbanites, 80 per cent men and 20 per cent women are affected by the mismatch bug. And about 20 per cent men and 80 per cent women match their clothes with good style, fit, colours and ensemble.

Each piece of garment you buy that does not match the executive image of the company you work for is an investment blunder. If you are unable to decide what's right and what's wrong in clothes selection, you must seek help either from people you know who have excellent taste in clothes or from an expert — an image consultant. Each time you wear clothes that are mismatched, ill-fitted, or out of sync with the occasion, you not only lose money on your wardrobe investment but also cut a sorry figure before others.

> *Success means having the courage, the determination and the will to become the person you believe you were meant to be.*
>
> Unknown

It is not only your body but your whole personality that is wrapped in the clothes you wear. The way you dress defines your style quotient. Your personality and lifestyle reflect your choice of clothing, hairstyle, accessories, shoes and their maintenance. In fact everything that you put on your body sends a message about your ambitions, expectations and achievements. It is imperative that you take into account your personality (as others will perceive you) by the clothes you wear to the office. Your office attire must make you look comfortable, confident and in control of yourself and enhance the image of the company you represent.

WARDROBE TIPS FOR MEN IN SEARCH OF SUCCESS

You have got to admit it: Men look best when they are dressed in formal attire. There is something about men in suits. They look so thoroughly well-groomed, appear smart, alert and walk with zip in their stride in their polished shiny shoes. In many industries that service high-end clients like multinational banks, deluxe hotels and international airlines, dark suits are the norm. There are some companies that do not insist on a formal dress code, yet their top honchos regularly dress in formal suits or blazers and ties. It has been researched that well-dressed men exude an aura of charm, sophistication and reliability. People readily trust those who are dressed sophisticatedly as compared to those who are dressed casually.

Formal Shirts

Colours and Patterns: Good-quality formal white shirts must be your first choice of investment. Some organizations permit colours other than white. Choose soft colours like pale cream and shades of blue to add to your white collection. Muted patterns and fine pin stripes will add to variety. Avoid checks, bold patterns, feminine prints, loud colours or dull and depressing colours as well as shirts with different-coloured collars and cuffs. For those just starting on a job and on a shoestring budget, a good-quality branded formal shirt may be beyond their means. Some export houses sell bulk 'export quality' shirts to vendors who sell them on city sidewalks at throwaway prices. At the cost of one branded shirt you could pick up four to six shirts on the sidewalk. All shirts, whether they are branded or export-quality, begin to look frayed at the collar and cuffs after two months of regular use.

Size Matters: Wearing the right-size shirt is very important. Sizes vary from brand to brand. When trying on a shirt, check the following:

i) **Collar:** Your shirt collar must be fused, flat and crease-free. Wrinkled collars look 'lived in' and are difficult to wear a tie. After you fasten the collar button, fit your fingers inside the collar. The fingers should move easily — one finger for exact fit; two fingers for comfort fit. When your collar fits you comfortably you will not have the urge to unbutton the collar.

ii) **Shoulders:** To avoid drooping shoulders, the seam of the shirt sleeves should be exactly where the shoulders end and your arms begin.

iii) **Sleeves:** Always wear a long-sleeved shirt when you put on a suit or jacket. Cuffs which are fused and wrinkle-free look elegant. To check the sleeves' length, keep your arms straight down and see that the buttoned cuffs end where the palm of your hand begins. Bring your hand up horizontally to check that the cuffs don't show your wrist bones. Nor should the sleeves flop over your arm because they are too long.

iv) **Buttons:** Make sure you fasten all the buttons on the shirt, including the small ones on the side of the sleeve at the cuff. The tiny buttons make sure that your arm doesn't get exposed at that point. Button-down collars also need to be buttoned. Fasten the collar button only when you wear a tie, and never wear a tie without the collar button fastened. You shouldn't wear shirts with missing buttons.

Your shirt pocket is not a pouch for knick-knacks. Do not stuff coins, pens, mobile phone, ticket stubs, sun glasses or reading glasses in your front shirt pocket. The best place for some of these items is the inside pocket of your suit jacket. If the weather is hot and you are not wearing your jacket, carry those items in a slim leather portfolio. Coins, ticket stubs and other knick-knacks should be put in the wallet. Wear your shirt smartly. Always wear a spotlessly clean and ironed shirt of the right size to feel comfortable and look good. Wearing the right shirt in the right way goes a long way in achieving the right formal image.

Formal Trousers

In companies that are strict about dress code, black, grey, and navy-blue dress trousers are considered as formal wear. Khaki, brown, beige and other sober-coloured (as opposed to red, purple, yellow and pink) trousers are considered as informal wear. Formal dress trousers are neither shaped like jeans nor worn on or below the hips. They are worn either on the navel or just below it — never above the navel. The length of your trousers, when you stand, must touch the upper heel-line of your shoes and never the floor as jeans do. If your socks are seen when you stand, the length of your trousers is too short. When you sit, about two to three inches of the socks will show. Always match your socks to the colour of your trousers. Most companies ban the use of jeans. If you must wear jeans, or pants cut in the shape of jeans, to the office, first check with the company's personnel or HR department if you are allowed to do so.

> *Your life is designed by three designers – circumstances, you and coincidences. Any one can be the chief designer at any particular moment.*
>
> Javed Akhtar

Undergarments

Remember the feeling when it was terribly hot and humid and your clothes were soaking wet with sweat? You felt you were walking in a wet raincoat all day. Don't blame the weather. Blame it on the underwear. You must know what type of undergarment to wear in which climate. People living in hot and humid climate should wear pure-cotton undergarments — no synthetic blends. Humidity makes the body sweat. The cotton underwear absorbs the sweat. The sweat absorbed by the cotton fabric acts like a ventilator and cools the body while the hot and humid air dries up the fabric — and the cycle goes on — keeping the body refreshed. Polyester and synthetic blends bring on the 'raincoat effect' since they do not absorb sweat. The sweat keeps the fabric wet and it clings to your sweat-damp skin like the raincoat. Since the fabric does not absorb the sweat, the hot and humid air takes forever to dry the sweat from the fabric and the body. Accumulated sweat generates bacteria, which also feed on the sweat. Bacteria generate foul odours. The result is you never feel refreshed and you stink. The weather literally wears you down. So now you know why you stink and feel tired! Men should always wear white cotton vests underneath their shirts. When you wear a cotton vest with a little sleeve to it, it not only helps absorb the sweat from the armpits but also prevents underarm sweat from staining the shirt. On the other hand, people living in cold climates should wear polyester-synthetic undergarments and socks which act as thermal wear to stay warm.

Socks

Your choice of socks either enhances your dress sense or becomes your Achilles' heel — a wardrobe *faux pas*. Most men don't pay attention to socks since they stay hidden inside shoes and are covered over by trousers. But when you sit, your trousers ride up, and the gap between the trousers and the shoes, even if it is two or three inches of socks that is visible, reveals a tale of either good breeding or poor taste.

Always match the colour of your socks with your trousers or shoes. White socks, tube and sports socks do not go with formal wear. Nor do bold designs and multi-coloured prints. Dark-coloured socks with either plain or muted self-coloured patterns are acceptable formal wear. Keep a good collection of socks for formal and informal wear so that you never have to repeat the same pair without washing them. Wear your socks that reach to your calves, and stay up. Socks that slip down and bunch around the ankles also pull your image down. While the texture of sports socks is thick, that of formal socks is thin. To get more mileage from a thin pair of socks, buy those with reinforced heels and toes. Never wear socks with holes; they should either be mended or thrown away.

Shoes

Most men look down on shoes and fail to realize how many people judge them by the shine of their shoes. It is time you put away those old pairs of shapeless, run-down, worn-out shoes in which you walk to the office every day. Get yourself a good pair of lace-up dress shoes polished to a mirror-quality spit-shine. When buying shoes see that the shine is mirror-like and not dull matte. Matte-finish shoes never give you the spit and shine you want from your office shoes. The life quality of your shoes depends on how you maintain them. You must get used to walking in a pair of brand new shoes before you wear them for an important meeting or a job interview. To prevent smelly feet and to increase the life of your shoes, you must have two pairs of shoes and rotate them every day. Before leaving home, make sure you polish your shoes to a mirror finish. Sneakers and sports shoes are not encouraged in many organizations. They smell badly in summers and must be washed twice a week and dried in direct sunlight. Before you attend office in sneakers and sports shoes, check with the management if you are allowed to do so.

Ties

Silk ties knot better, but are expensive. When buying a silk tie, pinch the tie gently to check the thickness of the silk. It is the silk fabric that must be thick and not the inner lining. The silk must have weight and fall smoothly, and not twist and turn, when you hold it up the full length from the narrow end. If it twists or turns, put it away. In choosing colours and patterns, observe the ties of top executives in your company and develop a similar taste. It's safe to choose conservative patterns over cartoon characters and psychedelic colours. Ties are never worn with a short-sleeved shirt.

The tie is a Western concept and getting it right can be a pain in the neck, especially in the mornings, when you are rushed for work. Ties have their advantage. They add colour to your ensemble and flair to your personality. If wearing a tie is part of your corporate dress code, you better learn to tie the knot and carry it off with style — sooner than later.

Tips to tie the knot

There are over a dozen different tie knots. The two most popular knots are (i) the Half-Windsor and (ii) the Windsor (or Double Windsor).

You should always wear your tie in front of a mirror to check each step. The mirror comes handy to check the length and adjust the knot to the centre of your collar.

Before you start putting on the tie, button up your shirt, including the collar, and flip up the collar. Also, the broad end is the part of the tie you will manipulate the most; hence, you should let it hang on the side of your dominant hand to facilitate the process. When you pull the knot up, the length of your tie should touch the top of your belt. Ties that are worn too short or hang below the belt present an unprofessional image.

Half-Windsor knot

The Half-Windsor knot is a modest version of the Windsor knot. It can be worn for any occasion. The Half-Windsor enjoys a professional and polished reputation. However, as it is not bulky, it makes for a better option for narrower collars.

6 steps to tie the Half-Windsor knot

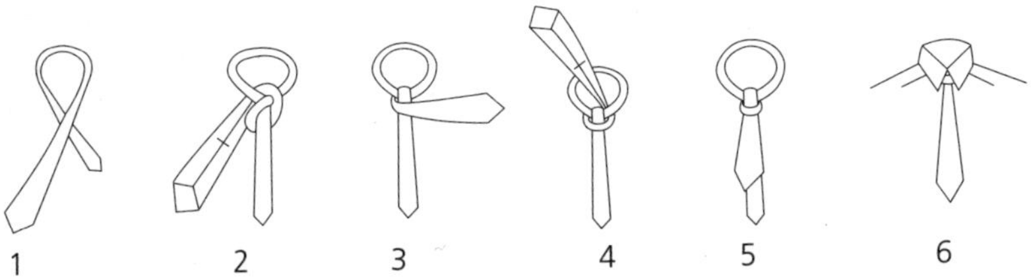

1. Face the mirror and place the tie around your shoulders, top side up, with the broad end hanging roughly 12 inches lower than the thin end.
2. Cross the broad side of the tie over the thin end to make an X fairly close to your neck (around the second shirt button).
3. Pull the broad end behind the thin end to the right, then up in front of it and down through the neck loop.
4. Pull the broad end over from right to left, overlapping your evolving knot.
5. Pull the broad end up through the loop again, behind what now looks like a nearly complete knot.
6. Bring the broad end back down and insert it through the knot.

You can finish your knot by tightening it. In doing so, you will see the beginnings of a natural dimple form. Press your forefinger to manually manipulate it to make the dimple as distinct as possible.

The Windsor knot

The granddaddy of them all, the Windsor is the most traditional knot. The Windsor and the Half-Windsor enjoy a professional prestige and polished reputation. However, the Windsor knot requires a slightly longer tie and drapes well when the inner lining is not thick. It makes a better option for narrow as well as wide spread collars.

8 steps to tie the Windsor knot

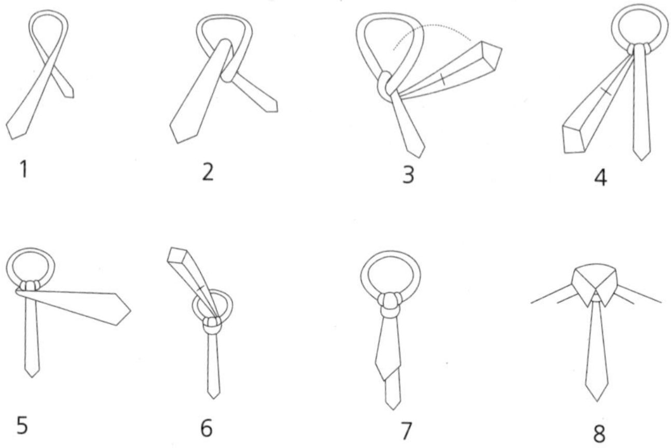

1. Facing the mirror, place the tie around your shoulders, top side up, with the broad end roughly a foot lower than the thin end.
2. Cross the broad end over the thin end to make an X fairly close to your neck (around the second shirt button).
3. Loop the broad end underneath the thin end of the tie and up through the neck loop. Drop it down so that it overlaps the thin end again.
4. Pull the broad end behind the bundle of cloth you have created to the left. Pull it up and drop it down through the neck loop again; then pull it to the left again.
5. Pull the broad end over from the left to the right, overlapping the first knot.
6. Pull the broad end up through the loop again, behind what now looks like a complete knot.
7. Bring the broad end back down and insert it through the knot.
8. Finish your knot by tightening it and don't forget to accentuate the dimple.

When you undo the tie, don't pull it off your neck, or bunch it as you would a coil of rope. Use both hands to untie it and hang it on the tie rack.

Belts

The colour of the belt must always match that of your shoes. A good-quality black leather belt is an essential item in your wardrobe. You may buy a brown belt later. Avoid cheap PVC or plastic belts with king-size buckles. Never leave home without the belt looped into your trousers. The buckles of your belt must be of good quality and standard size so that you could use the same formally and informally. For instance, dragonhead- and butterfly-shaped buckles may look good on women but do not complement a man's formal wear.

POWER DRESSING FOR WOMEN WHO DESIRE SUCCESS

On a lighter note, it can be said that few women keenly observe what men wear, while most men will never notice what fellow men wear. Most men keenly observe most women (no matter what they wear), while most women keenly observe what other women wear. Is it true then that more women are subject to probing eyes than men? And is it safe to conclude that more women are under the glare of probing eyes of both men and women? Even when you are alone, working and minding your own business, some eye is watching you. So you have to look your best all the time. Imagine the plight of men if they were under a similar glare and had to look their best all the time!

> *You don't get paid for the hour. You get paid for the value you bring to the hour.*
> Kareem Abdul-Jabar

You Are Judged by What You Wear

You work in a man's world. The corporate world is a man's fortress which he built for himself and is reluctant to share with you. He is jealous of his territory and protects it fiercely. He shares his territory with you grudgingly because he is threatened by your competence. You have a very strong brand USP; you have inborn managerial skills. Have you ever heard of a man asking for advice on how to balance home chores and a career? Never mind you cook his meals, clean his house, bring up the kids, keep his friends and family happy, especially at weddings, birthdays and festivals, and in spite of managing home so efficiently you have to prove yourself worthy of sharing his load at the workplace. Day after day and year after year, you have to measure up to some of the highest standards of corporate culture — rules compiled by men. Appropriate dress and appearance are essential ingredients for a polished and professional image for your business survival and corporate advancement. Hence, no matter what your age or designation, your business clothes and accessories must always complement your professional competence and the corporate image you represent.

Dressing for success includes more than just choosing the right outfit. You must consider accessories and personal grooming which will complement your professional image. A woman's professional appearance needs to support her professional accomplishments. Demonstrating that you care about your personal appearance communicates to the clients, investors and customers you are meeting with that they are important to you. Paying attention to the details of your appearance sends a message to others that you will also pay close attention to business details and to the needs of your customers and clients.

Clothes and Accessories to Avoid

The general corporate dress code for women is to stay within fashion limits and dress to impress — not to expose. Tight clothes that ride up when sitting or standing and shirts and tops that show skin in the midriff area and cleavage must be put away — away from the lecherous gaze of the corporate male. Clothes that are transparent, revealing or low-cut can put you in bad light in any company. In many organizations, women must have their arms covered. Sleeveless tops to the workplace are not accepted. If you wear sleeveless tops they must be worn along with a cardigan or a jacket. Your shirts, tops, blouses and pants should not be transparent. When clothes are tight they will be irritating, and you may have to tug, pull, itch or scratch, which is not something you will want to do in public consciously or unconsciously.

Don't wear tennis shoes, sneakers, slippers, sandals, stilettos, cowboy boots, or shoes that are uncomfortable to wear. Avoid fashion fads to the office. And don't put too many personal items in your handbag. When you look for something inside your handbag, it should not give you a disorganized look — like someone rummaging through clutter. Your make-up for the office should be light. Large handbags and other accessories like ostentatious jewellery, rings, nose rings, earrings, multiple necklaces, bracelets, bangles, heavy make-up and 'cheap' scented perfumes are frowned upon in most organizations, and so are visible body tattoos. Never let your hair down or streaked. Facial hair, legs and armpits must be waxed or shaved. In short, your dress and appearance must enhance your personal brand image while keeping in mind your high professional standards.

Clothes and Accessories to Consider

Saris, salwar kameez, business suits, dresses, a skirt with a dressy sweater, blouses, a jacket over a sleeveless blouse, and a long-sleeved blouse without a jacket are accepted office clothing. Many organizations ban the use of jeans, hip-hugging or low-hipster tight pants, but allow formal trousers and suits. It is safe to use black, navy blue, charcoal grey, khaki and white to the office. Image consultants point out that dark shades in fine pinstripes widely spaced give an all-time classic business look. Thick stripes close to each other may look trendier but are not right for formal office wear. Scarves are optional but must be conservative. Bowties and ties are worn with a dress shirt with the collar button fastened. Some organizations insist on a hose at all times when you wear skirts. Fine-quality waist belts and cummerbunds add grace and style to what you wear and are important accessories in your wardrobe. Your hair must be neatly groomed, pinned and tied — always. If you tend to sweat a lot, shampoo your hair every day. Your fingernails and toenails must be clean, trimmed and polished. The colour of nail polish must match that of your fingernails and toenails. Make it a habit to check the nail polish on fingers and toes every morning before leaving for work. Chipped nail polish will chip the shine off your corporate brand image.

Good-quality black and tan shoes are essential and must be polished to a high shine. Perfume, cologne and deodorant should be applied sparingly, evoking a subtle scent of expensive taste. Strong fragrances as well as inexpensive or 'cheap' ones assault the nostrils and turn on allergies, and are therefore considered inappropriate in corporate corridors. You should never smell of smoke (if you smoke in a car, your clothing and hair will always pick up the odour). When attending business meetings keep your business cards in your pocket for easy access. This will allow you to present your card without having to search through your handbag. At the end of the day, remove the cards and keep them in a cardholder so that they stay in good shape. If you attend meetings regularly, invest in a stylishly slim, feminine-looking bag to carry files and business materials.

Shoes

Stilettos are not part of the dress code in many corporate towers. In fact, heels higher than three inches are perceived as more suitable for a dance club than for an office environment, especially shoes with thin straps that expose more of the foot as well as shoes with very thin heels. The same applies to bright-coloured footwear. If you decide to wear a higher-than-three-inch heel, opt for the classic, closed-toe pump in a matte leather and neutral colour. You may also consider a platform style and wear pants or salwar of the same colour as your shoes to camouflage the height of the heel.

INFORMAL CORPORATE ATTIRE – MEN AND WOMEN

Some organizations, which include BPOs, advertising agencies, tuition centres, government-run offices and local banks, do not insist on a dress code, while some declare 'casual Fridays' when employees come dressed in casual wear. To dress casual for work may seem that the work climate is easy and 'everything goes'. But, in fact, the opposite is true since companies are run professionally and have to maintain their business image even on casual working days. It can be intimidating when you get to know that you are judged by what you wear, especially when there are no rules on what you should wear and not wear.

> *Success is a ladder that cannot be climbed with your hands in your pocket.*
>
> Unknown

Ironically, it is easier to comply with the 'corporate uniform' dress code than with the 'casual' dress code. In companies where casual clothes are the norm, employees are forced to exercise certain judgement on what they wear each day. A lot of valuable time is wasted each morning in deciding what to wear. Some organizations ask the personnel or HR department to set the guidelines for employees on casual-wear dress code according to the professional image of the company. To know what works best for your organization, watch what the senior executives wear and copy their style.

YOUR SUCCESS MANTRA: ALWAYS DRESS WELL

Are you the backroom worker or are you the front-office worker? Are you the company's workhorse, or are you its pride? Are you the kind of person who reaches office early and leaves late — and if that's not enough you carry the work home and burn the midnight oil, staring at the computer screen, poring over files past bedtime as you slog to meet deadlines? In fact, you are so obsessed with office work that you don't have time to eat, sleep, wash, bathe and groom yourself. The stubble on your face, the odour from your body, the crushed clothes you wore from yesterday, the gaunt look in your eyes make you a backroom worker — the company's workhorse —

indeed, a very valuable entity on the company's rosters. Though you work much harder than other employees, you are an embarrassment vis-à-vis the glamorous face of the company.

Balance your life — between work and good grooming, and between dedication to your work and dedication to building your brand image. Change your shabby habits quickly if you want to be recognised as the company's prized employee. Be image-conscious. Give yourself time to eat, sleep, wash, bathe and groom yourself, or else you will be told to ride the backroom service elevator to the office basement — into oblivion. All companies have dress codes. Some have them etched in stone; others are passed through word of mouth; some are formal while others are casual. Whatever be the dress code — formal or casual — it is absolutely mandatory for employees to dress appropriately (no matter how hard you work) and in the manner that enhances the company's business image.

CORPORATE HYGIENE

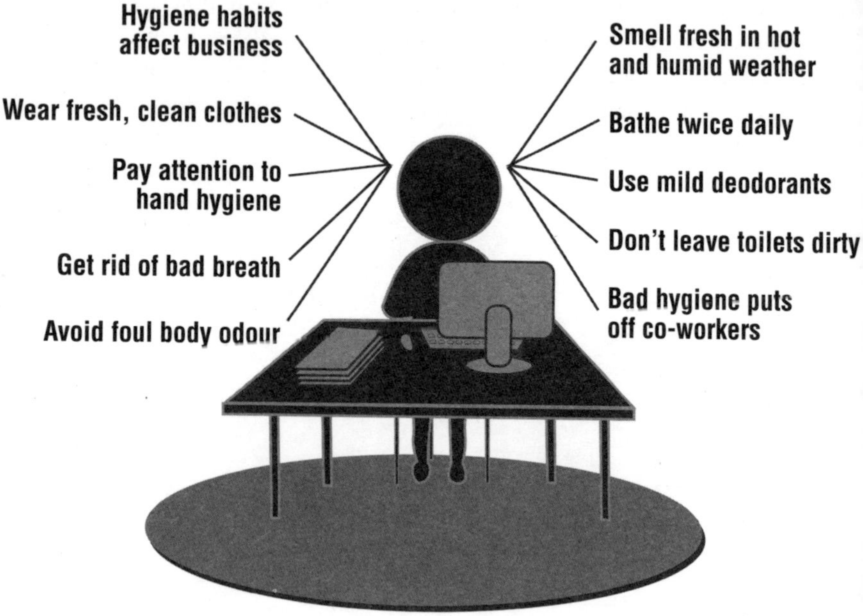

Chapter 6

ADD POLISH TO YOUR PERSONAL BRAND

CORPORATE HYGIENE

The corporate world is like a honeycomb that draws employees in swarms from all social classes, cultures, professions, castes, creeds and regions. An overwhelming number of people from small towns and remote countryside migrate into urban areas to colonize the corporate beehive.

Vijay was a software engineer. He shared a small room in a crowded chawl *with two out-of-town lodgers. He slept on the floor and lived out of a suitcase. Water supply was a problem in the area he lived. Fresh water was available when most of the world was asleep — between three and four in the mornings. Vijay bathed twice weekly and washed his clothes once a month. He never brushed his teeth.*

Every morning, swarms of employees buzz to their corporate beehives — and how! On waking up, Vijay chose clothes from the old pile that hung on his side of the clothes' rope. He wore clothes that smelled less rancid than the previous day, and rushed to the tea stall near the bus stop. He gobbled down an egg–bun with the tea and made a dash to the workstation. He reported to work after a visit to the office restroom, where he rinsed his mouth and also washed and dried his underarms with his kerchief.

Vijay must realize that corporate hygiene is not the same as rural hygiene. Ignorance or laziness could be the reason why employees show scant regard for corporate hygiene. When you disregard corporate hygiene standards, you hinder office efficiency. No matter where you come from or what your social background is, you must practise healthy hygiene habits, which are essential to rise above in the corporate world. There are no excuses to be lazy on cleanliness — you must act now.

Check the morning scene in any metro, city or town and you will see hordes of employees rushing to their workstations. On a fresh morning, many of them smell stale. Obviously, they rush to their workstations without bathing. Some people bathe but wear unwashed clothes, and some wear fresh clothes without bathing. Others dress shabbily. If you smell of stale, dried sweat and old deodorant, you are inappropriately dressed for the workplace, and you have only yourself to blame if you are branded 'smelly' or 'stinky', or if people avoid talking to you or coming close to you. Don't blame people for judging you harshly. When people prejudge you, don't simply conclude that they are jealous and prejudiced; maybe you need to improve your hygiene habits. The image people have of you, whether negative or positive, will remain etched in their memories. Your attitude shows through your hygiene habits and how you dress. If you cannot change your attitude, why do you expect people to change their opinion?

HYGIENE HABITS AFFECT BUSINESS

Spitting phlegm or a glob of *paan* is a common sight, and so is sneezing and blowing noses, urinating on walls and bushes, or throwing litter around. Isn't it a shame that so many adults, on the one hand, hold responsible jobs in reputed companies and, on the other, behave irresponsibly in the discharge of basic personal hygiene? Personal and corporate hygiene is the practice of keeping yourself as well as your living and working conditions clean so that you maintain good health and prevent disease.

It is not true that only people in low-paid and menial jobs are unhygienic. People from all walks of life, in spite of their education, sophistication and status in society, are found wanting in personal hygiene. Bad breath, body odour, unwashed hands, grit under fingernails, wax in the ears, stained teeth, smelly feet, and hair sticking out of bushy nostrils, ears and eyebrows point either to lack of awareness of or to conscious neglect of grooming and personal hygiene. Proper sanitary practices are important because these affect not only your wellness, but also your relationships with people as well as your self-confidence, self-esteem and business deals.

Social scientists will confirm that hygiene, grooming and appearance top the list of points on which people judge others. From job interviews to job performance, personal hygiene is the litmus test you must pass in order to succeed. People like to deal with clean, neat, tidy and pleasant workers. When you are judged otherwise because of poor hygiene habits, you lose many opportunities to succeed. Poor hygiene habits cancel out all other superlative work-related credentials you may have. People form positive impressions of those with good hygiene habits. Employees who make the effort to practise good hygiene habits are counted among those who are focused on career growth.

The following guidelines will help you get down to the nitty-gritty of personal and corporate hygiene. By practising these habits, you will add polish to your personal brand and achieve success in your personal, professional and social circles.

CORPORATE HYGIENE LESSONS

Many employees are unaware of good hygiene habits because in the hometowns they grew up in, such habits were not practised. Many practices which are a taboo in urban areas are rampant in rural areas. In rural areas, people chew tobacco and spit around; their body odours may upset you; and worse still, they scratch themselves in public. They belch after meals, and also blow their noses and sneeze without covering their mouths. And there are many other such habits which are frowned upon in corporate offices. Nobody in their right senses, who want to grow in their careers, will deliberately behave obnoxiously. The following points will remind employees of good hygiene habits so that they measure up to the high hygiene standards progressive business houses expect from their employees.

> *People who are unable to motivate themselves must be content with mediocrity, no matter how impressive their other talents.*
>
> Andrew Carnegie

Polish Your Brand with Cleanliness

Cleanliness is the best lotion to polish your personal brand with. There is no excuse for giving offence to others with sweaty, rancid body odours as you have ample opportunities for washing and bathing. A clean and tidy appearance is appropriate for all business and social occasions. A washed body dressed in fresh, clean and well-ironed clothes, a regular haircut and a daily shave ensure your grooming is appropriate and help make you feel 'connected' to the office image. You may want to pay attention to the following:

i) daily bath (morning *and* night)
ii) brushing of teeth and tongue, and cleansing the mouth
iii) clean and trimmed fingernails and toenails
iv) regular change of undergarments after bath

v) daily shave and regular haircuts
vi) regular trimming of facial hair, if sported.

Good hygiene habits form the cornerstone for laying the foundation of lasting first impressions. As you keep your body clean, neat and tidy, so also must you keep your desk, cubicle and cabin clean. The sight of your desk reflects the state of your mind. The untidy clutter on the desk reflects the clutter in the mind. A neat desk reflects a disciplined mind. A desk that is stacked with work files and a lunch packet, shelves and drawers crammed with knick-knacks, and an untidy cubicle strewn with litter reflect your cluttered work style.

When you mess with your corporate hygiene standards, you also mess with your corporate brand image. People quickly change their opinion of a first good impression into a bad impression. And they will forget the former, namely that the person used to have good hygiene habits earlier. But it takes a very long time for people to change a bad first impression into a good impression. And they will always remember the former, namely that the person earlier had bad hygiene habits.

Oral Hygiene to Stop Bad Breath

Your mouth is the area of the body most prone to collecting harmful bacteria and generating infections. Neglect in taking care of your mouth, teeth and gums will cause bad breath, dental problems and gum disease. Some people brush their teeth morning and night and still have bad breath. Some of the causes of bad breath are gum infection, food trapped in cavities, tartar deposits, and eating spicy foods, including onion, garlic and pickle. Keep your mouth clean to prevent bacteria from getting trapped between your teeth and on your tongue and causing bad breath. Brush your teeth and tongue after every meal. No matter how much you brush, some stubborn food particles will stay in crevices and cavities. You must floss to remove food that gets stuck in between your teeth. Avoid toothpicks; they severely damage the teeth. Gargle or rinse your mouth with water when it is inconvenient to brush after meals.

In the absence of a tongue cleaner, clean your tongue with your toothbrush. For, bacteria accumulate on the tongue and contribute to the foul smell when you breathe or open your mouth to speak even after you have brushed your teeth. Fasting also causes bad breath due to acidity in the stomach. It vanishes as soon as you eat some food. A dry mouth also brings about bad breath. Chew sugarless gum or suck sugarless mint to stimulate saliva from a dry mouth, but do this in private. Always carry a strip of gum for those times when you will not be able to brush, say after a round of cigarettes, whiskey, wine, beer or coffee. Brush your teeth at least twice a day, or better still after every meal. This will minimise the amount of bacteria in your mouth that leads to tooth decay, and will help you maintain a healthy and happy smile.

Hand Hygiene to Arrest Infections

You put your fingers into so many pies, so to speak. You use your hands and fingers in almost all activities, thereby putting your health in your hands, literally. For some reason, Indians are not hyper about hand hygiene. The most important way to prevent the spread of infectious diseases is to wash your hands as often as you can. Most infections, particularly common cold and gastroenteritis, are contracted when your germ-infested hands come in contact with your nose or mouth. In addition, infections are also contracted through contact with other individuals with whom you shake hands. Washing your hands with soap and water, especially after a visit to the toilet, is a must to keep your hands free of germs. It's not a pleasant sight to see someone nibbling at their fingernails. The sooner you stop the habit, the better it is for your image. If you must bite your nails, make an effort to clean your fingers, especially the cuticles, with soap and water before you start working on them.

Frequent hand washing reduces the spread of germs, bacteria and hand-to-mouth illnesses. Wash your hands with antibacterial soap, especially after sneezing and coughing and blowing your nose. When you apply soap, work up the lather for at least 60 seconds, making sure to clean each of the fingers, fingernails, cuticles and palms thoroughly. Rinse well and dry your hands with a fresh hand towel, paper towel or air dryer. Clean your hands frequently to avoid sweaty and sticky hands. You should always wash your hands before handling or eating food and before changing contact lenses.

Clean Fingernails

You must pay attention to your fingernails as well as your toenails. Some urbanites go to salons to have manicure and pedicure done by professionals. Most others, who self-groom themselves, should make sure the nails are always clipped low and even, and filed smoothly. Clipping them low reduces the opportunity for dirt to cling. This may mean that you will need a brush to wash your hands and fingernails, and a nail clipper with a file to keep your fingernails in good shape. Scrape away the dirt from under the nails with a nail cleaner which is attached to the nail clipper. As a habit, with every hand-washing opportunity, clean under the fingernails.

Women should check their nails, since they are painted, to see there is no dirt under the nails and the nail polish is not chipped. Shapely and polished nails add to your image quotient. Trim and file broken or cracked nails immediately or else they will irritate you the whole day long.

Most women footwear is designed to expose toenails. Generally, toenails are not given the same treatment as fingernails. Toenails should also be kept low, even and smooth. This is not only a hygiene tip but a grooming one as well. Ladies may opt to apply a clear gloss, if colour is not desired or allowed in some companies. Toenails that are trimmed, even and smooth and that are painted with clear gloss look healthy and attractive.

Bathe to Scrub Off Bacteria

> *People often say that motivation doesn't last. Well, neither does bathing; that's why we recommend it daily.*
>
> Zig Ziglar

Bathing twice a day is a good habit. Start the day clean, refreshed and rejuvenated with a bath, and as soon as you return home in the evening after work, wash off the day's fatigue, stress and bacteria. Sweat on the body is a breeding ground for bacteria and gives an offensive odour. Bathing twice daily reduces body odour and helps control itching, scratching and skin problems. In addition to bathing twice a day, it is a good habit to bathe after completing sweaty activities like jogging and workouts, since bathing reduces bacteria that contribute to body odour, particularly in the armpits, groin area and the feet. Bathing also ensures that your skin rejuvenates itself as the scrubbing of your arms, legs and torso will wash off dead, dry skin and help your skin stay healthy and refreshed.

If you have bad body odour, you should use antibacterial soap because it cleans bacteria better than perfume soaps do. Specialty soaps are available for specific body parts. There are foot as well as face soaps. Some areas require a more aggressive attack on bacteria. Choose one in each category to address the specific needs of those areas. After bathing, dry yourself thoroughly with a clean, dry towel to prevent bacteria growth. You must not share your towel or soap with others. Cross-infection is a risk that must be avoided, if possible.

Improve Your Body Odour

The main reason for bad body odour is the lack of attention to body hygiene. Body odour is usually caused by sweat that is produced under the armpits, groin and feet. Bacteria that feed upon the sweat are the cause for the stinking odour.

The food you eat enters your sweat through your diet. Reduce hot and spicy foods like pickles, garlic and onion. Tobacco and beer also have the same odorous effect. Bathe as often as you can when you are sweaty and sticky. To smell fresh in hot and humid weather, you need to spray a mild lingering cologne or antiperspirant after a bath, especially before you go to bed. Always use a clean, dry bath towel. What is the point in taking a bath and then rubbing yourself dry with a damp, smelly towel? Change your bath towel twice every week. The clothes you wear and the garments that touch your skin must be washed with antibacterial soap every day. In hot and humid weather, use only pure-cotton undergarments. Polyester and synthetic-blend garments do not absorb sweat. Sweat generates bacteria, and bacteria generate foul odour. The problem with foul body odour is that it penetrates into our psyche and we cannot tell how obnoxious we smell to others.

Get Rid of Smelly Feet

The nauseating stink of smelly feet is something you don't want to be associated with. Foul foot odour is caused when the sweat does not evaporate and bacteria feed on it. If you suffer from excessive smelly feet, pour a quart of vodka in a basin of hot water and soak your feet in it for 10 minutes. The hot water will open the pores, and the high alcohol content in the vodka will kill the bacteria hidden in the pores of your feet. When you bathe, scrub the soles of your feet and the spaces between your toes with an antibacterial soap and water regularly. Painful ulcers between your toes are usually caused by the use of synthetic socks on sweaty feet. In summers, wear pure-cotton socks to absorb the sweat. Avoid 'cotton mix,' 'cotton-rich,' 'cotton blend' or nylon-polyester-synthetic socks. Never share your socks with others. Always wear a clean pair of washed socks every day. Wearing unwashed socks will make your shoes and feet smell bad. Never wear the same pair of shoes every day. Choose the right pair of shoes. Sports shoes made of PVC and plastic material tend to smell foul when not washed properly. Wash and dry your sports shoes in the sunlight twice every week. Before going to bed, wash and scrub your feet and rub Vaseline, especially on the heels, where the skin is hard or calloused and tends to crack.

Keep Your Bed Fresh and Clean

Have you wondered why after bathing every night before going to bed, you still wake up in the morning, smelling like a furry animal? The reason could be found in the bed. Some people use their beds to lounge and laze, watch television, eat food, recreate with family and friends, do office work and also sleep. When you go to bed, do the pillows, sheets and covers smell fresh or do they smell of stale food and dried sweat? Do you have to dust off ants and other insects before you crawl into bed? When you sleep for six to nine hours wrapped in smelly sheets, quilts or blankets which are already infested with bacteria, you will naturally wake up with a foul body odour. Use the bed for what it was meant — to sleep in — and stop its misuse. Air the mattresses and pillows in the sun and wash the bed linen twice weekly. A freshly washed body in a clean bed will give you not only sound sleep but also a 'human' smell when you wake up.

Tips to Groom Your Hair

Washing your hair should be done anywhere from every day to once a week. But it should never be prolonged for more than a week. Hair is a trap for everything that is airborne. It traps dust and pollen, including all odours, cigarette smoke and food aromas. After a swim, you need to wash away the chlorine. Shampoo and condition your hair twice a week to ensure it stays healthy, strong and in good shape. Shampooing helps get rid of dandruff that is caused by dead skin cells. Oil your hair *before* a bath, never after a bath. Each of us has different hair types. Some have brittle and dry hair, which is difficult to grow and keep strong if washed everyday and becomes greasy when washed infrequently. Washing your hair too frequently also strips it of necessary nutrients required to keep it strong and healthy. After washing the hair, always use a conditioner for your hair type. It replenishes moisture to your hair and prepares it for combing and styling. If you omit the conditioner, your hair may have a dry or even brittle look. Conditioners keep the nutrients within your hair intact.

Regular haircuts give you a clean and tidy appearance. Getting your hair cut frequently is also critical to healthy hair. The length of your hair determines how often you get your hair cut. Men and women with short hair must get a haircut every six weeks to keep it trim and neat. If you have longer hair, you can go as long as ten weeks without a haircut, but not beyond that. It's healthy to have regular haircuts to get rid of dead, dry ends and to enable healthy hair to grow strong and quickly. Don't pluck hair from ears, nose and eyebrows in public. Set aside the weekends when you have more time to tend to ears, nose, eyebrows, armpits and chest hair. If you colour your hair it should flatter your personality, and if you choose to streak your hair first find out if your company policy permits it. Avoid caressing and playing with your hair in public places as it sends mixed signals. Men sporting long hair should tie the tresses tight into a ponytail.

In many cultures, shaving is an important part of cleanliness. For men, shaving the face enables it to stay cleaner and is a more acceptable hygienic practice, especially for those who work in corporate offices. Unless you have a well-kept beard or moustache, make sure you are clean-shaven and no scruff is seen on your neck, along your jaw line or near your sideburns. For women, shaving or waxing the legs and underarms also keeps the body cleaner with fewer places for bacteria to breed.

Smell Fresh in Hot and Humid Weather

Climate change has made summers longer, hotter and intolerable. While the human body is in the process of acclimatizing itself to the changing weather, you can do your bit by looking for new ways to beat the muggy weather and stay dry, fresh and cool. Spraying a deodorant–antiperspirant or cologne–antiperspirant will reduce underarm sweat and mask the bacterial odour. The perfume from the deodorant and cologne you use should not be so strong that while it masks your body odour, it makes others uncomfortable or turns on an allergy. Underarm roll-ons seem practical for many people. Perfumed and antibacterial powders also mask underarm odour. Foot powders containing antiperspirants, when sprinkled on the soles of the feet, help prevent smelly feet.

> *Some people dream of success while others wake up and work hard at it.*
>
> Unknown

Care for Healthy Skin

Skin is the largest organ of your body and acts as a barrier between germs and your body. It is tough and generally impenetrable to bacteria and viruses. On the other hand, germs can enter your body through other areas that are susceptible to bacteria such as your nose, mouth, eyes, ears or a break in the skin. Cover all cuts, burns and sores and change dressings regularly. Pay extra attention to any open wounds on hands, arms, legs and feet. Always carry clean handkerchiefs. It is safer to carry face tissues. Your face is exposed all the time to rough and inclement weather. It is important to wash your face often to remove the dirt and grime from eyes, ears, nose and mouth and wipe your face with a fresh, clean tissue or towel. This will keep your face free from pimples, which are the result of clogged pores. Eating plain yoghurt (*dahi*) at meal times will not only aid digestion but also reduce skin irritation and itches.

HOW TO USE CORPORATE WASHROOMS

Washrooms, restrooms, toilets and lavatories all mean the same. Like common property, washrooms are commonly used by employees without much care for fellow colleagues. There are Western- and Indian-style commodes. Whatever the style of the commode you are used to, '*Be Considerate*' is the style you should adopt. When you leave the washroom after use, leave it for others the way you would have ideally liked to find it: clean, dry, in working order, and ready for use. When you wash your hands and face, don't splash water outside the washbasin or on the floor. If you accidentally splash water outside the washbasin, find a way to make it dry. When you rinse your mouth after a meal, run the tap and wash the waste off the washbasin. Turn off the taps before you leave the washroom.

It is a sad reflection on the way men use common washrooms that women find it difficult to use the ones shared by men. Men should lift the commode seat and make sure droplets of urine don't fall on the seat or on the floor near the commode. Never throw cigarette butts and match sticks inside the pot. Always wipe the seat dry, flush the toilet after use, and drop the cover down gently before you leave. If you notice something broken, missing or not working, report it to the department concerned so that it can be repaired or replaced immediately, and in the meantime stick a warning sign to stop people from rushing in.

IMPLEMENTING CORPORATE HYGIENE POLICIES

If you have worked in close proximity with someone who had foul breath, peculiar body odour, unkempt hair reeking of cheap perfumed oil, smelly feet and dirty hands and fingernails, you know how painfully difficult it is to work with concentration, day after day and year after year, in the company of such persons. Many employees continue to work helplessly in the face of such assault since companies are silent on corporate hygiene policy. Unfortunately, co-workers cringe and squirm while they put up with these unbearable employees. They are afraid that the offenders may file complaints or even law suits for being harassed in a hostile work environment with gender, caste and creed overtones.

Personal hygiene habits cease to be 'personal' at the workplace. At a workplace where people from different social, cultural and economic backgrounds as well as from different genders, castes and creeds congregate, corporate hygiene policies (common to all employees) must be implemented. Making these issues a company policy keeps the problem from becoming personal. Unacceptable hygiene practices should be dealt with like any other employee behaviour problem — quickly and firmly.

And if the employee does not comply with the company policy, the supervisor should have the authority to take action.

HOW TO HANDLE ERRANT EMPLOYEES

When dealing with errant employees on hygiene, it is always advisable to approach the issue with utmost sensitivity. Don't leave hints as they can be misunderstood. Avoid putting toothpaste, soap, or hygiene items on the person's desk. The best way to approach the problem is to do it in person. Take a moment out for an informal conversation with the employee. The tone of the chat on corporate hygiene should be supportive and diagnostic rather than aggressive or disciplinarian. Approach the issue as a cool boss who allows freedom with limits, and make corporate hygiene a corporate issue related to business. You could tell them that their body odour or breath may be offensive to potential customers, or the cramped office space makes it difficult for fellow co-workers not to be distracted. By approaching the issue as a business concern, it would not appear to be a personal attack. You could also draw attention to their performance and how the issue of poor hygiene habits could affect their future career opportunities and that you don't want poor hygiene to get in the way of promotions or other opportunities. Lastly, it is best to be brief and to the point, but do so sensitively and with tact.

DON'T SLIP – WATCH YOUR STEP

To climb the corporate ladder and eventually reach the top, you have to be dedicated to your job and committed to developing your personal brand image. The company you work for will regularly evaluate your accomplishments and achievements along with your personality traits, which include exemplary hygiene habits. Many start out as high achievers when they join a company, but after a while they end up at the bottom of the ladder of frustration because they lose the competition to someone with impeccable grooming and personal hygiene habits. Treat this chapter as your coach and guide to build your brand value to beat the competition. If you have absorbed the lessons with a view to improving your personal brand image, it should not prove burdensome, and your brand image will serve as your personal valet to escort you to the top of the corporate ladder.

> *The greater part of our happiness or misery depends upon our dispositions and not upon our circumstances.*
> Martha Washington

POWERFUL FIRST IMPRESSIONS

Chapter 7

PRUNE YOUR BRAND IMAGE

POWERFUL FIRST IMPRESSIONS

It was nine-ish in the morning. Sabrina was waiting for the company's chartered bus to arrive. She saw a man, so early in the morning, swaying in a drunken stupor. The man was walking in her direction, dragging his feet with difficulty. He was unshaven. His lower jaw hung open and droplets of saliva drooled out. She turned to a colleague and asked him why people drank so early in the morning. Ram looked puzzled. With a nod, Sabrina gestured towards the drunken man. Ram told her that he knew the fellow and he was truly a walking wonder. Sabrina added sarcastically, indeed he was a walking wonder!

Ram told Sabrina the man's background. He had suffered a stroke and the family had thrown him out of his house. A social activist took up the matter. She found out that the family had transferred his property and money to their name and disowned him. The social activist filed a criminal case against the family and gave him back his home and money. The fellow fought through his paralysis all by himself and was now a walking wonder.

As she boarded the bus, Sabrina had a sinking feeling. She felt someone had driven a fist into her belly. She blamed herself for her uncharitable comments. She had been quick to judge the man by his first impressions. Had she known his background, she would have been kind in her judgement.

Gauging people by appearance is wired into our brain. When we meet someone, we analyse the person in a blink of an eye to form quick first impressions. Social anthropologists point out that the speed at forming first impressions is deeply rooted in our primitive survival instincts. Regardless of the advancement in human civilization, our brains automatically form split-second judgement of people.

Maybe we look upon the corporate world as a jungle and see everybody as an adversary. It is a dog-eat-dog mentality. You are instinctively scrutinized and judged by your dress and behaviour. To rise above and reign like a lion in the corporate jungle, you must train yourself to become a polished executive. Killer instincts matched with sophisticated corporate polish will give you a cutting-edge advantage over your adversaries.

"It's not fair," you screamed. And nobody paid attention. Your protest went unheeded because the universal rule is you are judged by your appearance. Of course, it's not fair, especially when your image forms 80 per cent of your personality. A paltry 20 per cent is attributed to hours of sweat and toil you put into your work. No matter how ambitious and talented you are, to achieve success your total image must also look the part. It truly pays to make powerful first impressions.

> *Every man's work, whether it be literature or music or pictures or architecture or anything else, is always a portrait of himself.*
>
> Elbert Hubbard

Generally speaking, when people think about first impressions, they think it is about fashion and style. But, in fact, first impression is about your image, which implies your total appearance — your clothing, grooming, corporate etiquette, and verbal and non-verbal communication. These are not only vital parts and pieces that complete your personality jigsaw, but also speak of your brand image and of the power it packs. Brand image is a powerful communicator. Good grooming contributes to lasting first impressions, and those impressions linger on. Long after people may forget your name, they will associate you with the image they have of you in their memories.

You have heard it said, India is the youngest nation on the planet and our youth are the new wealth creators. Yet, millions of employed and unemployed youth who invested their time and money to earn their degrees suffer from stress and depression because they are inadequately prepared or not job-ready. Studies show that they lack soft skills. Soft skills are a prerequisite to get jobs, to sustain them and to make a success of your career. Those among you who realized the importance of survival in the workplace picked up some relevant social skills and have managed to hold on to the job.

Consider your personality portrait like a jigsaw puzzle made of multiple pieces. Command over spoken and written English is one such jigsaw piece. Impeccable mannerisms, refined table manners, appropriate dress sense, personal hygiene, and many habits and characteristics are all jigsaw pieces that go on to make your personality portrait. Even if one piece goes missing or is misplaced, it will ruin the personality portrait. People will only look at the missing or misplaced pieces and form first impressions of you.

FIRST IMPRESSIONS LAST FOREVER

The beauty of the rose has been captured in innumerable paintings, poems and songs worldwide. For the rose to bloom in resplendent beauty, the rosebush must be nurtured with tender, loving care. The rosebush gets its strength and form after it is pruned. You are like the rosebush — prickly when not pruned. When the pruning and the trimming cut deep inside the structure of the rosebush, the roses bloom stronger and healthier and their beauty catches the eye of everyone passing by. You must learn new techniques to prune away all that is prickly, sloppy, shabby and mediocre in your personality so that your brand image outshines others' and people are attracted to you.

You worked your socks off to earn your professional degrees. You are also diligent and hardworking. But your career is going nowhere. You are stuck at your workstation like a dependable mule. The world is changing and changing fast. Professional degrees combined with an appetite for hard work are great personal assets of an era gone by. The need of the hour is to package your brand image so attractively that your brand value is appreciated, recognised and rewarded by your supervisors and employers. Why waste time and feel sorry for yourself when you can improve your soft skills? There is no time to lose over lost opportunities. Look ahead and act fast. You must quickly practise the art of making positive first impressions.

TURN ON YOUR CHARM

Have you noticed that when you first entered a room, or a business meeting, and the introductions were made, you had that one great moment when everyone gave you their undivided attention? During that moment of introductions, you were also being evaluated (clothing, cologne odour, social graces, language proficiency, tone of voice, etc.) and instantly minds were being made up whether to accept or reject you. In most cases, people take a decision about a stranger in a matter of seconds. If you lose out on the magic of that moment, you will have to try much harder for a second chance to make that positive first impression.

The common saying is, you never get a second chance at making good first impressions. It is a make-or-break situation. The other common saying is, first impressions are lasting impressions. Both sayings reinforce the fact that 'first impressions' are the life blood of business and professional people. Careers are made or destroyed, deals are won or lost, and relationships are bonded or broken — all in a matter of minutes or seconds — on the basis of first impressions.

GOOD FIRST IMPRESSIONS GENERATE BUSINESS

Why is it that so many people in business and everyday life seem to be clueless about the importance of making a good first impression? Many people routinely wake up each morning and rush to work without bothering about first impression and how it will impact the minds of colleagues, clients, vendors or business rivals. Whether intentional or not, there is no excuse for losing a business deal with a client because of your casual attitude. As an employee of an organization, you must strive to cultivate the skills to develop positive first impressions, which are crucial for forging profitable, sustainable, long-term partnerships and help build the business and keep it thriving.

> *One must forever strive for excellence or even perfection, in any task however small, and never be satisfied with the second best.*
>
> JRD Tata

Sizing up people is instinctive. Just as you measure up people instinctively, others too measure you up. It takes you perhaps a quick glance to evaluate someone who you met for the first time. In this short time, you form an opinion of the other person on the basis of dress, appearance, body language, words, voice, tone, mannerisms, and body odour. Similarly, at every new encounter, you are evaluated and another person forms an impression of you. First impressions are difficult to reverse or undo and they set the tone for the relationship that will follow. Making a positive first impression is important for building relationships with clients, vendors, customers and even co-workers.

ORIGIN OF FIRST IMPRESSIONS

When we meet someone, our brain instantly analyses that person. The eyes and ears quickly pick up data about the person's physical appearance, behaviour and attitude and send it to the brain for analysis. However, the speed of forming first impressions is deeply rooted in man's primitive survival instincts. The footprints of first impressions can be traced to our primitive ancestors. The ability to use appearance and behaviour to gauge intentions was a priceless resource when confronted with a wild boar in the forest. Regardless of the advancement in human civilization, our brains have yet to outgrow that automatic split-second judgment.

Though humans have evolved from the Neanderthal to the present techno-savvy executive, his brain still carries imprints of his origins. On the one hand, he is a suave corporate executive; on the other, his existential habits reflect primitive survival instincts. Assessing, analysing and evaluating intentions of fellow human beings to form first impressions are instinctively primitive and at the same time sophisticated and cultured. Let us simplify a complex process to understand how first-impression data is stored in the brain's memory bank.

The part of your brain where memory is located can be compared to a library. Books in the library are stored in categories like Fiction, Medicine, Engineering and Architecture. The 'Fiction' section is further divided into specific categories like poetry, prose and novels, and these are further divided into periods, regions, etc., for quick and easy identification and recall. The brain too organizes its data and stores information into slots and labels them into categories for ready reference. For instance, data on people would contain personality traits and characteristics such as achiever, organizer, industrious, waster, loser, cheater, lazy, liar, etc., relating to behaviour patterns already stored in the brain.

From the moment you see a person, your sensory organs send data on appearance and behaviour to the brain, which analyses the data by matching with what it already possesses from previous experiences and files it within milliseconds in categories like 'drunk', 'aggressive', 'needy', 'hardworking' and 'cultured'. The moment the data is filed under a specific category, the person gets labelled. And that label will impact present and future interactions. In categorizing people, we all take shortcuts, and first impressions about people often turn into long-term perceptions and reputations, which are good for people who make *positive* first impressions, but bad for those who make *negative* first impressions.

YOU CAN GET PEOPLE TO RESPECT YOU

People form an impression of you from the way they perceive you. And the way they perceive you depends on the external aspects of your personality such as your communication skills, mannerisms, behaviour and actions. Are you aware that people in authority look you in the eye when they talk, and look away when you talk to them? In fact, when you talk to people in authority, you look past them or elsewhere — rarely in the eye. You smile when you speak to your superiors; they don't. They speak in a strong voice; you speak with hesitation and uncertainty. They stand tall with chin jutting out while you hunch your shoulders, almost bending, when you stand. They close the gap when they speak while you keep a 'distance' when you talk. Of course, you do not tell the office to treat you like a doormat; your mannerisms, behaviour and actions do. You give the impression that you can be 'used' by the office as a doormat.

You could be that executive who is looked upon as polished, well groomed and respected. When people look at you, they make judgments about you, based on what they see, not on who you really are. The way you live in the privacy of your home may reveal another story altogether, but that does not matter. You could be untidy and cluttered, yet people see you and think of you as a neat and tidy person, because that's the picture you presented to others. They may judge your ability and disposition by that first impression. In short, it is your appearance that creates a positive or negative picture of you, and not who you actually are. By changing your external appearance such as hairstyle, grooming or clothing, you can change the image others have of you to the image you want them to have. Appearance can be a powerful and useful tool in controlling the kind of message you send to others.

Physical appearance matters a lot. The people you meet for the first time do not know you, and your appearance is usually the first clue they have to go on. They say a picture is worth a thousand words, and so the 'picture' you first presented says a lot about you to the person you are meeting. Is your appearance saying the right things to help create the right brand image you want? The key to a good brand image is to present yourself in the best light possible.

TAKE A LESSON FROM GATECRASHERS

People want to be seen with other people and feel 'connected' in order to get something out of that association. Birds of the same feather flock together in season for a reason — their identity and strength lie in flocking together. For humans, to hang out and be accepted by the people we want to be seen with, we have to appear and dress like them. You have heard of gatecrashers (who otherwise could be casual wage earners) attend big fat wedding receptions by copying the dress code of invitees. Unknowingly, the hosts welcome gatecrashers, whose first impressions are that they are special invitees, and end up paying for their food and drinks. Gatecrashers connect with high-society invitees with their dress and appearance and indulge in all the extravagance the party provides. It's a lesson you can learn on how first impressions impact the goals of gatecrashers. You don't have to gatecrash any party or office. All you have to do is make the right first impressions with your dress and appearance, and you will succeed in achieving your goals.

Once a positive first impression is formed in the minds of people, it becomes a solid foundation for the way people will perceive you in the future. If you have established a positive brand image, the foundation for a successful business relationship is set permanently. To keep the wheels of your personal brand image speeding in the direction of your future goals, you are expected to deliver on two fronts:

1. Excellent interpersonal skills
2. Avoid stepping on social landmines

The following pointers will help you brush up on your interpersonal skills and guide you to sidestep social landmines so that you reach your goals successfully in the quickest possible way. Twelve basic pruning tips have been offered below. When practised regularly, they will put your personal brand image on the fast track to make memorable first impressions.

BASIC PRUNING TIPS

1. Have a Positive Attitude

Nothing works better at the office than a positive attitude. Enthusiasm spreads all around when people work with a positive attitude. Though it is difficult to maintain an upbeat manner and an infectious smile, you must try to be positive even when you are criticized. Do not carry your home issues to your workplace. Using your co-workers as therapists not only hurts productivity but also damages your credibility. It can affect your professional image even if people appear sympathetic.

2. Dress to Impress

Your corporate attire must be appropriate at all times. Your company expects that each employee's dress, personal appearance, and personal hygiene project a professional image. Good grooming and appropriate dress inspire customer confidence and help create a pleasant work environment for all. You are expected to present an authoritative, conservative and competent image. Professional business attire includes business suits and polished shoes. It does not include casual attire, such as blue jeans, T-shirts, cotton leggings, shorts, sandals, sneakers, lycra or spandex clothing. You must keep in mind you are the *brand ambassador* of the company at all times.

3. Shine Your Shoes Every Day

People will look you up from head to toe literally. If your shoes are not polished, the client will wonder whether you pay attention to other details. Shoes are the last thing you put on before you walk out of the door, but they are often the first thing some people notice.

4. Walk Briskly

Studies show that people who walk fast are considered to be fast thinkers and are viewed as energetic people — the type clients would want to do business with. If you want people to have an impression of you as a plodder, drag your feet when you walk. Otherwise, walk briskly with an alert stride. You never know who is watching you.

5. Good Manners Always Impress

Holding the door open for others to pass, offering your seat for someone older than you in age or rank, anticipating others' needs, and performing a host of little deeds make you good-mannered, polite, attentive and courteous. It goes without saying that good manners help make a good first impression like nothing else does. In fact, anything less can ruin the one chance you have at making that first great impression. So be on your best behaviour and give it your best shot! One modern menace that threatens to destroy positive first impressions is the mobile phone. Put your mobile phone on silent mode and keep it out of sight when you attend meetings.

> *People become really quite remarkable when they start thinking that they can do things. When they believe in themselves they have the first secret of success.*
>
> Norman Vincent Peale

6. Listen More; Talk Less

Listen, listen and then listen some more to what the client says. Never interrupt them or act like a know-it-all and complete their sentences. The idea is to communicate to them that you are there to listen to them and help your organization achieve success. You don't want to get the reputation as someone who always has the last word. You will impress the client further when you pull out a note pad and begin to jot down points.

7. Speak with Clarity

Talk slowly and clearly when you speak formally. It is very annoying to listen to people who mumble under their breath or speak too fast. Train yourself to speak at a moderate pace in a well-modulated voice with proper pronunciation. When you speak, let your smile light up your eyes and your voice. People respond with warmth when they *feel* the warmth in your voice. Avoid slang words ('dude', 'bloody', 'damn', 'yaar', 'sh*t') and abusive words. To speak grammatically correct sentences, you must train yourself to speak in short sentences and to the point. If people cannot understand what you are saying, they will disregard you and your organization.

8. Your Handshake Is Important

Even though employees are aware that a good business handshake should be a firm one, yet time and again people offer a limp hand. You can be assured of giving an impressive grip and getting off to a good start if you position your hand to make complete contact with the other person's — web to web. Once you have connected, close your thumb over the back of the other person's hand and apply gentle pressure —never a tight squeeze. You may have the beginning of a good business relationship.

9. Maintain Your Carriage and Poise

A smile or a pleasant expression tells people that you are glad to be with them. Eye contact says you are paying attention and are interested in what is being said. Leaning slightly towards the person makes you appear engaged and involved in the conversation. Use as many body language signals as you can to look interested and interesting. Your body speaks a language much louder and more authentic than your words. Try to maintain proper posture when you stand, sit and walk. Mind the way you carry your body. You should walk with your body erect but relaxed, head up and shoulders even. Do not slouch or hunch your back; be gracefully at ease. When you sit to meet people, you must sit properly. Proper sitting means that you must not sprawl in a chair with feet extended, nor slouch with your back curved. Both feet should be placed on the floor, though crossing the legs when one is sitting on a straight-back chair is allowed, provided the soles of your shoes and the heels in particular are not visible to anyone. In some cultures, it is considered an insult if the soles of your shoes point towards the person sitting beside you.

10. Be on Time

Never make anyone wait, be it an employee or employer, or a business acquaintance. Never be late for a meeting or for work. Many first good impressions get trashed into the bin of 'bad impressions' even before the meeting begins, because you are running late. Someone you are meeting for the first time is not interested in your 'genuinely good excuse' for running late. Always plan to arrive a few minutes early. And allow flexibility for possible delays in traffic or taking a wrong turn. Arriving 15 minutes early is much better than arriving five minutes late, and it is the first step in creating a powerful first impression.

11. Keep Business Cards Handy

Your business cards and how you handle them contribute to your total image. Have a good supply of them with you at all times since you never know when and where you will meet a potential client. Keep your cards in a card holder where they are protected from wear and tear. That way you will be able to find them without fumbling around, and they will always be in good condition.

12. Never Lie

Customers in particular and people in general hate being lied to. A single lie can destroy the reputation you have built over several years. The mobile phone and the internet have revolutionized communication like never before. Talk is cheap and instant, and so are the impressions you leave on the minds of people. Phone calls, voice messages and e-mails must be attended to immediately. Don't procrastinate. Don't lie about being busy when you are not. Being truthful will enhance your personal brand image and the company's business.

YOUR COMPANY'S MORAL IMAGE COUNTS

Companies hire employees who not only are professionally competent but also have a clean image and possess high moral values. People with criminal backgrounds are not hired. Just as companies run a character-check on employees, the time has come for employees to run a check on the moral image of the company and its promoters. Each day more and more companies are 'exposed' for their wrong doings — companies that have lost the moral compass. Primarily, you have a responsibility to yourself. You have to care for your reputation — your personal brand image. What will people think of you if you work for a company that is caught on the wrong side of the law? What impression will people have of you and what explanations will you offer to your clients, customers, vendors, friends and family when your company's promoters and executive directors are sent to jail for unethical and illegal practices? Won't your personal polish lose its sheen and your corporate image take a beating? Will your clients, customers and vendors trust you? Won't they trust their instincts and go by the impression they have of you and treat you as a person who represents corrupt practices?

To work or not to work for such companies is the choice you will have to make. There are two factors to consider: either you stake your image on your reputation or you stake your image on the money. If you choose the former, you will keep away from companies engaged in shady and criminal activities. And if you choose the latter, you can always seek higher remuneration for the loss in reputation you may suffer.

Corporate houses may appear to be faceless monoliths but they have an image to live up to or strive for. Positive first impressions of your company, its top executives and employees can have a significant impact on its brand image. Brand image is everything because it speaks volumes about your organization's reputation based on values, achievements, work ethics, and professionalism.

FIRST IMPRESSIONS ON WORKPLACE CONDITIONS

If a customer or visitor happened to walk into your office right now, would you be embarrassed over the state of your office surroundings? Your desk is completely covered with files, stationery and other stuff. There are files which have been moved to the floor (temporarily, of course). Losing items has become a daily occurrence. Your current projects are rarely in order and many a time you discover misfiled documents. You cannot find a place to keep the customer's new tender documents because your computer table at the corner is also covered with loose papers and file folders. If truth be told, you are operating in panic mode most of the times.

The overall appearance of your workplace has a huge impact on how your customers perceive you and the way your company does business. As a company representative, your behaviour impacts the company's brand image. They say you only have one opportunity to make a first impression. While most people think that the phrase pertains to how we are groomed or how firmly we shake hands, the truth is that it also applies to how we maintain our workstations. Check your desks, shelves, drawers, floors, everything. Make sure your office is organized with files, documents and papers neatly stacked, stored and labelled for efficient access. Desks, computers, etc., should be cleaned every evening before you leave the premises, and food, drink and other personal items removed. All file folders (only important ones) that remain on your desk should be easily accessible and organized.

A clean, well-organized workplace should be made compulsory to enable employees to work in a structured manner, so compliance must be enforced. When it comes to creating a work environment that appears pleasing to the eye, a company policy must be put in place and made mandatory for all employees to adhere to. The policy should be detailed and specific so that employees know what is expected of them and of their role in promoting the company's brand image. First impressions are lasting impressions — always.

BUSINESS ETIQUETTE

Chapter 8

EMPOWER YOUR BRAND VALUE

BUSINESS ETIQUETTE

Harish was the regional marketing manager in a multinational company. He had a head for numbers and was glib with words. He could reel off statistics with the same ease as kindergarten teachers do multiplication tables. But he did not care much for business etiquette. "Women — a woe to men!" was the kind of jokes he stooped to in order to poke fun at co-workers. He conveniently bypassed company policy which called for executives to wear a tie when they met clients.

When talking, Harish habitually used expletives and slangs. He considered brash behaviour contemporarily modern. To justify his crude manners and vulgar talk, he gave the example of his 21-year-old son, who questioned societal customs and practices. He told colleagues and clients to listen to the youth since they made up 55 per cent of India's population. He exhorted them to talk and act like the youth in order to stay relevant in modern times.

Harish had it wrong. Business etiquette is the oil that lubricates the corporate machinery to keep it running smoothly. It is about corporate manners that govern workplace behaviour. When you do not practise it, you project yourself as an unprofessional boor. To rise above the competition, employees must realize that business etiquette is appreciated by all.

Business etiquette empowers your personal brand, while lack of it obstructs growth. Everything you do and say affects not only you but also your organization. You are expected to practise good manners and follow traditional social customs in business. Make it a habit to indulge in business etiquette; it is the lubricant for success in the corporate world.

Business etiquette is absolutely essential to succeed in the business world. Your colleagues, clients and superiors will always compare your etiquette standards with how good you are at the job and how well you perform on the etiquette scorecard. More than the hard work you put in, it is your behaviour traits that are weighed either in your favour or against you. Your Etiquette Quotient must add to your brand value and complement your work, and not pull you down. You work hard and it comes natural to you because you are well endowed with technical skills. You must also learn to work smart and use business etiquette in your workplace. By doing so, you will develop a strong brand value and stay ahead of the competition.

In fact, business etiquette is today's buzzword. By following some basic social and business etiquette tips, you will be able to ensure that your actions send the right messages to the right people all the time. This chapter will show you how to use social skills with poise and grace and transact business with thoughtful consideration for others' welfare.

LUBRICANT FOR RAISE AND RISE

Business etiquette can broadly be defined as socially acceptable workplace behaviour. It is the lubricant you must use to earn your raise and rise in your organization. By getting in the habit of behaving in a manner consistent with the principles related to the best in business etiquette, you will be more likely to make an excellent impression on the people you encounter in your professional, social and personal life.

> *Four steps to achievement: Plan purposefully. Prepare prayerfully. Proceed positively. Pursue persistently.*
>
> William A Ward

Committing mistakes in business situations can harm your reputation and ruin your career. For instance, did you send an email or post something on Facebook that you later regretted? Did you insult a client by using humour inappropriately? Did you lose out on concluding a business deal because you took a call on your mobile phone at the most crucial moment? Did you avoid conversing with an important client because you forgot the person's name? These and many other "mistakes" have a tendency to slow you down or pull you down. You may choose to brush them under the carpet and go on as though nothing serious happened, or you may choose to master the skills of human interactions so that in future you will never trip on the corporate carpet.

MASTER THE ESSENTIALS OF BUSINESS ETIQUETTE

There are many aspects of business etiquette, depending on corporate functions, purpose, products, culture and vision. For the sake of clarity, we will club business etiquette pointers under two subheadings: (a) office customs and practices, and (b) business communications. Under these two subheadings you will find many big and small etiquette pointers which probably remain overlooked due to office workload. The aim is to help you avoid offensive habits that annoy people and learn easy and quick ways to conduct yourself appropriately in the workplace. You will also learn the use of etiquette in business communication and how to introduce people in business situations. The practice of these etiquette norms will help you acquire confidence in business and social situations and build strong rapport with colleagues and customers in a manner that is appropriate and professional.

A. OFFICE CUSTOMS AND PRACTICES

Equality among Colleagues

In the business arena, men and women treat each other as colleagues and share an equal status. In social situations, men are expected to open the door for women to pass first, assist them in carrying packages, step aside for them to enter the elevator first, or even pay for lunch. In the office environment, none of the above courtesies is expected. Whoever gets to the door first opens it and goes through it. Whosoever, be it a man or woman, has their arms full as they approach the door, common sense would dictate that the person be given assistance. In a social situation, a woman initiates the handshake; in a business situation, either a man or a woman may initiate the handshake.

Ranks Are Supreme

In the business arena, customers, clients and superiors are treated with courtesy. You have to wish them, hold the doors open for them to pass, assist them in carrying packages, and step aside so that they enter the elevator first. The boss will extend the courtesy to customers and clients.

Tips to Treat a Lady

- When accompanying a lady on the street, a man should walk on the outside, closer to the road.
- When going through the revolving door, a man should precede a lady.

- When ascending an escalator with a lady, a man should allow the lady to precede him.
- When descending an escalator with a lady, a man should go first.
- At a business luncheon with a lady, a man should offer to seat her by holding her chair.
- If a lady excuses herself from a business meal, the man who is seated closest to her stands up to acknowledge her departure from the table, and he must stand up again when she returns to the table.

ANNOYING AND OFFENSIVE OFFICE HABITS

Wherever people congregate to work or recreate, common sense dictates that you have to be accommodative. If you do as you please, you will be a nuisance to others. Rules of etiquette ensure that everyone enjoys equal opportunities to exercise their rights and duties to congregate in an atmosphere of mutual respect and cordiality.

> *Before everything else, getting ready is the secret of success.*
>
> Henry Ford

The closed-door office culture is the privilege proprietors, chief executive officers, managing directors and presidents enjoy; the rest of the employees work in open spaces and cubicles, where the atmosphere is open, relaxed and also annoying. If the nature of your work demands privacy or quiet time for thinking, your work quality suffers because of the background chatter and other noises of co-workers. There are certain habits you may have developed and no one told you how annoying or offending they can be to co-workers. Check yourself on the following points:

Loud Laughter

A good hearty laugh is always welcome but it should be under control at all times. Loud, high or shrill laughter is an indication of something more than pure pleasure — that manners are not under check. Also, avoid talking to someone across the cubicle or across your desk, however important it is. Walk over to the person to have the conversation in soft tones.

Irritable Noises

You should never drum your fingers on the table or desk. Do not crack your knuckles, whistle, sing or hum. Keep your mobile phone on 'silent'/'vibrate' mode. Alternatively, set the ringtone on a low volume so that others are not disturbed. Avoid talking on speakerphones. When someone is talking on the phone or sending an email don't start talking and waving your hands, using sign language or talking loud. You are interrupting the person speaking on the phone as well as disturbing others.

Boorish Mannerisms

During conferences and meetings, do not distract yourself and others with the mobile phone, make calls, play games and receive or send messages — these are considered to be bad habits. Scratching the head or any other body parts, nose picking, sniffing, clearing the throat and sucking in the phlegm, coughing, belching, breaking wind, spitting, blowing the nose loudly and then examining the contents in the handkerchief or paper tissue are disgusting habits.

Eating and Preening at the Desk

Don't leave old and stale food in your cubicle, shelves or desk as the persons sitting at adjoining desks will find it nauseating. Food left overnight decays quickly and begins to stink. For the same reason, don't bring food with really strong odours to eat at your workstation. Your cubicle is not your dressing room or a place to put on make-up, trim or file fingernails and brush your hair. Use the restroom for preening purpose.

Respect the Privacy of Others

You should not enter your colleague's cabin, cubicle or room without permission. Knock before you enter. Once inside, don't pick up anything and put it in your pocket just because the area is open and the person is away. Don't snoop, check or access data from the computer or read/copy files and memos without being invited to do so. These matters are private or personal, and to read them or copy them in someone's absence is certainly unethical, if not immoral.

Do Not Be Curious or Intrusive

In the way you speak with others, be sure that any question you ask will not embarrass the person you are speaking with. For instance, do not ask about matters of religion, health or family that are strictly private. Never ask the age or the wage of a person. Do not try to fish out information which is personal and private. When speaking with your boss, do not ask questions about someone else which is confidential. If you have to ask your boss for permission, do so when only the two of you are there. Asking for permission or concessions when the group is present may put the boss in an awkward situation.

Do Not Spread Gossip

When you come across personal and confidential information about someone which will show that person in bad light, you must restrain yourself from spreading gossip and cheap talk, even if that person be a rival. Actions which compromise or harm another person's good name must strictly be avoided. Defamation of character is a legal offence. In this whole matter of privacy, much depends on your ability to sense when people are offended and when they are not. Do not address your superiors by their first name unless they have personally told you to do so. And do not give nicknames to your colleagues and superiors which could in any way offend them.

Mind Your Language

Conduct yourself at the workplace as a professional at all times. Avoid using any form of profanity, vulgarity or swearing during business meetings or when you are in the company of business associates. Also, avoid jokes that discriminate against genders, castes, religions and regions. Making inappropriate remarks or using language that is inappropriate in a professional environment sends a negative message about your professionalism.

Stop Complaining and Whining

Complaining is negative. Negative vibes, complaints, gossip and comments definitely don't create a congenial work environment. Negativity spreads like wildfire, infecting not just your work life but your home life too. People get tired of listening to the same negative comments about someone or some issue over and over again. If you have an issue with another person, talk directly about it and get it over with; don't complain to others. Negative talk leaves negative impressions. You do not want to keep complaining about

> *Criticism of others is futile and if you indulge in it often, you should be warned that it can be fatal to your career.*
>
> Dale Carnegie

how you lost out on a promotion, how jealous some co-workers are or how prejudiced your boss is. People will steer clear of you to avoid listening to your depressing comments. Constant whining or complaining will make people wonder whether you speak negatively about them behind their backs.

Antisocial Habits to Avoid

Sharing lewd jokes and vulgar pictures through e-mail, Facebook, SMS and MMS to embarrass fellow colleagues; shoulder-slamming people near escalators, elevators and revolving doors; bullying, teasing, ganging against or harassing someone; and rushing into elevators without allowing people to exit first — these not only show lack of common courtesies but also go against the norms of social and civil decency.

Don't Be Physically Intimate with Colleagues

Getting intimately involved with a colleague or subordinate is not only setting yourself up for trouble but also suicidal for your career. Of course, you won't know the kind of trouble you will be in until you are already drowning in it, such as stalking behaviour (yours or theirs), sabotage at work (yours or theirs), or jealous partners (yours or theirs). Plus, it is just not a professional way to make your work environment professional, efficient or productive.

Quick Tips on Office Etiquette

If you open it	CLOSE IT
If you turn it on	TURN IT OFF
If you unlock it	LOCK IT
If you break it	REPAIR IT
If you can't fix it	CALL IN SOMEONE WHO CAN
If you borrow it	RETURN IT
If you use it	TAKE CARE OF IT
If you make a mess	CLEAN IT UP
If you move it	PUT IT BACK
If it belongs to someone else	GET PERMISSION TO USE IT
If you don't know how to operate it	LEAVE IT ALONE
If it doesn't concern you	DON'T MESS WITH IT

B. BUSINESS COMMUNICATIONS

E-mail Etiquette

> *Most of what we call management consists of making it difficult for people to get their work done.*
>
> Peter F Drucker

The internet is the biggest communications revolution of our times. One doesn't have to be a 'techie' to access the internet to receive and send electronic mails (e-mails). While e-mail communication has come of age, many companies have not realized how important it is and soon lost their competitive edge to rivals. Such companies either ignore e-mail queries, or send them late with replies that don't merit the effort of opening them.

Many companies, on the other hand, train employees to use appropriate, businesslike language in all electronic communications to enhance their professional image. People who run the most successful companies are also the most responsive. When you leave a voice message or send an e-mail, these individuals get back to you immediately with information, whether they are at thc office or travelling. Rekha Awasthi, who oversees 5,000 employees, makes it a policy to respond to e-mail within 24 hours. She says her responsiveness provides a model for her employees. If she responds quickly to employee questions or concerns, they in turn understand the importance of getting back to customers in a short time.

There are many etiquette guides and many different etiquette rules governing e-mail usage, depending on the nature of business or its corporate culture. Listed below are 10 basic guidelines on e-mail etiquette that apply to almost all companies and individuals:

1. *All messages should be short and concise.* If the message is of more than a few lines, divide the text into paragraphs for clarity and better visual impact. Remember that reading an e-mail is harder than reading printed communications, and a long e-mail can be very discouraging.

2. *Use a meaningful subject line.* If a busy executive cannot figure out from the subject line what the e-mail is about, the message usually gets ignored or deleted.

3. *Answer all questions.* An e-mail reply must answer all questions and pre-empt further questions. If you do not answer all questions in the original e-mail, you will receive further e-mails regarding unanswered questions. This will not only waste your time and the customer's but also cause considerable frustration.

4. *Use proper spelling, grammar and punctuation.* Never attempt the SMS format for e-mail. The use of proper grammar, spelling and punctuation not only makes the message more easily understood but also enhances your image and the company's. Virtually all e-mail programmes have a spelling and grammar check, so there is no reason not to use it.

5. *Keep all messages relevant.* All messages posted must be relevant to the subject at hand. When replying to someone, quote the parts of the original message that pertain to your reply.

6. *Project the company's professional image.* In a business e-mail, avoid sending jokes, quotes and punctuation faces.

7. *Answer swiftly.* Customers send an e-mail because they wish to receive a quick response. If they did not want a quick response they would post a letter. Therefore, each e-mail should be replied to within 24 hours at most and preferably within the same working day. If the e-mail is complicated, respond by saying you received it and will get back to them soon. This will put the client's mind at rest.

8. *Avoid attachments.* Include the message in the body of the e-mail. With viruses being rampant, many people do not open attachments, no matter what size. Large attachments can take a long time to open, and many busy executives do not have the time to wait.

> *It's not the employer who pays the wages. Employers only handle the money. It's the customer who pays the wages.*
>
> Henry Ford

9. *Do not write in CAPITAL letters.* IF YOU WRITE IN CAPITALS IT IS INTERPRETED AS IF YOU ARE

SCREAMING ON THE INTERNET. This can be highly annoying and might trigger an unwanted high-voltage response.

10. *Deleting e-mail.* Remember an e-mail is not gone when you delete it. A deleted e-mail is permanently stored on the magnetic tape in the hard drive of your computer. An employee's e-mail is a company's asset and can be reviewed at any time by the employer.

Telephone Etiquette

Like the internet, the mobile telephone is the next most important communication revolution of our times. It has many advantages and a great many disadvantages. The biggest disadvantage for mobile telephone users is the lack of training in telephone etiquette. Whether you are eating a quiet meal in a restaurant or waiting for your turn in the common waiting area of a hospital, clinic or office, you are forced to listen to the loud and inconsiderate conversation of someone who is completely oblivious of the inconvenience caused to people sitting or standing nearby.

At the workplace, impoliteness or rudeness to others when speaking on the phone is totally unacceptable from employees. Every connection an employee makes with a customer or client is vital to the profits of the company. So many companies lose out on business deals when they fail to connect because of untrained employees, who lack proper telephone etiquette, and poor customer service standards, which ultimately result in business losses.

> *We should be treating the customer in the same way that we would want to be treated as customers. I think we have a lot to learn on this front – and a lot to change.*
>
> Ratan Tata

Taking care of customers over the telephone and making them feel looked after, well-informed and appreciated is essential to each and every business. Whether you are the front office receptionist or executive secretary or you work in an organization with the responsibility to make and receive calls, the following 10 telephone tips must always be followed:

1. *Speak audibly.* The caller on the other end of the phone can only hear you, not see your face or body language. Put a 'smile' in your voice and speak clearly, slowly and distinctly. Always sound professional, positive and polite when you answer the phone.

2. *Use your normal tone of voice when answering a call.* Don't speak with a pretentious accent. If you have a tendency to speak loud or shout, avoid doing so on the telephone.

3. *Always identify yourself properly.* When calling a client or customer always identify yourself properly by providing your name, the company's name and the contact telephone number. Before you proceed, ask the client if it is convenient to talk or you should call later.

4. *Don't answer the phone while you eat, drink or chew gum.* Your words will be inaudible, slurred and muffled when you speak while eating and drinking.

5. *Avoid slang words.* Respond clearly with a "yes" or "no" when speaking. "Yep", "Yup", "Yeah" and "Okay" are slang words. Avoid swear words or abusive language. Always use the *magic words*: "Please", "Thank you" and "Sorry".

6. *Address the caller properly by his or her title.* Never address an unfamiliar or business caller by the first name. For instance, you will say, "Good morning, Major General D'Souza" or "Good afternoon, Ms Sharma". Thereafter, use the honorific "Sir" or "Madam".

7. *Listen to the caller's message.* The ability to listen well is a quality lacking in most people but it is important to listen carefully to what the caller has to say. It is always a good habit to repeat the information back to the client when you are taking a message. Verify with the caller that you heard and wrote the message accurately. To be efficient, always keep a notepad and pencil handy by the telephone.

8. *Be patient and helpful.* If the caller is irate or upset, listen to what they have to say and then refer them to the appropriate resource. Never snap back, talk rudely, or disconnect.

9. *Always ask if you can put the caller on hold.* If you are responsible for answering multiple calls at once, always ask the caller politely if you may put them on hold. Never put the client on hold for

more than a few seconds or they may become upset. You must learn how to handle several callers simultaneously with ease and charm.

10. *Return calls promptly.* Calls left on the voice mail or answering machine must be attended to promptly. Even if you don't have an immediate answer, acknowledge receiving a voice message within 24 hours or less, and let the person know you're considering the request or taking action on it. Never call the client's home between 8 p.m. and 8 a.m. unless you have specifically been instructed to do so.

Stop Improper Mobile Phone Usage

One of the most prevalent etiquette problems in the modern business world is related to mobile phone usage. Too frequently, people, including top executives, breach proper business etiquette by leaving their mobile phones on during meetings and conferences and divert attention from the matter at hand and onto the device. Some people thoughtlessly answer calls during meetings with clients, co-workers and supervisors. You can hear loud conversations in office elevators. It is disrespectful and inappropriate to inflict your telephone conversation on other people. The gap in etiquette training also shows when people whose business is to provide services either lie outrageously or disconnect calls rudely and never bother to return the client's call or send a message.

With the widespread adoption of mobile phone usage, many people have lost sight of the fact that the person in whose presence you are deserves your full attention. Ignoring the person who is in front of you and instead taking a call from someone else is downright rude and conveys lack of respect. Learn to use the 'silent' mode on your mobile phone so that you know when others are trying to contact you, but the people around you will not be disturbed. If you want to make a positive impression on your clients and enhance the professional image of your company, you should limit your mobile-phone conversations to times and places where they are not disruptive or intrusive to others.

C. BUSINESS INTRODUCTIONS

The basic practice in business etiquette requires that you know how to introduce people — a skill that should not be overlooked. It is said that the most important thing about introductions is that they should be done. Almost any error you make will be forgiven; what may not be forgiven is failing to introduce someone at all, because that person was left to navigate the choppy waters of social introductions in the sea of unknown people on their own without any help from you. Fortunately, knowing how to introduce people gets easier with practice.

The first step in making introduction is to determine who should be introduced to whom.

1. Introductions in business are based on rank. *The basic rule is that the name of the higher-ranking or older person should be said first.* In a business situation, the customer or client is always considered higher-ranking. "Mr Anil Prasad (your client), I would like you to meet Ms Anita Kelkar, executive director, sales and marketing of YAWN Inc."

2. Unless you are in an informal setting, introductions should be made using the first and last names, as well as titles such as "Dr" and "Professor" when appropriate. If someone does not have a professional title, use the honorific title "Sir" or "Madam". If the person you are introducing has a clear relationship to you, this should be made clear. For instance, "Pooja Marwah, I'd like you to meet my friend Natasha Jain." (Pooja is older than Natasha). "Dr. Ranbir Gupta, please meet my husband, Professor Praful Singh Bedi." (Ranbir is senior vice president of the company).

3. A peer of your company is introduced to the peer of another company. Say the name of the person outside your company first.

4. The name of the official or dignitary is said first, such as "Major Arvind Deshmukh, I would like you to meet Ms Jayanthi Rao, a social activist."

5. All guests, unless they are dignitaries or elderly, are introduced to the guest of honour.

6. In a group setting such as a party, you should introduce a person to the group first. For example, "Kishore, these are my friends, Shiva and Aashima, John and Namita. Everyone, this is Kishore, an old friend visiting from Germany."

7. If someone has forgotten to introduce you, there is nothing wrong

in introducing yourself and explaining how you know the host if you are at a party. Give your first and last name clearly without a title, such as "Mr" or "Dr". Also, it will help others remember your name if you give some information about yourself.

When You Are Introduced — *Quick Tips*

a) Unless you are elderly or disabled, men and women must rise to be introduced to anyone. (Some authorities affirm that while men must stand up when being introduced, women should stand only when introduced to dignitaries, persons of rank, or older gentry.)

b) If you are meeting someone in your office, stand up, walk around your desk and initiate a handshake. The desk should never come between you and the guest.

c) If you have forgotten someone's name, it is more polite and less awkward to simply acknowledge the fact than to avoid an introduction.

d) If you are being introduced to a group of people, you are not required to say something after each introduction. Always repeat the person's name. It adds a touch of personal interest as well as helps you remember the name.

BUSINESS ETIQUETTE – YOUR BRAND AMBASSADOR

Business etiquette empowers your brand value by adding equity to it. In the narrow sense, 'equity' applies to profit-and-loss spreadsheets and to stocks and shares. In the broad sense, 'equity' is the value attached to the brand image of the company or the person and it has nothing to do with stocks and shares. For example, in the first and second IPL (Indian Premier League) cricket seasons, Kolkata Knight Riders fared badly as a team on the field, but their brand equity was the highest when rated among other teams which had performed brilliantly on the field. One man's charisma led the brand. Shahrukh Khan single-handedly marketed Kolkata Knight Riders even when his team failed to win matches. In brand equity, Kolkata Knight Riders was on top of the charts and not the teams that won the IPL championship.

You can learn from Shah Rukh Khan. If he can make something out of failure, so can you. Your department could be on a losing wicket or you could be surrounded by a bunch of losers. Why would you let your reputation, built over years of good performance, get flushed down the drain? Do you have to dress shabbily because your co-workers dress sloppily? Do you have to be rude to co-workers because the managers are ill-mannered? You owe allegiance first to yourself, then to the company — not to a bunch of losers in the department who are ready to take you down with them.

Motivation is the art of getting people to do what you want them to do because they want to do it.
Dwight D Eisenhower

Business etiquette will help you keep your pride and dignity, especially when others have lost it. You must work in a way that will enhance your brand value. You have to cultivate business etiquette so that you can add value to your personal brand. The more skills you have, the more value you add to your personal brand. The more skills you develop, the more equity your brand earns. Your equity rests on the formidable reputation you earned. Your brand equity, which is linked to your image, enhances your brand value personally, professionally and socially. You have to work on yourself and improve mannerisms and behaviour to become a valued asset. The more you focus on business etiquette, the more assets you will develop. These assets will enhance your personality and add more value to the professional image of your organization.

TABLE MANNERS

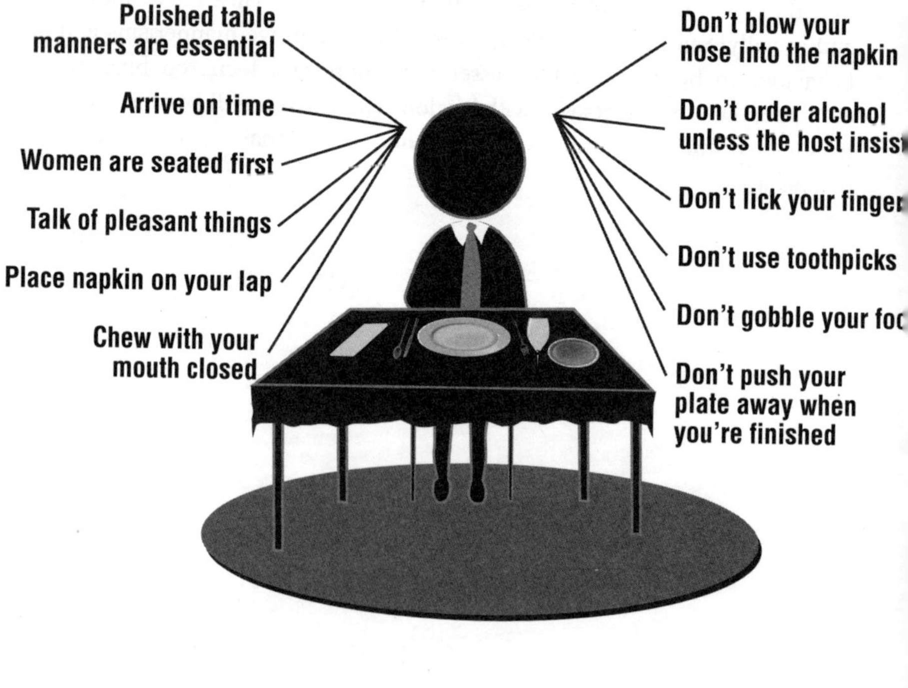

Chapter 9

GARNISH YOUR CORPORATE BRAND

TABLE MANNERS

Bosco never enjoyed business lunches or dinners. He hated his job each time he had to represent his company at a business meal. The formal trappings of table manners made him uneasy and self-conscious. He was a foodie who loved to eat what he liked and not what was served to be eaten in the way convention demanded. "Can you enjoy fried mackerels made in Goan vindaloo masala *or to-die-for Bombay duck curry with a knife and fork?" he said. According to Bosco, food must be eaten in the way it was meant to be — with fingers. He also cleaned the curry off the plate with his fingers or mopped it up with bread. He occasionally let out small belches to signal a satisfied meal.*

Now, Bosco should have realized that the goal of business meals was to seal business deals. The company pays for the meal in order to promote business and not purely for experiencing gastronomic delights. He must learn to enjoy business lunches and dinners with his mind on business negotiations and off the food.

In today's competitive business climate, table manners play an important role in business encounters. Garnish Your Corporate Brand *offers you gilt-edged tips to wield the spoon, fork and knife with effortless ease to help you cut through business deals — without scaring you on formal lavish-style banquets. Competition in the business arena is fierce and companies are looking for executives who not only handle themselves professionally in the boardroom but have also mastered the art of dining etiquette when accompanying business clients to the restaurants. To rise above, you must apply your mind and learn to eat your way to success with polished table manners.*

It is a worldwide phenomenon. A lot of business is conducted and many business deals are concluded at the dining table. Today, more and more companies indulge in cut-and-dry business meals to break ice with potential clients, conduct job interviews, wrap up contracts and sign up new partners and mergers. Every little detail from the way you sit, what you order, how you use the fork, to the conversation you have, shows your table manners and professional polish. If you are under the impression that everyone is busy eating and no one notices table manners, or that you are so good at your work that no matter how you eat is nobody's business, think again. Gulping down your drink and bolting down the food will not only give your clients a bellyache but also choke business orders.

To have impeccable table manners you have to be consistent with your habits. You cannot have two standards of behaviour — one at home and the other at the office. For instance, you cannot eat like a boorish Hun at home with family and friends, and later behave like a polished executive at the corporate table, even when the service is buffet. The slip shows — and how! People who eat boorishly in casual gatherings usually end up as an embarrassment at formal dining.

POLISHED TABLE MANNERS IS BUTTER FOR BUSINESS

> *When I let go of what I am, I become what I might be.*
>
> Lao Tsu *aka* Lao Zi

Business executives are expected to have excellent table manners. But with television meals and finger foods doing the rounds, table manners are no longer practised in everyday life. To avoid embarrassment to the company, it is necessary to teach business executives acceptable dining etiquette before sending them out to represent the company at a customer lunch or business dinner. There are definite rules of dining etiquette, and having a working knowledge of these turns an executive into a poised marketing representative of the company. Proper use of utensils plays an important part in making a favourable impression.

Whether you are dining informally or formally, you always come to the table well groomed: hair combed, hands and fingernails cleaned, clothes fresh and tidy. However appetizing the meal is, you do not give the impression that the main thought on your mind is the food you are eating. To stave off hunger pangs, eat a light snack before leaving home for a business dinner. While the body is being nourished, your mind must be occupied with the conversation or other activity that may be going on at the dining table. Do not discuss the food except to make an appropriate modest compliment. Insincere flattery or criticism is always out of place.

Are you a picky eater — the one who chooses a particular morsel from the common dish and will not be satisfied with what first comes to the spoon? Of course, there are certain foods that may not agree with you, or sickness may require a special diet. These cases are easily understood and do not draw unfavourable attention the way picking and choosing does. When you accidentally eat something steaming hot or chew on pungent food, never spit it out on the plate. Quickly sip water and wash it down. If a fishbone gets stuck in your throat, eat plain bread and swallow it. If the problem persists and you may need to use your finger, excuse yourself from the table and go to the washroom.

Sitting at Table

It is always advisable to wait to be told by the host where to sit. When you sit down, do not sit too far from the table; otherwise you will have to bend the head too much while eating. On the other hand, do not sit too close to the table, for if you do, you will have trouble using the knives and forks properly. Your chest should not touch the table. Sit in such a way that the four legs of the chair are on the floor — not tilted — and that your two feet are on the floor, though you may cross your legs at the ankles if you find it more comfortable. Do not twist your feet around the legs of the chair. When you sit at the table, the elbows should never be on the table in any position. You may rest your forearms on the edge of the table. The contact with the table takes place near the wrist rather than near the elbow. The hands are not kept under the table, except when you are eating an Indian traditional meal, in which case the left hand is kept hidden from view.

Use of Napkins

When the host starts to unfold the napkin, it is a signal for you to do the same. Usually, you should put the napkin on your lap within the first 10 seconds after sitting down at the table, and don't remove it till you are ready to leave the table. However, follow the host's lead. If you notice the napkin is in the goblet, this is usually a signal from the restaurant that the server will place the napkin into your lap. Unfold the entire napkin if it is small; unfold it half if it is large. Do not wipe your plate or polish the utensils with your napkin. This is very bad manners and a real insult to those who have prepared the table for the meal. Should a plate or utensil be soiled, inform the server quietly and ask them for a clean one. The napkin is provided so that you can gently wipe your lips and finger tips and protect your clothing while you eat. Never use the napkin like a handkerchief to wipe your face, blow your nose or sneeze into. If you have to sneeze suddenly, turn your head away from the table and from all others, if possible, and put your handkerchief or hand over your mouth and nose. If you must blow your nose, excuse yourself from the table. If you cannot be excused, turn your head away and do it quickly and quietly into your handkerchief and put it away without examining the contents.

Do not suspend your napkin from the collar like a bib. Women should try not to get lipstick on cloth napkins. Use the napkin to blot, not wipe, your mouth and lips; do not hold the napkin stretched wide and then move your mouth back and forth on it. Rather press the mouth with a small part of the napkin. If you excuse yourself during the meal, place the napkin on the left hand side of your plate or on the chair. This signals the server that you are not done. When done, place your napkin on the right of the plate to signal the server. The host will signal the end of meal by placing the napkin on the table. Don't crumple your napkin and leave it on your plate; fold it loosely and leave it *beside* your plate.

Be Considerate Towards Others

Do not roll up the sleeves or push them back when you begin to eat. Learn to eat in such a way that your clothing does not get soiled by the food. A meal is a social event, not manual labour. When you wish something that is not in front of you, ask the person sitting next to you to pass it or to ask for it. Never point to it; pointing with the finger is always impolite. Since there are many dishes on the table, your pointing will often be misinterpreted and will cause much more confusion than a simple verbal request spoken softly but distinctly. Never stretch out your hand to get something at a distance. You must be especially careful not to pass your hand or arm over the plates of people sitting next to you. There is never an excuse for this action which people consider as barbarously uncouth. Avoid making gestures while you are holding a knife or a fork in your hand.

To avoid making awkward noises, chew with your lips closed. There is no need to chew with your mouth open. Secondly, do not suck food off the spoon or fork. Liquids are sipped quietly from the side of the spoon. Solids such as rice, puddings, and breakfast cereals are removed from the spoon by closing the lips over it. They are not removed by the teeth or 'dumped' into the open mouth. All of the above points are part of being considerate to others. This consideration is even more directly shown in the matter of taking food from the serving dishes and seeing that those near us at the table have their share of what is served.

FORMAL BUSINESS MEALS

When you see the table that is set for a formal business meal, it can send cold shivers down your spine even if you are a well-heeled diner. Which utensil to choose from a variety of silverware that is laid out on the table can churn your belly and make you lose your appetite. The array of stem glasses can be a daunting sight.

Setting the Table Right

A - Serviette (napkin)	B - Dinner plate
C - Soup bowl on plate	D - Bread & butter plate with butter knife
E - Water glass	F - White wine
G - Red wine	H - Fish fork
I - Dinner Fork	J - Salad fork
K - Dinner knife	L - Fish knife
M - Soup spoon	N - Dessert spoon and cake fork

In fact, it is not as difficult as it may look. Usually, there should be no more than three of each type of utensil beside your plate. You simply start from the outside and work your way in, using one utensil per course. When fish is served, your fish fork is on your outermost left, followed by your dinner fork; if fish is not served then the salad fork takes its place. Your soup spoon is on your outermost right, followed by your fish knife and dinner knife. Your dessert spoon and fork are above your plate. If you are still unsure, don't panic; follow the lead of your host, who will begin first or watch the person sitting next to you. It is polite to wait for your host to begin eating before you do, unless the host tells you to go ahead and eat so that your food does not get cold.

Drink from the Right Glass

Wine connoisseurs agree that each type of wine needs a particular type of

glass and the right way to hold it to bring out the distinctive bouquet. Using a narrow glass for a rich Burgundy, for example, won't allow enough room to swirl it around in, and it's the swirl that brings out its bouquet. The glass also needs to taper properly towards the top so that it captures the bouquet and yet allows for sipping. In general, the stem of a glass should be long enough to keep hands from touching the bowl, which can affect the wine's temperature, and therefore its bouquet.

a. **Water**: full body glass with *short* stem. *Hold it by the stem or the bowl.*
b. **Brandy**: brandy snifter. Roll the snifter between both hands and then *cup it in one hand* — warming the glass brings out the bouquet in brandy.
c. **White wine**: slightly smaller glass with wider bowl to capture the bouquet. *Hold the glass by the stem* to preserve its chill.
d. **Burgundy Red and Pinot Noir**: a wide bowl to bring out their complexity. *Hold the glass at the bottom of the bowl.* The glass is slightly taller than the white-wine glass.
e. **Champagne**: a narrow fluted glass which reduces the wine's surface area to keep the bubbles from dissipating.
f. **Red wine**: the biggest of the wine glasses. *Hold the glass at the bottom of the bowl* where it meets the stem.

FINE-TUNE YOUR BUSINESS MEAL MANNERS

Hold Forks and Knives Properly

The fork may be used in either the right or the left hand. If you keep it in the left hand, as Europeans do, the convex surface is kept up and the prongs are pointed down. When the fork is used in this way, the knife is used to pile the food on the back of the fork. To eat this way with ease requires a good bit of practice. Few people can do this with ease, so it's worth your while to practise this skill. If you keep it in the right hand, as Americans do, the concave side is held up and the prongs are normally pointed up. In this case the knife is not used to push or pile the food on to the fork, for the knife is never used in the left hand. In general, the knife is grasped around the handle by the thumb and the last three fingers, with the first finger placed along the upper edge.

All the other utensils are held pretty much as we hold a pencil, with the handle resting on the web of the skin between the thumb and the first finger. Do not grasp them by circling the fingers around the handle for this makes it very difficult to use them with ease and without raising the elbow into an ungainly position. Used knives and forks are kept on the plate, not on the table. They are never propped at the side of the plate in such a way that the handle rests on the table and the rest of the utensil on the plate. Rather they are kept flat on the upper edge of the plate when not in use. As a rule, the elbow is kept near the side and not raised. This becomes easy provided the knives, forks and spoons are held and handled correctly. The general rule is, do not call attention to yourself. It is bad table manners if the way you eat

(a) makes a mess;

(b) makes a noise; or

(c) calls attention to the fact that you are determined to stuff yourself.

How to Serve Yourself

When a dish is served to you, do not look around for the best or the biggest piece. Take what is nearest you. Of course, if a certain serving is too much for you, you may take a smaller one, or if something does not agree with you, you may pass the serving without taking anything, but do not be too choosy about what you take. Do not put too much food on your plate at one time. Take a moderate helping and then after finishing that much, if you wish more ask for it. It is bad manners to take food in your plate and then not eat it. If you are not sure you are going to like something, take a small helping and then ask for more if you like it. What is taken should be eaten. It is even worse manners to pile so much food on your plate that others at table do not get a fair share or even have to do without it.

> *When you reach for the stars, you may not quite get them, but you won't come up with a handful of mud either.*
>
> Leo Burnett

When taking food from a serving dish, lift it from that dish with a serving spoon and place it on your own plate. Do not spill, push or rake it from the common dish into your plate. Leave the serving dish neat. Do not let your own fork or spoon touch the serving dish. Except for bread and the like, all food is taken with a spoon or fork — never with the fingers.

Passing the Dishes

You may not like some of the dishes that are served, but be sure to pass them to others at the table. While you must not stare at the other's plate or watch anyone in the act of eating, you should have your eyes open to other's needs and pass what is needed, even without being asked. If one item is asked for, pass what goes with it. For instance, if coffee is asked for, pass the milk and sugar also; if bread is asked for, pass the butter too. If someone at the table asks for a second helping, do not stop it on the way to take something for yourself first. You may ask for the dish after the person has taken a helping. If there is a variety of fruit or any other serving, do not take all of one kind for yourself, thus limiting the choice for others. The common dish should be to the left of your plate or in your left hand as you help yourself from it. When you pass the food to another always use the right hand.

Eating with Grace

Eat at a moderate pace — neither so slow that others have to wait till you finish, nor too fast, bolting your food down. Of the two faults, eating fast gives the impression of greediness. Let your movements be graceful, not jerky. And try not to do too many things at once. There are people who are chewing with the mouth, stirring coffee with the right hand, reaching for a serving plate with the left, and engaged in a serious conversation, all at the same time. Do not take too much food into the mouth at any one time, and do not drink while there is food in the mouth. When you drink, never swish the liquid in your mouth — unless you are called upon to taste wines at the vineyard.

Eat slowly and chew your food well. Keep a control over your bodily functions. Involuntary sneezes, hiccups, burping, belching and breaking wind must be kept under check. If you know it is coming up, excuse yourself from the table, but if it creeps up suddenly while you are eating, have the grace to apologize.

Keep separate foods separate on your plate. Don't make one big heap of everything. This obviously applies to dishes of types other than rice, curry and dal, which are generally meant to be placed one on top of the other or in separate small bowls when provided. Sauces and chutneys may be put right on the food they will be eaten with, but butter, jam, pâté and things of that sort are first put on the plate and applied to the bread, toast or crackers just before the morsel is put into the mouth. When sugar or salt is put on solid or semi-solid food, for instance, cereals at breakfast, it is generally sprinkled evenly on the top of the food but not stirred into the food. If you must stir it in, do it in the least obtrusive manner.

Inedible articles such as bones, seeds or stones from fruit, or anything else that cannot be swallowed may be removed from the mouth in two ways. You may remove them with your thumb and forefinger, keeping the mouth closed as much as possible, or you may slip them from the mouth onto your spoon or fork and put them back on the edge of your plate. You should never drop them directly from your mouth to the plate.

ADD A TOUCH OF CORPORATE CLASS

Breaking Bread

The acceptable practice is to break a morsel of bread, naan, chapatti or roti with both hands, using the thumbs and forefingers, but the breaking is not done all at one time. Place a slice of bread or bread roll and the butter on your bread plate, and then pass the breadbasket and the butter dish to your right. Tear off a small piece of bread or break the roll into half, butter it and eat it. Bread is never eaten in whole slices unless it is toast or garlic bread. Bread is not eaten with a fork. There is only one exception to this rule. If there is gravy or dal which you wish to take with a fork, small particles of bread may be dropped into it and then the bread and gravy may be taken with the fork. In fact, these pieces must be taken with the fork, for the bread should not be used as a mop with which you clean the plate.

Naan, chapatti and roti are never eaten with a fork. Nor are they used as mops with which to clean the plate. If no special butter knife is provided and you have to use your own knife to take butter from the butter dish, first wipe the knife on the piece of bread you are going to butter and then take the butter from the dish and put it on your bread plate. It is glaringly offensive to butter a whole slice of bread, then rest the elbow firmly on the table and bite half-moons into the bread. Do not pass bread, naan, chapatti and roti with your fingers or on the end of you knife; pass the breadbasket with your right hand.

Cutting Fruit

Stewed fruit is eaten with a small spoon. Fresh fruit that is not bite-size is first cut and then eaten. Cut the fruit and eat it with your fingers, unless the fruit is very juicy, in which case a spoon or fork may be used. As with all other food, the fruit should not be cut all at once, but as and when a piece is wanted it should be cut from a larger portion. Softer fruits such as bananas should be cut on the fruit plate. Harder fruits such as guavas, pears, apples and perhaps some peaches are best cut in hand. Papayas and melons are eaten with a small spoon or fork. So are mangoes and similar fruits after they have been cut through the middle without peeling them.

Finger Foods

Being large in size, club sandwiches are best eaten with the knife and fork. Otherwise use your hands. Potato chips are eaten with fingers. French fries, when eaten with finger foods such as hotdogs, burgers and sandwiches, are eaten with fingers. However, when eating French fries with other foods, cut and eat them with a fork. Garnishes such as carrots, cherry tomatoes, parsley, radishes, pickles and olives are all finger foods. Pizza is best eaten with your fingers, but use your fork for the first few bites. Use caution when squeezing lemons; you don't want to squirt yourself or anyone else. Hold your hand over and around the lemon as you squeeze, or shield the lemon with your spoon to prevent the juice from hitting someone.

Scooping Soup

Spoon the soup away from you. Lean forward, but don't hunch forward when bringing the soup to your mouth. Sip the soup quietly from the side of the spoon, not from the tip. Between sips, the spoon is placed on the under-plate. You may drink only thin soup from the soup bowl, provided the soup bowl has handles, and after taking a few spoonfuls first. Thick soups or soups containing chunks of vegetables or meat are always eaten with a spoon. When tipping the bowl to get the last few drops of soup on the spoon, tip the bowl away from you. When you are finished, place the soup spoon on the right side of the under-plate or leave the spoon in the soup bowl when there is no under-plate.

Drinking Beverages

Ordinarily the cup or glass is held in the right hand (but there may be exceptions). Stem glasses are held by the stem. Do not drink while there is food in your mouth. Swallow the food and then drink. Before using the glass, wipe your lips if they are soiled so as not to leave a mark on the rim of the glass. And if you feel you want to dry your lips after drinking, do so, but always with the napkin — not with your hand. The best way to consume bottled drinks and carbonated beverages is to drink them from a glass. Your second option is to drink them from a bottle with a straw. Never drink straight from the bottle. Avoid gurgling noises while you are drinking. Do not drink all the contents at once; nor drain the glass or cup empty. While drinking, keep your eyes lowered, not looking about.

Sipping Tea and Coffee

If you happen to be drinking tea or coffee standing, hold the saucer in the left hand in such a way that the liquid does not fall on your clothes or on the floor. Stir sugar into the tea or coffee with your right hand. The stirring should be done noiselessly and with a slow rather than rapid motion. Remember that a liquid can only dissolve a certain amount of sugar so that if you put in more than that amount, the sugar will settle at the bottom of the cup and you will have to stir it more than once to avoid wasting the sugar. Do not consume the tea or coffee by taking it in spoonfuls from the cup; rather, drink it from the cup. Tea or coffee should never be poured into the saucer to cool and it should not be drunk from the saucer. Do not blow on it to cool it. Moving it slowly with the spoon is about the only acceptable way of cooling a liquid that is too hot to drink. Keep the spoon on the saucer, not in the cup. Bread, biscuits, cookies and the like should not be dipped into tea or coffee and then eaten.

> *I forgot what I was taught. I only remember what I've learnt.*
>
> Patrick White

EATING WITH FINGERS

You must be dexterous eating with your fingers, especially when you are invited to a traditional Indian meal. These meals have their own rules. Use the fingers of your right hand to break bread and take the food to your mouth without soiling the palm of your hand. (The left hand is considered 'unclean' and is rested on the lap and out of sight.) The host may choose to personally serve food on your plate; you are required to put your hand out, palm down, over your plate as a signal for the host to stop when sufficient food has been served. Soiled fingers are never sucked or licked. Use the finger bowl at the end of the meal (a small bowl with water in it is meant for washing the fingers). First dip the fingertips into the water and then wipe them on the napkin. If a napkin is not provided, wipe your fingers on your handkerchief without calling attention to the cleaning-up operation. Never use your shirt, coat and trousers to wipe your hands.

TWO GENERAL REMARKS

1. *Your Face:* Keep your face away from your plate. This means that you will not bend your head to take the food but will raise the food to your mouth with the hand doing about 85 per cent of the moving. We can concede the head the other 15 per cent. Do not sniff the food to see how it smells; nor blow on it to cool it off.
2. *Your Teeth:* Never clean your teeth at the table. This means that toothpicks are not to be used at the table and fingers are to be kept out of the mouth. Nor should one take a drink of water and then swish the contents around in the mouth to cleanse it at the end of the meal. If food particles are stuck between the teeth, go to the washroom or somewhere else after the meal where you can clean your teeth without others having to watch the process.

Eating may not quite be the simple task it might seem to be if one wants to do it with real consideration for others. All the do's and don'ts mentioned above have one motive behind them — that we should not offend the eyes, ears and general sensibilities of others. If you are convinced of the need for good table manners, you will want to cultivate good dining habits in order to gain a competitive edge by adding polish to your personal brand as well as find it natural to eat in a way that will always make you a pleasant dinner partner and a valuable asset to your company.

SECTION III

MASTER BUSINESS COMMUNICATION SKILLS

Chapter 10
INTERACTIVE SOCIAL NETWORKING
Art of Conversation

Chapter 11
EFFECTIVE BRAND POSTURING
Get Fluent in *Bodytalk*

Chapter 12
BLOW YOUR BRAND TRUMPET
Speak like Steve Jobs

ART OF CONVERSATION

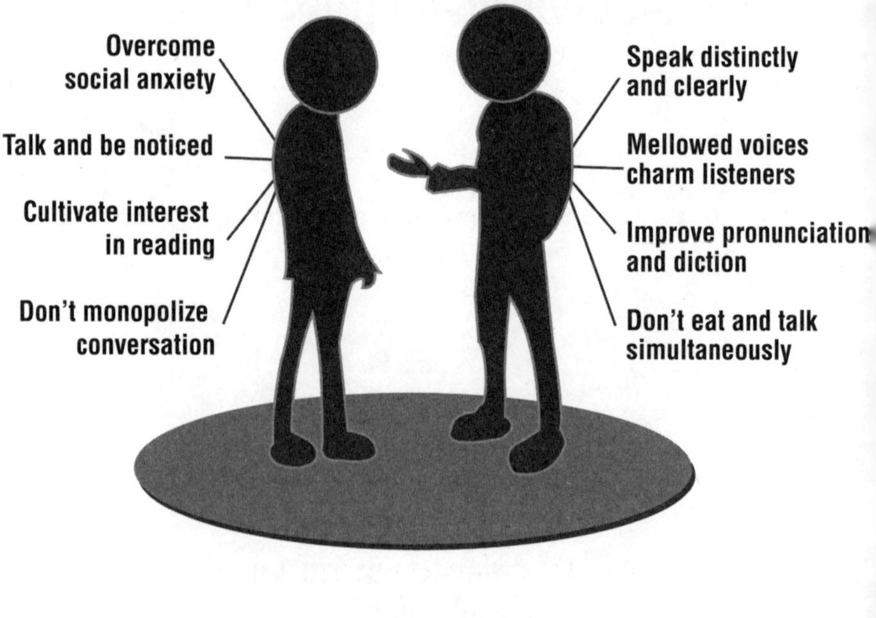

Chapter 10

INTERACTIVE SOCIAL NETWORKING

ART OF CONVERSATION

Rajesh was a gentleman. His face creased into a smile each time he spoke. The smile from his lips touched his eyes and his voice. He was a warm person, people said, as they warmed up to him. He had a way with words — he spoke slowly, gently, and held your gaze, which made you feel important. He never interrupted you; he allowed people to finish what they wanted to say. At the office, subordinates never felt ticked off by the boss because Rajesh would call them in his cabin, talk about their strengths and tell them how much the company depended on their efficiency, competency or punctuality. They left the cabin ready to prove they were worthy of his respect.

A polished, well-spoken gentleman, Rajesh spoke English, Hindi and Punjabi fluently. He had made a lot of effort to cultivate this fluency. He lost his father when he was a child. His mother brought him up along with two other siblings. They studied in the neighbourhood government-run school where his mother was a teacher. When he was at school and later at night college, Rajesh spoke English with difficulty. He thought in Hindi and then attempted a quick mental translation while he groped for the right English words to fit the 'native' idiom. Most people stop making the effort, but Rajesh was determined to reach the top. He observed people he admired and copied their mannerisms. He listened to newsreaders on television and emulated their style. Rajesh practised English drills night and day — and succeeded.

English conversation at the workplace can be difficult to learn. Office towers are like the Tower of Babel, where you meet people from different continents, countries, regions, cultures and backgrounds. People talk English so differently because they speak English in their native idioms. However difficult you find it to understand and converse in English, don't be frustrated and don't make fun of people. To improve your conversation skills you must rise above, like Rajesh did. Business English is the language of commerce. To fast-track your career to the top, you will have to take the 'English' elevator.

Many people think that today's youth are bold and are not afraid to talk, because they constantly yak, yak, yak on their mobile phones. You got it wrong. The truth is that the youth are mortally afraid to speak in formal gatherings. Most of them get so nervous that they avoid making contact with people. Such people are said to be affected by social anxiety.

DON'T BE 'VICTIMIZED' BY SOCIAL ANXIETY

One of the manifestations of social anxiety is your inability or disinterest to strike a conversation with people. A niggling fear in the remote recesses of your brain keeps you tongue-tied. This can be a major handicap for you when social anxiety spills into the workplace. At meetings and conferences you keep your thoughts to yourself and abstain from contributing to the discussion because you are fighting a mind war. Let us say you have an idea and want to share it, but a tiny voice inside your brain tells you to keep quiet because you will make a mistake and people will laugh at you. While a part of your brain worries about *how* to say it, the other part of the brain worries about *when* to say it. Yet another part of your brain cautions you that it could be a silly idea and your boss would frown at you. In the meantime, mediocre ideas from colleagues are praised by the boss while you struggle with your internal complexes.

Is your anxiety people related or speech-related? For instance, you worry about what others will think of you. You want people to think well of you and their opinion of what you say matters a lot to you. You are also afraid of making mistakes in front of others. If that is the case, you could be afflicted by social phobia. On the other hand, if you are afraid to speak in English because of poor delivery, poor grammar, fractured sentences, bad pronunciation and unpolished diction or if you are afraid that people will make fun of you, you could be suffering from linguistic phobia.

And there are males with feminine voices and females with masculine voices. Whether your voice is high-pitched and squeaky or deep-set and gruff, you are so embarrassed by your voice that you keep your mouth shut at conferences and meeting and you let go of the opportunities to speak because you are afraid what people will think of you. For no fault of yours, you are stuck with a poor voice and you do not know how to enrich your voice quality. There is no need to despair. Take heart for you can enrich and improve your voice quality by doing some exercises at the end of this chapter.

TALK AND BE NOTICED

Each time you hold back sharing your ideas at meetings and conferences, you bypass an opportunity for recognition. Social anxiety can come in the way of your promotion. To be a team leader, you first have to be a team player. To succeed in the workplace, you must identify the barriers that hold you back from speaking informally and formally. Is it social phobia, or is it linguistic phobia? Once you are able to identify the trigger, you will be able to overcome the barriers. Run through this checklist to identify the barriers that pull you down.

> *You learn to speak by speaking, to study by studying, to run by running, to work by working... All those who think to learn in any other way deceive themselves.*
>
> Anatole France

- Are you a shy person?
- Do you believe people are generally smarter than you?
- Is your English grammar and pronunciation bad?
- Are you uncomfortable with the way you look: dark, short, tall, fat, pimpled, skinny, broad, bald, spectacled or whatever?
- Are people more fashionably/attractively dressed than you?
- Do you believe people are snooty or snobs?
- Do you think most colleagues and friends are hypocrites?
- Do you think people look down on you because of your poor English?
- Do you get tongue-tied when office seniors join your group?
- Is your voice too thin, gruff or squeaky?
- Do you feel inferior to people who speak English fluently?
- Are you affected by people's wealth, status or position?

These are just a few pointers to get you started. Maybe you could jot down some specific barriers which make you anxious. Write each 'barrier' on a piece of paper and imagine placing them in different boxes — one box for each 'barrier'. Now imagine a person carrying those many boxes to the workplace or to a lunch meeting with an important client. How would you rate your success under the weight of so many boxes (social barriers)? When burdened under the weight of so many social barriers, where is the chance of having a relaxed, enjoyable, intelligent and engaging conversation with anyone?

Social phobia has a way of catching up with you when you are an adult. The seeds of 'silence' could have been sown in your early childhood. Maybe you were less communicative, or shy of strangers. You mostly kept to yourself and played on your own. You rarely spoke to people, and whenever you did, you spoke in monosyllables. So, the seeds of silence may have been sown at home. As you grew up into an adult, your habit of being silent also grew with you. At meals, you shared the table but not your thoughts with the family — working the laptop, using the mobile phone, reading newspapers or watching television was a regular habit whenever you were at home. At office, it was usually 'functional' shoptalk in soft monosyllables. If this is your profile, you will need to seriously work on developing conversation skills. Social networking has come of age.

BE A PEOPLE'S PERSON

It's a fact of life that the degree of happiness and success depends to a great extent upon your ability to carry on a conversation — light-hearted or serious, silly or intelligent, depending on the situation. It's also a fact of life that you don't need a Master's degree in linguistics for that. People who converse confidently not only receive salary increases and promotions but are also popular at social gatherings.

Merely chatting with office colleagues or strangers at airports or on planes and trains is not going to get you an office raise or a promotion. But not being able to generally chat with people makes you an introvert. And to be perceived as an introvert is not an attribute you want on your office record. On the other hand, the practice of chatting with people will grow into a habit, and this habit gets more and more fine-tuned as you develop confidence. With confidence comes the ability to spontaneously strike a conversation with people of all ages, no matter how approachable or standoffish they are. Practice makes perfect, we are told. Whatever your attitude towards chatting with people is, whether inhibiting or exhibiting, by your practiced skill you perfect the art of being either an introvert or an extrovert.

Not wanting to chat with people is the first roadblock you have to get over in order to be a good conversationalist. This roadblock is caused by two barriers — one is mental; the other physical. In the case of both the barriers, the mind agonizes over the many hypotheses it churns out, usually making huge mountains of tiny molehills. For example, a mental barrier occurs when you tell yourself, "If I say something, people will think I'm stupid. It's better to be quiet and listen." This happens when you are low on confidence and self-esteem. On the other hand, you are hesitant to speak because you are not comfortable with English usage. That is a physical barrier. Your mind is agitated, warning you of dire consequences, "If I speak I'll stammer and sputter words, making a fool of myself. Sit tight. Don't say a word!" This happens because you are uncomfortable speaking in English. You need to improve your language skills — quickly. Or, on the other hand, you may behave like a snob. You consider the audience so below your social standing that you think it would insult your intelligence to converse with them. You would choose to spend a quiet evening by yourself in a place full of people rather than converse with them because they are below your status and they have nothing in common with you.

> *If you don't create your reality, your reality will create you.*
>
> Lizzie West

YOU CAN CONQUER INHIBITIONS

The best way to learn how to swim, they say, is to make a splash in the pool. The best way to learn English is to randomly converse with people. The more you converse in English with family, friends and co-workers, the more fluidly your tongue will move when you speak English words and phrases. Of course, you will make mistakes but that is no excuse not to speak in English when you are with family and friends — in your personal comfort zone.

Also, ask yourself: What is the purpose of having a conversation? (Some find the word *conversation* formidable, while the use of the word *chat* is easy on the mind and the tongue.) Do you want to impress people with your oratory skills? Is it to convince them to your point of view? Do you want to impress others that you can argue with logic and conviction? Do you want people to know how well-read and well-informed you are? Or is your idea of a conversation to have a good time?

People spend a lot of time preparing, dressing and grooming themselves before they leave home for work, outings and parties. Seldom does anyone spend any time on running a mental check by 'preparing' topics of conversation or questioning its purpose. When you put the purpose in focus, you'll understand the dynamics of conversing with people in an interesting and engaging manner. Once you know its purpose and utility, you will find it easy to engage people in small talk, which is the starting point of every conversation.

You will enjoy exchanging pleasantries with people and conversing with them when you realize that the primary purpose of conversation is to express, not to impress. There are other forums to 'impress' people like when you participate in meetings, discussions, seminars, presentations and speeches. In those forums you draw attention to yourself. Your aim is to make a point as lucidly and effectively as possible and people compliment you on your language and delivery skills. So you prepare and rehearse your body language cues, apt choice of words and phrases, ideas arranged in logical order, mellowed voice and appropriate dress with smart accessories — the works! In short, when you have to impress, go out and impress 100 per cent. While on the other hand, in restaurants, clubs, cafeterias, pubs, theatres, social functions and public places, when the purpose is to enjoy the moment, conversations are held in a casual, relaxed and friendly atmosphere, whether the people are known to you or complete strangers.

USE HUMOUR IN CONVERSATION

People enjoy the company of those who make them laugh. Some have a natural talent for telling jokes. When you add fun and light-heartedness to an otherwise dull or morose conversation, people will naturally be attracted to you. To tell a joke with a straight face is a skill you must develop. You cannot laugh and tell a joke at the same time. There is a humorous side to most situations and you must train the quirky side of yours to spot it. RK Laxman's cartoon clips on the social, economic and political situations kept the country craving for more. Comic relief is a welcome diversion at conversations.

> *A lie gets halfway around the world, before truth has a chance to get its pants on.*
> Winston Churchill

When sharing humour, there is also another point to consider. Some people make fun of others to show how smart they are. In jest, they damage their characters. The art of conversation is not about ridiculing people; comedians do that to make a living by making fun of celebrities. To be funny and humorous, you need to have excellent communication skills. If you want to share a joke with your audience, it should not be directed against any particular person, caste, creed, region or nation. A person who can poke fun at himself is a person to be admired.

CONVERSATION KILLERS – THE *DON'TS*

Don't Be Silent

Common courtesy demands that you speak to people. If you are a chronic listener, people will assume you are either dull or unfriendly. Many guides on conversation will caution you of its first rule — listen; don't talk. Follow that advice if you are garrulous. But all those who hesitate to speak, haven't you spent so many agonizing years listening in silence? Haven't you been waiting all the while wondering when you should speak up? Your time has come. It's time you made your contribution to the pool of conversation without drawing negative attention to yourself.

Don't Fidget with Your Phone

When you fidget with your mobile phone, others get the impression that you are eager either to make or receive calls, or send or receive messages. You cannot carry on a conversation with people while you keep glancing, looking, peering at the phone in your hand. It is bad manners to listen to music, play games, send or receive messages, or make or receive calls without first excusing yourself. It is not only rude but also an offence to photograph people on your mobile phone without their consent.

Don't Smell Foul

Sweaty body odours (from head to toe) are huge barriers. Hot and humid summers in any part of the world are a challenge to stay cool and fresh. Unwashed PVC shoes and synthetic socks give a nauseous odour; so do sweaty clothes. Your kerchief shouldn't look like a kitchen rag. Unwashed hair smells bad and looks greasy and unkempt. And most importantly, don't assault your listeners with a stench from your mouth. Watch what you put in your mouth: whiskey, beer, wine, cigarettes, garlic and onions. Remember: burping and belching give out disgusting odours. Bad breath due to poor oral hygiene habits or gingivitis drives people away instantly.

Don't Eat and Talk at the Same Time

When you talk, don't fill your mouth with food. When you dig and explore your teeth with a toothpick in public view, people consider you uncouth. Never speak, laugh and chew your food simultaneously — your listeners will spend many anxious moments worrying about particles of food from your mouth spraying over them and their plates. Take a small bite and chew gently when someone else is doing the talking — it gives you time to listen to others. After you've swallowed down the food, dab your lips with a napkin or tissue and then speak — without jumping into the conversation headlong or cutting others midway.

Don't Monopolize the Conversation

If you talk non-stop and do not allow others to express themselves, you will learn nothing from interacting with people. You are not an encyclopedia. Flitting from one subject to another without giving others the opportunity to comment will turn people away from you. Nobody is in the mood to listen to lectures, homilies and sermons at social gatherings. Pause to catch your breath and wait for others to react and share their opinion. Everyone has an opinion on something. Listening to what they have to say is an essential part of social courtesy.

Don't Interrupt Others

> *The best way to succeed in this world is to act on the advice you give to others.*
> Unknown

The surest way to kill a conversation is to interrupt the speaker mid-sentence. You walk to the group, recognise a face and shout, "Hi, how are you? Long time, huh?" Other kinds of interruptions begin with "That reminds me of..." or "Have you heard this before...?" or "By the way..." It's rude to ask the speaker "Have you finished?" While interruptions from old buddies are accepted, those by 'outsiders' are not. People will judge you to be insensitive, ill-mannered, rude or authoritarian and avoid you.

Don't Interrupt Interruptions

You have the group's attention; the doorbell rings, a new arrival joins the group and you are interrupted mid-point. What should you do? Very politely, keep quiet. While the new arrival is being introduced, remember to repeat the newcomer's name and give your name slowly and clearly. After the introductions are over, don't continue with your old story — unless someone in the group found your story too exciting and asked you to complete the story. When asked to continue, do a quick synopsis for the newcomer's benefit and then continue the story. On the other hand, if you are not reminded to carry on, it could be because the story was not going anywhere, or the newcomer would not be interested in your story. Allow time for someone else to pick up the conversation.

Don't Be Pretentious

Be polite; be courteous; but don't be pretentious. When you pretend to be something you are not, you invite people's ridicule. Pretentious people also engage in 'one-upping'. You said you recently bought some new accessories. She quickly said she picked up some very valuable accessories for half the price you paid. Pretentious people believe that their stories reveal their superiority — that they are smart shoppers while others are stupid. The one-upper is a very annoying conversationalist.

Don't Cut Anyone Off

Don't talk to only one or two persons when conversing in a group because they are 'known' to you. Never speak in regional (foreign) languages when others in the group do not understand. Whenever you speak in a language everyone does not understand, quickly translate what you said. You cut people off when you converse on subjects which others have no interest in or knowledge of, or when you share 'inside' jokes or stories related to your job that only your office buddies understand. You must converse on common topics and in the language everyone understands so that everyone can participate.

Don't Be Piggish

When you are introduced to people or when you greet others, don't pick your nose, bite nails, cough or sneeze in your hands, lick the food off your fingers, scratch yourself, run your hand through your hair, or leave the toilet without washing hands and extend the same hand to greet people.

ART OF CONVERSATION CAN BE LEARNT

According to Dr Peter Marsh in *Eye to Eye*, "The art of conversation involves intricate skills of social coordination. Showing interest and being interesting, starting conversations and ending them, taking your turn or interrupting, bring all our communication resources into play."

Casual conversations usually begin when one person remarks, "Nice weather, isn't it?" or asks some other clichéd question. Conversation openers are rarely original. The anxiety of making the first approach does not generate creative thought, but that does not matter. What matters is that those openers are recognised for what they really are — attempts at starting a conversation. The *words* are not important; the fact that they have been *spoken* is. So don't rack your brains to come up with something original or startlingly shocking.

Conversing with people is an art and not a science. Sciences like physics, chemistry, algebra and geometry are governed by strict rules and formulae. Two plus two will add up to four under any conditions, and never to four and a half. On the other hand, even after strictly following whatever 'rules' of conversation there are, the results here are unpredictable. Though conversation is verbal, it relies heavily on non-verbal cues. When non-verbal expression contradicts verbal, the speaker loses credibility. Conversation is not just an 'art'; it is a *dynamic* art. It becomes a dynamic art when topics and reciprocity move fluidly from one person to another in smooth synchrony.

Conversation is not simply the content of your speech; it is about timing as well, and this is where the *real art* comes in. To know when an opening line is welcome will depend on the nonverbal cues you pick up from the person you want to talk to. For instance, you rushed to your friend to share the good news of your promotion, but you found him pacing back and forth anxiously. You stopped yourself and held back the news of your success because the timing was not right.

Anticipating what others will say and do is fundamental to good conversation. It involves a whole series of signals — some in spoken language; others from pronunciation, intonation, hesitations, pauses, grammar and diction; and still others from body language: overall appearance, eye movements, postures and gestures.

MELLOWED VOICES CHARM LISTENERS

How we sound to others is something that never bothers us, because we are the ones speaking. The hapless person is the one who is at the receiving end of our 'conversation'. When you are asked to repeat a sentence, you take it for granted the other person missed hearing you or has a language problem or a hearing problem. You never think that the way you speak could be the problem. To know how you sound to others, record a video of you talking, or send yourself a message on voicemail and listen to it the next day. To check your voice quality or the content of your recording, you must never listen to it when the text is fresh in your mind. The following day when you have forgotten the exact content of your message, listen for clarity and meaning of the text you recorded the previous day. In all probability you will be surprised to hear the quality of your voice or the content of the recording. Your recorded voice will sound so different to your ears. Watch the video recording and see yourself speaking. Observe closely and make a note of your facial expressions, gestures and body language cues — are they distracting or are they appropriate?

> *Motivation gets you started. Habit keeps you going.*
>
> Unknown

The audio and video recording will be your wake-up call to self-improvement. When you do the exercise mentioned above, the following tips will be helpful:

- Don't mumble when you speak.
- Don't drop your voice or trail off at the end of the sentence.

- Don't speak too fast — it may bring on a stammer (some television anchors stammer when they speak extempore). Speak in the manner the listener understands and remembers what you said.
- Pronounce words correctly, and speak grammatically correct sentences.
- Smile when you talk, and talk with a 'smile' in your voice.
- Don't use fillers: "um", "huh", "uh", "ah", "I mean", "you know", "like", etc.
- Don't twitch, fidget or shuffle your feet or make nervous gestures.
- Don't gobble down food or gulp your drink when talking.

MAKE YOUR VOICE SEXY AND ATTRACTIVE

At social get-togethers or at the workplace, men and women are attracted to a sexy tone of voice. A sexy voice is one that sounds deep with velvety overtones and has a good and clear resonance. It is a proven fact that women are more drawn to men who have a baritone, and men are more drawn to women who have a seductively husky voice. Research shows that men and women who have these types of voice respectively demonstrate self-confidence, trustworthiness, credibility and mysteriousness, and are much sought after. The Bachchans have excellent voice quality for you to learn and copy. Amitabh Bachchan is a role model for men and Aishwarya Rai Bachchan is a role model for women. Both superstars have deep, velvety and sexy voices worthy of emulation. When they speak, you will notice words smoothly glide out from their lips slowly; they are well articulated — a treat to the ears.

A high-pitched squeaky voice is a roadblock to your social and career advancement. You should invest some time to improve a dull, weak voice. Improving your voice quality will make you more attractive and boost your self-confidence. It's no longer a secret that people with high-pitched voices miss a lot of opportunities and are most of the times not listened to. On the other hand, if you have a deep voice, you automatically get so much more from life. For example, people with deep voices appear to be respected more and they are listened to more often, since men and women think deep voices are appealing and sound sexier. No doubt such people are more likely to be chosen to occupy better positions in some companies.

Don't sound disappointed if your voice is high-pitched, squeaky or weak. Ninety-eight per cent of humanity has to work to improve their tone of voice, while two per cent has it easy. The obvious way to increase your chances of getting back your confidence or the promotion you want is by improving the quality of your voice, which is possible provided you are determined. There are techniques and exercises that you may have to adopt to train your voice to make it sound deep and have better resonance. But these techniques and exercises might take weeks or months to set in before you achieve the desired effect.

TIPS TO IMPROVE YOUR VOICE QUALITY

Whether your voice is hoarse, crackly, gruff or simply not deep enough, there are a number of things you can do to improve the sound of your voice.

> *Nothing worthwhile comes easily. Work, continuous work and hard work is the only way to accomplish results that last.*
> Hamilton Holt

- **Quit smoking and cut down on alcohol.** A hoarse smoker's throat and the gruff growl of a whisky voice are caused by badly inflamed vocal cords, which could be permanently damaged.
- **Get plenty of sleep.** If you do not get enough sleep, your voice will sound hoarse, will crackle, and the pitch will generally be higher than normal. A minimum of seven hours of quality sleep each night will ensure your voice is at peak performance.
- **Eat a healthy diet.** Your diet does affect the sound of your voice. Icy cold drinks 'freeze' vocal chords. Eat fresh fruits and green vegetables to provide your body with vitamins, proteins and antioxidants to help strengthen the vocal cords.
- **Avoid shouting.** Shouting is not good for your vocal cords. Prolonged shouting and screaming cause damage to them and they can become permanently impaired.
- **Watch your posture.** Posture plays an important role when it comes to the sound of your voice. If your chin is down and you are constantly in a slouched position, your voice will suffer. Simple techniques like pulling your back straight up, sticking your chest out and lifting your chin will immediately make you notice an improvement in voice quality.

EXERCISES FOR A SEXY VOICE

Men and women love deep sexy voices: Getting yourself such a voice is as easy as deep breathing — literally. Take a deep breath and fill your lungs to full capacity, and hold the air in your lungs for some time. Then, breathe out loudly with a slow but steady speed, saying "haaaaa..." Note that it should only be heard as "ha", and from your lowest pitch possible. Do it over and over every day for about 10 minutes or so.

Recite a poem in your regular voice: Don't rush through it. Say each word of the poem fully and completely in a loud voice. When you are done, say it again, but drop down one note. As you keep going, drop down another note, and repeat that a few times — in a loud voice, without shouting. The idea is to eventually be able to drop down to your lowest note possible without feeling strained or forced.

Exhale slowly while you are speaking: Learning to do this will give you excellent control over your voice. Many people working on their voice have a tendency to hold their breath when speaking. That does not sound natural. Make sure you never do that.

Practise singing loudly in the shower: Most people make the mistake of speaking too softly and not using enough variation in pitch. Singing is a sure tonic for improving inflection in your tone of voice as well as to improve your mood. If you are shy to sing in public, sing loudly in the shower.

Practise humming regularly: Hum tunes till you feel a vibration around your nose and mouth area. This is your optimal pitch; try and keep your voice at this level. Hum a lot during the day to get used to this pitch. If you feel your voice drop or go higher, try and correct it. The more you hum, the quicker you will develop a deep sexy tone of voice.

Breathe through your belly: You should feel your belly expand each time you breathe in. The air should go down to your diaphragm. Breathe from your diaphragm. Practise long and controlled exhalations.

Speak slower than you usually do: Most men and women talk far too quickly. You must often remind yourself to speak in a slow, relaxed way. To learn to speak slowly, you must l-i-n-g-e-r lovingly on the vowel sounds.

Articulate every word: Pronouncing the consonants so they are crisp and sharp makes your voice sound better and easier to understand. Use your lips to the full extent in forming words. Practise saying every word as if you meant it. Speak aloud all the single- and double-letter words. This is the essence of a confident voice. Try exaggerating your lip movement to reduce mumbling. Practise exaggerating vowel sounds.

> *High expectations are the key to everything.*
> Sam Walton

Laugh and learn: Tongue twisters add fun to learning. Become an expert at articulating them as quickly and crisply as possible. Focus on the ones you find difficult. According to the Guinness Book of World Records, the world's hardest tongue twister is "*The sixth sick sheik's sixth sheep's sick.*" Practise it and prove them wrong! These types of wordplay exist in every language. Test yourself by articulating the following with clarity — and three times faster than the first!

Peter Piper picked a peck of pickled peppers.
Did Peter Piper pick a peck of pickled peppers?
If Peter Piper picked a peck of pickled peppers,
Where's the peck of pickled peppers Peter Piper picked?

She sells seashells by the seashore.
The shells she sells are surely seashells.
So, if she sells shells on the seashore
I'm sure she sells seashore shells.

CONVERSE WITH POISE AND CONFIDENCE

You may talk yourself into believing that social networking is not for you because you are focused on your job. And also convince yourself by saying: Where is the time for distractions like chatting with people? What are you — a mole in the hole? Moles are busy rodents who keep burrowing endlessly. People watch your habits and label you. Social networking is not only recreational but also increases your database of contacts who will promote your brand image. If you avoid people, thinking it is a waste of time, the 'mole' aptly describes your job profile and brand image. It sums up your life's struggle. Why be labelled as a 'loner'?

Research points out that introverts also use social networking sites to make contacts. You should also — at least to get started. Isn't it time you trashed the 'mole' image? To change your image, you will have to change your habits. You will have to dedicate time to improve your spoken English skills and be friendly and approachable to people in the office and outside it. To achieve your dream of making it big with a million bucks in your bank, you will have to put your money where your mouth is. Don't shy away from training yourself to be a suave communicator. Work hard at it and you will be able to match your spoken English skills with your professional brand image. You have to be perceived as a valuable asset — a bankable brand for the company to bank on.

GET FLUENT IN *BODYTALK*

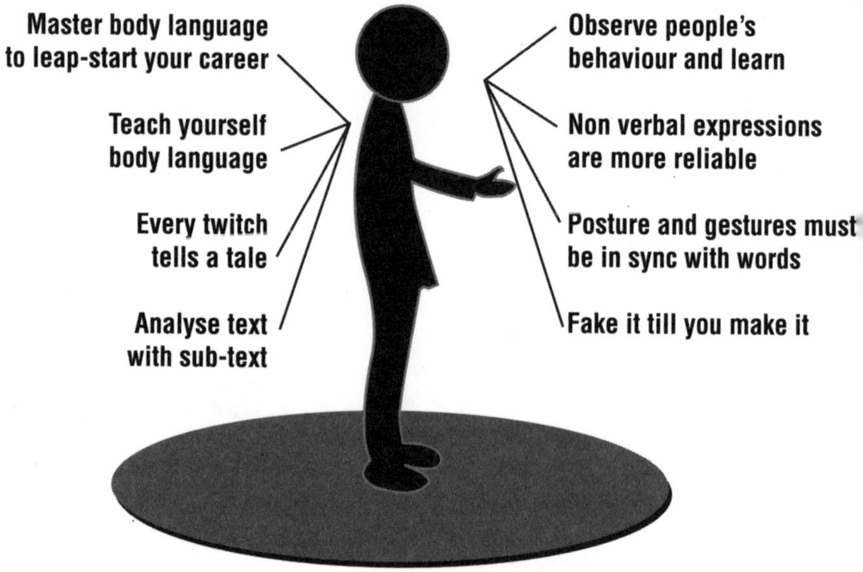

Chapter 11

EFFECTIVE BRAND POSTURING

GET FLUENT IN *BODYTALK*

Doraiswamy remembered the lecture on Body Language he attended as a student at the IIM. A decade later, he could recall the professor's observations on the White House video his class had been shown. "Less is more," the professor had thundered while showing the clip on Power Dressing. President John F Kennedy in the Oval Office was dressed in white shirt with sleeves rolled up, while all the officers were dressed in formal suits and full military uniforms. On the subject of Power Posture, Kennedy stood with his feet apart and spoke with his hands stuck in his coat pockets with thumbs jutting out. Since Doraiswamy never wore a suit to the workplace, he wore his shirt sleeves rolled up and stuck his hand in his trouser pockets with thumbs jutting out. His colleagues wondered what would have happened had Doriaswamy seen clips of Kennedy's toddlers running around the Oval Office, playing games with the father, or Kennedy sitting with his feet propped on the table top while conducting business with his staff.

To master power games, you must first master the basics of body language. There are many written and unwritten rules which govern corporate behaviour. It is easier to understand written and verbal communication; it is difficult to understand and interpret body language accurately. Doraiswamy cannot ape leaders blindly, however influential they were in their time. To rise above, he will have to imitate effective modern-day role models.

When talking is as easy as breathing, what makes business communication so frustratingly complex? Well, we communicate with much more than words. In fact, research shows that most of our communication is nonverbal. Nonverbal communication or Bodytalk *includes our facial expressions, gestures, postures, how fast or how loud we talk, how close we stand, how we sit, how much eye contact we make, and even the tone of our voice and the rate of speaking. The way you look, move and react tells people whether you care and how well you listen. The nonverbal signals you send either produce a sense of interest, trust, and desire for connection or generate disinterest, distrust and confusion.*

Effective Brand Posturing *will help you communicate effectively and build better relationships professionally and socially. You will learn how to understand and use* Bodytalk *as a powerful tool to connect with colleagues and clients and navigate your way to the top.*

Are you taking full advantage of body language? Whether you are at a job interview, conduct a briefing, talk to a client, or try to motivate your staff, your body is also 'communicating' as you speak. And if by some chance your body language happens to reinforce your message, you are likely to be much more successful at communication than others. "Isn't that what happens — naturally?" you will say. To the first part of the statement, the answer is 'yes' — your body also sends out messages when you speak. To the second part, body language seldom works in sync with what you say.

Man has chewed his way through centuries, ripping clean with his teeth barks of trees and animal bones with whatever care for teeth was available. It was only in 1840 that the world's first college of dentistry was established in Baltimore, US. Similarly, body language has been around since prehistoric times when man first planted his foot on this planet, and language evolved from an exchange of grunts and growls. It was only recently (in the 1980s) that body language awareness was introduced in corporate lectures to give executives a business edge over their rivals and competitors. Many people still refer to the workplace as a corporate jungle.

USE *BODYTALK* TO LEAP-START YOUR CAREER

Since the 1990s, body language has been the flavour of corporate training. More and more companies realized that body language awareness not only gave diplomats and business executives an edge when negotiating but also launched the business successfully overseas. Soon globe-trotting executives lined up to attend body language classes to bridge cross-culture barriers and learnt to respect customs and traditions of people from across the globe. The rewards were immediate. For instance, if you could read key body language signs of your counterparts across the globe and could interpret them accurately you had an ace up your sleeve. You were able to understand the subtle behaviour traits of your customers and used that advantage to quickly close the deal.

You can see why body language became the hot property of the corporate world. When body language skills were so important, why was it never a classroom subject, you will ask. One reason could be that it is not a reliable science. When interpreting body language, two plus two does not add up to four — the answer could be something else. The second reason is that most people undervalue the importance of body language until they are looking for a deeper understanding of human behaviour in a personal relationship, or to gain an edge in a competitive business situation.

DEVELOP THE 'STREET SMART' INSTINCT

Did you miss some lectures on body language? There is no reason to fret over a lost opportunity. Even now it is not late to teach yourself how to use effective body language techniques to give you the added edge to succeed in your career. Have you noticed how street vendors and beggars, at traffic light junctions, use body language techniques to perfection in their trade? Both get their patrons to shell out money. Interpreting body language is a skill you can teach yourself at any age, provided you are determined. You can use this skill with the finesse of a master craftsman to be an effective communicator as well as to better understand people in business and social situations. Understanding and interpreting body language will accurately give you the power to see the truth beyond what another person is trying to tell or hide. You don't have to enrol for body language workshops to master the subject. With some clues from this chapter to get you started, you can practise and develop your body language skills by engaging in people watching, either sitting at home or lounging outdoors.

ANALYSE TEXT WITH SUB-TEXT

Have you watched people struggle to wriggle out of tight questions on TV channels? You felt they got away lying. Did that make your blood boil? Don't be furious. Get curious and learn the subtle art of body language while you entertain yourself. Watch interviews of important people in public life on television channels and learn to spot the truth from the lies through their body expressions. Comedy that is low on words and high on body expressions makes great entertainment as well as a quick way to learn body language.

Here is a tip: to learn body language, split the sentence into two parts — text and sub-text. The *text* is the verbal expression. Ask yourself, does the text answer the questions raised or are the answers evasive? Is the text repetitive? Then move your attention to the *sub-text*, which is the nonverbal expression. Like, when the interviewer throws tough questions at the interviewee you see a silly grin pasted on the face (sign of nervousness) of the latter and the facial muscles are taut; there is a change in voice quality. The tone of voice is strained; at times there is a sudden fit of stammering or hesitation in articulating a word — the interviewee is at a loss for words. In fact, the interviewee is trying hard to tie loose ends (lies) to the truth. Watch the eyes — are they glazed, unfriendly or intense? And there are the hands and feet to observe. The hand usually rubs the nose. When a person lies, blood rushes to the nose (Pinocchio effect). All this is the matter of *sub-text* for you to observe, consider and evaluate. To get to the truth of the matter, you have to compare the *text* with the *sub-text* and draw your conclusions. That's *edutainment* for you!

EVERY TWITCH TELLS A TALE

You must observe movement because it is an important part of study for students of body language. There is a lot of information you can pick up by studying how the person moves and acts. Different types of movements have specific meanings, and how the person stands as well as little gestures can tell you a lot. Body language includes body movements and gestures (legs, arms, hands, head and torso), posture, muscle tension, eye contact, even people's breathing rate, perspiration, tone, pronunciation and pitch. These reveal clues about a person. If you pay close attention to the people around you, there are times when you can be aware of many unspoken cues and signals. Body language reveals many 'unspoken' clues.

WATCH HOW PEOPLE BEHAVE OUTDOORS

Another place to learn body language is to observe people in public places like malls, airports, buses, trains, cinema halls and restaurants, and notice how they act and react with each other. Don't be afraid to study people in common areas — you are not intruding on anyone's privacy. Spot the body language signals. Watch how they play out. See what signs are most effective or least effective. Make mental notes or write them down on a notepad. Then try them out.

As you watch people, try and determine how they feel about each other, whether they are friends, family, or just plain strangers. Try to guess what their relationship to each other could be or what they are saying to each other, or try and get a sense of what is going on between them, and see how many clues you can pick out right. Even if you do not get the chance to check whether you are correct in your assessment, you will be developing observational skills. The more you practise, the better your body language will become. It will help you fine-tune your own body language skills and pick up vital signals when you interact with your boss, colleagues, customers, friends and family.

POWER WALK YOU CAN IMITATE

To grow in your career, your office is an excellent place to observe power postures. Watch the way top senior-level executives walk. People who exude power exhibit a purposeful style and confident mannerisms that give the impression they are the power centres. The same applies to how generals and politicians walk. Now watch how Robocop and other actors who project raw power on the screen, walk — slowly, deliberately, elbows slightly jutting out. Arrogant grace is one of the most effective weapons in the power walk. With every self-assured step, you exude an aura of confidence and power. Eyes from all around the room are drawn to you. Yet, it doesn't look like you are trying to attract attention. To gain confidence in the corporate corridors, learn how to walk like the top bosses in your office. You must walk slowly, deliberately and purposefully and not scurry through the corridors like some office squirrel. Have a plan, and if you don't have one, make one and follow it.

To imitate the power walk of the top executives, you will have to do it with grace and style. In copying their physical movements, you should not end up being ridiculed as the office clown. Worse still, you may get censured for making fun of the boss. So beware! Observe closely and you will notice that the power walk is supported by a cluster of other subtle body language nuances and attributes which you have to observe, study and practise. A straight posture when you stand, sit or walk, good hand gestures, eye contact, an appropriate dress, proper tone of voice, pitch and pace of words — these are some of the body language characteristics you will have to master in order to achieve the aura of leadership charisma in the workplace.

PROPS PROMOTE POWERBASE

There is more to the power walk of people in authority than meets the eye. Some people are born with leadership aura, while others depend on props to broadcast it. A person who exudes natural authority does not rely on the size of office, desk or executive chair to broadcast authority and power. But, people who are not confident about their leadership aura rely on external power symbols such as the name plate with designation on the office door, the size of the office, the large desk, and the high-back, over-stuffed swivel chair. Similarly, the government uses the 'humble' white Ambassador car with a red beacon (power vehicle) accompanied by heavy security as a symbol of power. Without power symbols many people in power feel powerless.

TIPS TO IMPROVE BODY LANGUAGE

There are no fixed rules on how to use your body language signs and signals. What you do might be interpreted in several ways, depending on the occasion and who you are talking to. Your body language will be different when talking to your boss or co-workers compared to when you talk to a girl or guy you are interested in. As you take your first steps in learning about body language, here are a few tips on how to quickly improve your *bodytalk* skills.

Be Aware of Your Body Expressions

Whenever you make a verbal mistake, you can easily correct yourself because you can hear your own words. Since you cannot see your gestures and postures, the most distracting body expressions go uncorrected. You cannot change body expressions which hurt your image, unless you know they exist. In order to change your behaviour, you must be aware of how your body communicates itself. Train yourself to be more observant of your body expressions. Notice how you sit, stand and walk. Watch how you use your hands and legs and what you do with them while talking to someone. If you attend drama classes and practise mime and dance, you are better equipped to study your body expressions and move to the next step.

Practise in Front of a Mirror

Many people who train in public speaking begin by practising in front of a mirror. The mirror is a practical learning aid for beginners. In the privacy of your room, the mirror tells you how you come across to other people. The reflections of your gestures, posture and facial expressions give you instant feedback from the mirror, and this will help you improve your body language.

Use Your Inner Eye

Close your eyes and visualize how you would stand, sit and move to feel confident, open and relaxed when you want to communicate. This exercise helps you fill your mind with positive energy and success thoughts. Use your inner eye to see yourself move and act like a successful executive. Then try it out. In other words, if you look and act like a winner, the chances are you will likely become one.

Fake It till You Make It

Changing your postures, gestures, facial expressions, voice, pitch and tone calls for a radical makeover from your old habits and may seem pretentious as it is not the real you. But if you keep the practice going for long enough, the new body language will replace the old drag, slouch, ticks and twitches that you were used to. Some people are belligerent; they habitually snap, snarl and shout for no apparent reason. Your new body expressions will help you change your moods also. Body language is usually a reflection of what you are feeling. And it is also true that if you change your body language, your feelings will begin to change as well. That is why, when you feel yourself dragging after a lunch, a brisk walk can rejuvenate you. You also tend to feel better when you put on fresh clothes or if you just smile. When you smile more, you will feel much happier. If you sit up straight, you will feel more energetic and mentally alert. If you slow down your rate of speech and your movements, you will feel calmer and more in control. Your feelings will actually reinforce your new body language behaviours.

> *Are you bored with life? Then throw yourself into some work you believe in with all your heart, live for it, die for it and you will find happiness that you had thought could never be yours.*
>
> Dale Carnegie

CAUTION: BODY LANGUAGE CAN BE MIS-READ

A single word has multiple meanings, and the word has to be understood in the context of the sentence it is spoken. Similarly, a single gesture can have multiple meanings, and the gesture must be interpreted in the context of other body expressions. A single gesture can mean any number of things, or maybe even nothing at all. The key to accurately reading nonverbal behaviour is to look for the cluster of signals that reinforce a common point. If you place too much emphasis on just one sign out of many, you might come to an inaccurate conclusion about what a person is trying to communicate. For instance, a firm handshake indicates a strong personality while a weak handshake is taken as a lack of fortitude. This example illustrates an important point about the possibility of misreading nonverbal signals. A limp handshake might actually indicate something else entirely, such as arthritis. Yes, there could be more than one meaning when you see a person sitting or standing with arms crossed. Suffering abdominal discomfort could be one reason while another could be the person is 'defensive' or 'closed'. Each person is unique, and their signs and signals might have a different underlying cause from the ones you guessed. Always remember to look for the cluster of gestures or the group of behaviour acts. A person's overall demeanour is far more telling than a single gesture viewed in isolation.

BODY LANGUAGE HAS MANY LAYERS

There are many layers of body language. The gestures you make, the way you sit, how fast or how loud you talk, how far or close you stand, how much eye contact you make — not only do these send strong messages but they are also physical manifestations of your emotional state. The way you look, move and react reveals whether you care or not, and how well you are listening.

> *I've learned that people will forget what you said, people will forget what you did, but people will never forget how you made them feel.*
>
> Maya Angelou

Successful nonverbal communication depends on your emotional state as well as on an understanding of the cues you are sending, along with the ability to accurately interpret the cues others are sending to you. This requires your full concentration and attention. If you are thinking what you're going to say next or daydreaming, you are almost certain to miss nonverbal signals. As a student of body language, acquaint yourself with how your eyes, face, hands, feet, and tone of voice connect or disconnect when you are communicating. It will help you fully understand the moment-to-moment experiences your whole body is wrapped up in and how alert you have to be to actively participate in the communication process.

OBSERVE HOW THE BODY SPEAKS

To study how different parts of the body communicate, let us peel off a layer at a time, especially those layers where most of the action takes place as we continuously give and receive countless wordless signals when we interact with others.

Our Eyes

Eye contact is an important part of communication, but it is also important to remember that good eye contact does not mean staring fixedly into someone's eyes. Too much eye contact can seem confrontational or intimidating. The way you look at someone can communicate many things, including interest, affection, hostility, rage, attraction or contempt. Eye contact is also important in maintaining the flow of conversation and for gauging the other person's response. How can you tell how much eye contact is correct? Some communication experts recommend intervals of eye contact lasting four to five seconds.

- In some cultures, looking at someone in the eyes is a sign of disrespect, so they avoid making eye contact.

- In many cultures, when people fail to look others in the eye, it can seem as if they are evading or trying to hide something.
- People who look to the sides a lot are nervous, lying or distracted. However, if a person looks away from the speaker, it could indicate submissiveness.
- Looking sideways generally means the person is distrustful or unconvinced.
- If someone looks down at the floor a lot when speaking, they are probably shy or timid.
- If their eyes seem far away, it usually indicates that a person is in deep thought or not listening.

Our Face

When we make facial expressions, we are essentially transmitting a variety of signals that can be received, read and interpreted by others. By contracting or expanding our facial muscles in different degrees and combinations, we can produce thousands of different messages that provide clues to (1) our overall emotional state, (2) our short-term feelings about our immediate environment, (3) our mental well-being, (4) our personality and mood, (5) our physical health, (6) our credibility and (7) whether or not we view others as being credible. Approximately 43 facial muscles are at work to form expressions of happiness, sadness, anger, surprise, fear, disgust and more.

Facial expressions are great indicators of what you are thinking. They are not always easy to read though. As Dr Paul Ekman, who did extensive research in body language, said, "In a sense, the face is equipped to lie the most and leak the most, and thus can be a very confusing source of information." The face is able to signal emotions in a second, and it is able to hide emotions just as well.

Most of us carry stress on our faces. Tensing your jaw, brow or forehead activates the muscles in your neck and shoulders and creates further tension in the whole body. Your face reflects your approach to life. If your face is relaxed and your posture is straight, you will instantly be perceived by others as more likeable, friendly and attractive. A genuine smile lights up the face and gives warmth to the eyes. Smiling lifts the face and makes you look youthful, friendlier, more confident and more attractive. So no matter what your mood is, relax your face and smile — people are watching you!

Our Hands

Our hands convey so much more than words in any given situation. They are used in greetings. You join your palms, thumbs and fingers pointing upwards, and say *Namaste*. Another most common form of greeting is shaking hands. A firm handshake is always preferred to a limp one, but a firm handshake is not always a reliable indicator of a confident person with a firm character as many believe it to be. Seasoned businessmen realize that people value a firm handshake and train themselves to shake hands firmly. Some people in their enthusiasm squeeze harder than it is appropriate. Handshakes that are uncomfortably firm show lack of respect or awareness when used in Asian cultures, where firm handshaking is not normal.

Other than *greetings*, hand gestures are used for the following: *Asking:* palms offered upwards are a common gesture, as if asking for alms or asking a question. *Receiving:* outstretched palms denote receiving and giving as well. Open palms of both hands also show that you have concealed nothing. *Weighing:* Up-and-down movement of cupped hands indicate weighing. Cupped hands also signify delicacy, such as offering a fragile idea. But you grip your hand tightly to show a situation under control. Gripping hands tightly can show possessiveness, ownership and desire — the tighter the fist, the stronger the feeling.

Our Feet

Feet offer genuine body language clues. Amazing as it may sound, 'feet talk' is completely unconscious. Generally, people work so hard on controlling their facial and hand expressions while communicating that they forget about the feet. The reason could be that the feet are placed so far away from the brain that they go unnoticed.

In fact, the feet communicate exactly what we think and feel more honestly than the other parts of our bodies. For instance, look which direction the person's feet are pointing when talking. If they are both pointing towards you or the rest of the group, the person is interested in the conversation. If one of their feet is pointing towards the exit, it means they would rather be somewhere else — the person subconsciously wants to leave, even if their body is turned towards you. Some people may point their feet to the direction of their interest. If they purposely touch their feet to yours, they are flirting! If the person is sitting, feet crossed at the ankles, it means they are comfortable and at ease.

Fast-tapping the feet or shifting of weight from one foot to the other will often mean that the person is impatient, excited, nervous, scared or intimidated. Note though that some people with ADHD will constantly jiggle their legs. It doesn't mean anything; it is entirely subconscious and cannot be stopped. Also consider that when people sit for half an hour or more they tend to change their leg positions, which can include leg crossing purely for comfort reasons. Again, allow for these concessions when interpreting signals.

Our Voice and Tone

"It's not what you said, it's how you said it" tells you how important it is for you to pay attention to your voice and tone. The way you talk can have a particularly profound effect on how others interpret what you say and how you feel. People communicate with their voices even when they are not using words. Nonverbal speech sounds such as tone, pitch, volume, inflection, rhythm, and rate are important communication feeders. When you speak, other people 'read' messages in your tone of voice in addition to listening to your words. These nonverbal speech sounds provide subtle but powerful clues into your true feelings and what you really mean. Your tone of voice can reveal emotions and feelings. It can indicate sarcasm, irritation, anger, affection, superiority, submissiveness or confidence.

Your tone of voice can convey a wealth of information ranging from enthusiasm to disinterest to anger. In order to improve your tone of voice, first, you should start observing the way your tone of voice affects how others respond to you, and second, try using your tone of voice to emphasize ideas that you want to communicate. For instance, if you want to show genuine interest in something, express your enthusiasm by using an animated tone of voice. Softer tones and pitches are associated with friendliness; also, softer tones are seen as being non-aggressive and helpful. A rising intonation is used to pose a question or ask for help, while a higher tone is generally used to request information. To effectively project a confident, knowledgeable and credible tone of voice, it is important to sound upbeat, warm, controlled and clear.

Our Space

How close is close enough for you for comfort? Edward T Hall mentioned three zones: personal, social and intimate. But these zones come with a rider: Space is culture-dependent. What is considered close in one country is far in another. Have you ever felt uncomfortable during a conversation because the other person was standing too close and invading your space? Did you feel the urge to be closer to someone, for whom you had warm feelings? When you moved slightly closer to them, did they move slightly away? That meant they did not want the meeting to be any more personal than it already is. But if they did *not* move away from you, they were receptive to your move. And if they responded by getting even closer to you, they probably really liked you or were attracted by you. The farther away that someone is, the less they actually care, since they maintain their 'distance' between you and the situation. When relations break down, have you noticed that the first thing couples demand is 'space' from each other?

We all have a need for physical space, although that need differs, depending on the culture, the situation, and the closeness of the relationship. You can use physical space to communicate many different nonverbal messages, including signals of intimacy, aggression, dominance or power. Corporate spaces are allotted to executives, depending on their positions of power in the office hierarchy.

USE BODY LANGUAGE TO INFLUENCE CUSTOMERS

As a company employee, you are in the business of selling. Your vendors, customers, clients (whatever you call them) are buyers of your company's products or services. They patronize your products and services for a number of reasons. As a seller, you are never the 'king'; the customer is king — and he knows it! The customer literally pays your salary. You cannot pay lip-service to the 'king' and get away with it. He will take away the business to your competitor. The customer not only knows he is king, but also demands to be treated as a 'king', which unfortunately many service providers are loath to accept. You will have to pamper your egoistic 'king', who can be moody, distracted, forgetful, irritable or offensive, when he is unhappy.

> *There are two kinds of people: those who do the work and those who take the credit. Try to be in the first group; there is less competition there.*
>
> Indira Gandhi

The following suggestions will prepare you to treat your customers the way they want to be treated — with respect and grace:

(a) **Exude positive energy.** Before meeting your customer, prepare yourself to look and feel energetic by using positive body language. Tell yourself that your personality and charm is wrapped around the company's product and services. Let your aura of positive energy touch your customers.

(b) **The customer is not your buddy.** A firm, brief handshake is always acceptable for greeting someone you are meeting professionally. Never attempt to embrace or hug your client. Do not address clients by their first names (unless the person told you to do so) or show undue familiarity. Touching or patting the client's head, hand, shoulders, back, legs, etc., is unprofessional and inappropriate.

(c) **Maintain professional distance.** From the moment you greet customers, watch where they stand. This will tell you how close to approach. If they back away a bit after the handshake, don't move forward to close the gap. If the customer begins to lean closer, expressing positive energy towards you, it is a signal for you to lean closer as well — though not too close. On the other hand, the customer may incline the head closer towards you to hear what you said. This is the signal for you to speak louder and not to move closer.

(d) **Don't be rushed for time.** You may have a very busy calendar, but do not show haste. The customer should never feel he is being squeezed for time, especially when the meeting was agreed upon through an appointment.

(e) **Watch your customer closely.** Observe the customer's body language carefully. During the meeting, if you think a more enthusiastic tone is desirable, change your body language gradually to be more enthusiastic in order to influence the way the customer feels.

(f) **Timing is of essence.** Always make positive transitions in your body language while the customer is speaking. This shows you support the customer's ideas and feelings. If you make changes when you begin to speak, it may show that you are trying to take control.

UNDERSTAND GLOBAL CLIENTS BETTER

More than two-thirds of the effectiveness of a negotiation is determined by nonverbal communication. Body language provides valuable insight into a person's feelings and attitudes. But they are often misleading due to cultural differences in the use and interpretation of nonverbal cues. It is therefore important to understand and recognise differences in the use of non-verbal cues so that the body language of customers, especially of those from other cultural backgrounds, is not the cause of costly misinterpretation.

The world has shrunk to the size of a few fleeting hours. At the speed of a jet plane, executives are overnight in corporate lobbies across continents, wheeling a deal — and how! Cross-cultural negotiation is a specialized field that requires body language training. Cross-cultural body language training helps you get an added edge over your competitors. You learn about many factors that can influence the process and proceedings of negotiations. To understand the importance of cross-cultural negotiations, take a look at three interconnected aspects.

EFFECTIVE CROSS-CULTURAL NEGOTIATIONS

Business of Relationships

Most European and American businesses are contractual in nature. Relationship-building is seen as unhealthy because it could cloud objectivity. Emotions complicate the deals. In India and much of Asia and Africa, business is personal. Partnerships will only be made with those they know, trust and feel comfortable with. It is therefore necessary to invest in relationship-building before conducting business.

Negotiation Styles

Negotiations differ from culture to culture. For example, in India, decisions are usually made by the most senior figure or head of a business family. In the Middle East, negotiators discuss issues simultaneously rather than sequentially. In China, negotiators are highly trained in the art of bargaining. The Japanese negotiate in teams and decisions are based on consensual agreement. In Germany, decisions can take a long time due to the need to analyse information and statistics in great depth. In Britain, pressure tactics and imposing deadlines are ways of closing deals.

Be Culturally Correct

There are other factors to consider in cross-cultural negotiations. For instance, should you address a person by the first name, surname or title? Do you shake hands or not? Is small talk part of the proceedings or not? Is it appropriate to give gifts? In some cultures, strong and direct eye contact conveys sincerity, trustworthiness and confidence. In others, it is considered rude and dominating. In some cultures, people are time-conscious, and latecomers are considered rude and insulting. In others, being on time is not considered important or essential.

Cross-cultural ignorance is no excuse to cut a sorry figure of yourself and your company. Training can update your knowledge on the niceties and pleasantries of different customs and traditions. By tailoring your behaviour to win people's admiration from across cultures, you will succeed in maximizing your social and business potential.

SPEAK LIKE STEVE JOBS

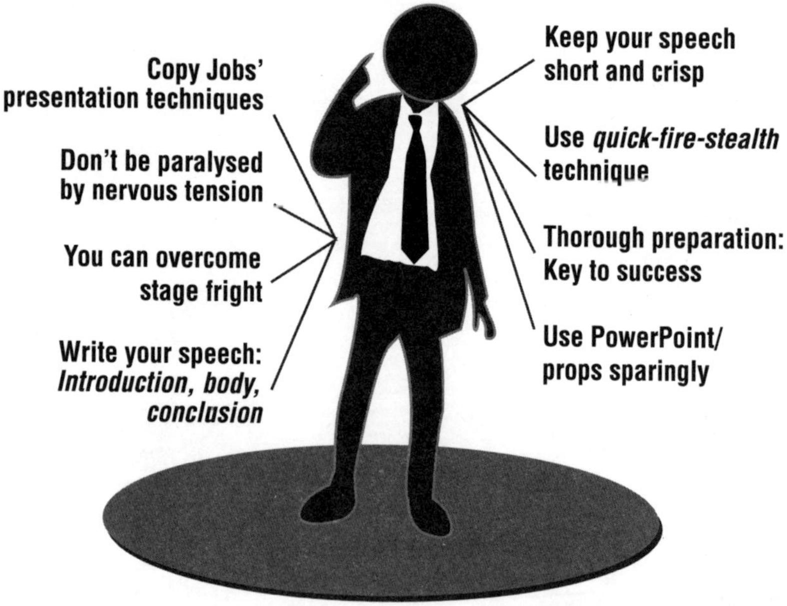

Chapter 12

BLOW YOUR BRAND TRUMPET

SPEAK LIKE STEVE JOBS

Adithi enjoyed presentation assignments. She remembered a speaker had once said that the audience retained 2.5 per cent of what was said and forgot 97.5 per cent of what they heard. Adithi used that information to plough her way through company presentations. When the audience remembered only a fraction of what they heard, why waste time on preparation? Adithi's boss, who was also her father-in-law, was impressed with her anglicized accent. Words tripped over the gloss of her red painted lips with the confidence of a Chinese speaking Ching-lish *in a singsong Cantonese accent.*

PowerPoint and the internet were the most trusted allies of a techno-savvy and gizmo-dependent Adithi. Together they made a winning team. Visuals accompanied by paragraphs boxed in fluorescent colours kept the audience's attention riveted to the screen. She numbed the audience's brain with a jab of jumbled statistics. Like a hypnotist, she manipulated their eye movement; she used the laser beam to direct the audience's eyes up, down, left, right and centre of the screen.

Adithi had got her facts completely wrong. Statistics had indicated audiences' reaction to ineffective speakers. Only 2.5 per cent were effective and inspirational speakers, while 97.5 per cent were ineffective speakers who bored the audience with poor content and bad performance. Have you noticed that most presentations contain an overload of irrelevant information — poorly presented and of no practical use in the workplace? Adithi represented those 97.5 percent of speakers who believed the audience was numb-brained.

Beware. Never undermine your audience or insult their intelligence. Don't brazen it out like Adithi, but don't be scared either. You could die of many things, but not of stage fright. Blow Your Brand Trumpet *will show you how to prepare, rehearse and deliver presentations without hitting the panic button. The world applauded the master communicator Steve Jobs. To rise above, learn from this guru.*

Steve Jobs was a compelling and passionate public speaker. With all the expectations on his shoulders as a dynamic CEO, he lived by that reputation and delivered inspirational speeches — so unlike the boring speeches we hear from other CEOs. He was the supreme master in the use of visuals; he elevated PowerPoint to its exalted position as a visual aid. With hard work, if Steve Jobs could be the world's finest orator, so can you!

If you think you've got problems or you are stuck in a miserable job, or worry what to do with your life, you should watch the videos of this iconic man. After he quit college, Steve Jobs struggled hard to stay alive. *"I didn't have a dorm room, so I slept on the floor in friends' rooms, I returned Coke bottles for the 5¢ deposits to buy food with, and I would walk the seven miles across town every Sunday night to get one good meal a week at the Hare Krishna temple."* People all over the world remember the 2005 Stanford University speech in four words: *Stay Hungry. Stay Foolish.*

People were madly excited to listen to Steve Jobs presentations because they knew something wonderful would enfold. Jobs did not disappoint them; he kept his audience insanely hungry for more. He packed excitement, emotion, enthusiasm and passion in the stories he told. Whether it was a product, feature or service, he believed in its amazing powers and spoke about it in the common man's language that connected him instantly with his audience. You will want to know the secret of Steve Jobs' presentation skills. How did he weave his magic? The answer is: He used some very simple techniques — the four big ones are listed below.

STEVE JOBS' SPEAKING TECHNIQUES

1. Capture Audience Attention

Jobs knew that he was there for the audience, and he showed his awareness by focusing on the crowd. It is critical to understand why the audience is listening to you so you can tune your presentation in a manner that makes them receptive listeners. He waited for them to finish their applause and then began, *"I am honoured to be with you today at your Commencement from one of the finest universities in the world. I never graduated from college. Truth be told, this is the closest I've ever gotten to a college graduation."* When designing the opening of your presentation, your goal is not to beat about the bush. Your goal is to capture audience attention. A controversial statement, with a touch of humour, works wonders.

2. The Rule of Three

Jobs recognized that the human mind could not process a mountain of material in one speech. So, he divided his presentation into three parts. To the Stanford grads in 2005, he said, *"Today I want to tell you three stories from my life. That's it. No big deal. Just three stories."* Jobs was aware that the Rule of Three was one of the most powerful concepts in dramatic writing. During Macworld 2007 presentation, when he launched the iPhone, he said, *"Today we are introducing three revolutionary products. The first is a wide-screen iPod with touch controls, the second is a revolutionary mobile phone, and the third is the breakthrough Internet communication device."* For added emphasis, Steve Jobs repeated the three products three times. He then delivered the knockout punch: *"These are not three separate devices. This is one device! Today Apple is going to reinvent the phone!"*

3. Focus on the Benefits

Jobs focused on the benefits of the products he launched rather than on the technology that made it possible. His focus was more on what technology could do for you. For example, when he launched the 30GB iPod, Jobs explained how the audience would benefit — they would be able to carry 7500 songs, 25000 photos or 75 hours of video! When introducing iTunes movie rentals, Jobs said, *"We think there is a better way to deliver movie content to our customers."* Jobs explained the benefit by saying, *"We've never offered a rental model in music because people want to own their music. You listen to your favourite song thousands of times in your life. But most of us watch movies once, maybe a few times. And renting is a great way to do it. It's less expensive, doesn't take up space on our hard drive..."* Your audience always asks themselves, "What's in it for me?" Answer the question and don't make them guess. Like Jobs, you must clearly state the benefits of every service, feature or product you present.

> *Consult not your fears but your hopes and your dreams. Think not about your frustrations, but about your unfulfilled potential. Concern yourself not with what you tried and failed in, but with what it is still possible for you to do.*
>
> Pope John XXIII

4. Rehearse, Rehearse and Rehearse Again

Steve Jobs could not pull off an intricate presentation with video clips, demonstrations and outside speakers without hours of rehearsal. People working inside Apple said Steve Jobs would practise the entire presentation aloud for many hours for several days. Nothing was taken for granted. The entire presentation was coordinated for many hours over many days. Steve Jobs presentations looked effortless because they were exceptionally well-rehearsed.

When you listen to Steve Jobs' earlier speeches and presentations, you will see how the early years' speeches lacked in finesse which his later years' speeches had. The journey he began as a novice speaker eventually led him to become the master presenter who was lauded the world over. You may or may not become another Steve Jobs; but you surely can try and emulate his presentation style so that you can master his techniques to reform yours and in the process carve your own niche to be a master presenter. This chapter will take you on that journey which will help you reach your goal in the quickest possible time.

EFFECTIVE SPEAKERS EXUDE LEADERSHIP QUALITIES

So, you get nervous, tense, and butterflies flutter in your stomach. It is a common phenomenon to feel nervous, but it also cramps your style as a suave speaker or it may negatively impact your career. Perhaps, you are not the person chosen to lead office delegations, receive VIP clients or make presentations and hobnob with the high and mighty in the company. Or, if you are the chosen one, you probably cut a sorry figure because of nervous tension. Most companies choose those with strong personality appeal, self-confidence matched with a touch of class, mellowed voice, good diction and pronunciation, and who are well-groomed and appropriately dressed. Employees who are team players with the ability to manage people, and also have the ability to bridge relations with superiors, colleagues and clients, are sought after; they negotiate deals, and they can think and speak rapidly on their feet in conflict situations. Were they born that way? Of course, not! People like Steve Jobs worked hard at it. While we played the fool, they spent days, weeks, months and years, perfecting the art of being master craftsmen in presentation skills.

> *You have a very powerful mind that can make anything happen as long as you keep yourself centred.*
>
> Dr Wayne W Dyer

Effective speakers are not born; they are made. After comparing Steve Jobs' earlier speeches with his recent ones, you will realize that making effective presentations is an art which can be mastered. And you can do it provided you are ready to work hard at it. Just as there are a number of factors involved from the first step of preparing the speech to the final step of its delivery, so also there are many facets of your mind and personality that require tweaking and polishing before you can be acclaimed a master presenter.

NERVOUS TENSION CAN PARALYSE YOU

Nervousness brings on anxiety. Anxiety activates the sympathetic nervous system to release adrenalin into your blood. The moment anxiety hits you, the reptilian brain located at the base of your head instantly activates the body's defence mechanism. The war sirens come on. There is a battle raging inside you. Your mind is in turmoil. All your systems are put on high alert to protect the body from physical danger. You are in *fight-or-flight* mode, which means that, like our prehistoric ancestors who either had to dig in their heels and fight the tiger or outrun the beast, you are in a state of primal alert mode.

MAKE NERVOUS TENSION WORK FOR YOU

Treat It as a Mind Game

Truth be told, it is a mind game, literally. Nervous tension cripples you because you allow the mind to respond to anxiety signals, and you lose the battle to stage fright. You are the master of your body, so stay in control. Let us find out how the enemy (anxiety signals) enters your system. It uses 'propaganda' or negative messages to destroy your confidence. You allow negative suggestions to invade your mind. You believe that you have many shortcomings and no matter how hard you try you will never succeed. You also readily believe in the enemy propaganda that the audience is hostile, superior and critical. You feel inferior in front of the audience's superior might. Negative inputs not only strengthen self-doubts but also weaken mental resolve. Confused signals destroy your confidence.

Fill Your Mind with Positive Thoughts

Act like a confident general and not a confused foot soldier, and take charge of your mind and body. This is your chance to act like a master strategist. You can turn this propaganda around through counter-espionage. Use the same route the enemy used and beat it at its own game. Feed the mind with 'conquest' messages. Plant success thoughts: you are a hard worker, very intelligent, and you will charm the audience with your confidence. Remind yourself that you are the 'Achiever' and you will carry the battle to the finish and prove to the audience that you are 'Better than the Best'!

This is fantastic 'propaganda' to boost your morale. But don't stop there. To beat the enemy, you need superior arsenal. Your ammunition lies in your preparation. You will dedicate a lot of your time (like Steve Jobs did) to practise, rehearse, practise, rehearse and practise till you master your presentation. When negative suggestions can bring about failure, why can't positive suggestions and the will to win empower you to succeed?

Use *Quick-fire–Stealth* Ammunition

As a master strategist, you will urgently require to stock up on *quick-fire–stealth* ammunition to prepare yourself to speak before an audience with confidence, clarity and polish. Tips on quick-fire preparation have been laid down below in six sections (A to F). Once you have mastered the *quick-fire–stealth* technique, you will not only develop faster ways to prepare your presentations but also perform to the best of your ability with considerable ease, no matter how stressful the situation.

> *One important key to success is self-confidence. An important key to self-confidence is preparation.*
>
> Arthur Ashe

The *stealth* ammunition lies in the E and F sections, which give you advance information on how your audience will evaluate (critique) you and your speech. As a strategist who takes the war to the enemy camp, it is important for you to know the type of ammunition the audience will use to evaluate you. The old saying is, "Forewarned is forearmed." Apply the *stealth* ammunition at the time you rehearse your presentation and you will surely conquer the hearts and minds of the audience!

TIPS ON *QUICK-FIRE–STEALTH* PREPARATION

A. How to *Plan* a Speech

1. Know who your audience is: AGM, daily/weekly office briefing, product launch, keynote, client presentation, economic forum, Rotarians, sports club, etc.
2. Choose the topic quickly. A lot of valuable time is wasted 'thinking' of a suitable topic.

3. Choose the right subject. You must be passionate about the subject and want to talk about it.
4. Churn the subject matter in your mind: turn it around, look at the pros and cons, argue for and against it.
5. Don't consider PowerPoint visuals at this stage.
6. Write your speech in the order of: *Introduction. Body. Conclusion.*

   Introduction: i) inform the audience what you are going to say.
   ii) make it startling; make them want to listen to you.

   Body: The audience will listen to you when the subject matter is important, interesting, controversial or novel. Hence

   + present arresting facts or startling statistics.
   + sprinkle the talk with human-interest stories and humour.
   + arouse curiosity and high expectations.
   + use props — OHP, PowerPoint, live demo — only when essential.

   Conclusion: Your audience must know you are concluding your speech. They must remember the main points of your talk and be stirred to action.

   + be brief.
   + conclude with a forceful argument.
   + say 'thank you' with meaning and feeling.

NEVER

- let your talk run downhill, or fade off at word-endings.
- make an apology.
- exit the podium while saying the last few words.

B. How to *Write* a Speech

This is the toughest part: *Writing Your Speech!* Don't we all wish we had a magic wand to have a ready speech placed in front of us? Let's stop daydreaming and get down to work.

1. Don't waste valuable time surfing the net for ideas. Not yet. You need ONE idea.
2. Don't gather picture slides and quotes.
3. Jot down points at random of what you already know (think-tank).
4. Make a selection of points you put together.
5. Arrange the points in the following order:

   Body: Use the points to cohesively build the 'body' of your speech.

   Introduction: Put down something startling to capture audience attention.

Conclusion: This is the icing on the cake. Your aim is to leave a lasting impression on the minds of your audience.

6. Embellish the *Introduction*, *Body* and *Conclusion* with interesting information and
   (a) give what the audience wants.
   (b) clarify your points.
   (c) make points memorable — add humour.
   (d) add interest to your speech with anecdotes.
7. Use a variety of 'connectors' for emphasis: examples, quotations, statistics, anecdotes, human-interest stories, definitions, comparisons, contrasts, and audio-visual aids.
8. If you are still short on ideas, talk/discuss with your friends, family and peers about the topic.
9. If you are still low on information, surf the net, visit the library and tap other sources (archives, journals, newspapers, magazines, etc.).
10. Your speech should NOT exceed the time allotted to you. Keep it short.
11. Do not cram too much information in your speech. Build on ONE idea.

> *The person who risks nothing, does nothing, has nothing, and is nothing.*
>
> Janet Rand

C. How to *Rehearse* a Speech

1. Go over your speech at least four to six times daily for several days!
2. Practise to remember ideas, not words.
3. Prepare note-cards, and practise from your note-card, not your actual script.
4. Don't chop rehearsals. Go through the entire speech at each practice.
5. Pay attention to eye contact, gestures, posture, inflection and pauses.
6. Rehearse standing if you will deliver the speech standing.
7. Concentrate on your MESSAGE (it should be convincing and easy to follow).
8. Speakers are nervous because they are afraid they will make a mistake. Never plant negative thoughts in your mind. If you are nervous because you have not prepared well, you only have yourself to blame.

9. Reading from notes kills audience interest. You may want to write the main points on a small note-card for reference.
10. Video-record some of the rehearsals and review your practice sessions objectively.
11. Time your speech. NEVER exceed the time allotted to you.
12. Be willing to take criticism from people who will evaluate your speech.
13. Find someone at home to help critique and improve your delivery.
14. Care about how you say and what you say, otherwise no one else will.
15. If you use PowerPoint, rehearse with the team which will assist you on the final day.

D. How to *Deliver* a Speech

1. **Connect with your audience.** Audience contact is the most essential part of public speaking. So, right from the start, you must secure their ATTENTION and RESPONSE. Tell yourself that you are about to transfer your ideas to the minds of your audience. And you are going to achieve this definite object in a limited time by giving them
   i) a deeper understanding of the subject matter, and
   ii) a desire to act positively.

   Hence you have got to be *alert* to audience reaction and response. Are they
   (a) interested and intent?
   (b) distracted and bored?

   Keep assuring yourself that you will dazzle the audience with the power of your ideas. Remind yourself that people can never recall a speech verbatim, but they can recall a speech seamlessly well delivered with effortless ease. That is why people remember Steve Jobs the presenter.

2. **Make nervous tension work for you.** This is your moment. You prepared your presentation well and rehearsed it many, many and many times over. You are fully prepared; like a spring, you are fully wound up — tight, taut and ready to unwind. You have a clear idea of what you are going to say. Your mind is on the subject and you stay focused on the content. As you walk to the podium, you breathe slowly to unwind and make nervous tension work for you. All players and athletes do it. Players use nervous tension to focus on the game — on winning the match. You must focus on the delivery.

When you focus on what you are going to say rather than on yourself, you will be able to use your nervous tension to speak effectively. Remind yourself that people can never recall a speech verbatim, but they can recall a speaker who spoke with simplicity and sincerity. That is why people remember Steve Jobs the presenter.

3. **Breathe, relax and look friendly.** Your time is NOW. Feel friendly. Look friendly. Sound friendly. Walk to the stage/podium confidently; don't rush. Breathe in slowly and deeply and breathe out slowly. The air should go right down to the pit of your belly. Then, slowly squeeze your belly in to gently breathe out the tension inside you. Don't shuffle pages at the podium. Don't start your speech the moment you reach the mike. Smile to the audience and make eye contact. Pause. Smile again as you slowly and gently breathe in and out — long, deep breaths. Remind yourself that you are there to charm the audience. Look at your audience and greet them in a strong, clear, pleasant tone — with a 'smile' in your voice. You have begun the delivery! Remind yourself that people can never recall a speech verbatim, but they can recall a charming and disarming speaker. That is why people remember Steve Jobs the presenter.

4. **Put your best foot forward.** You must be appropriately attired for the occasion — shoes polished, hair in place, and well groomed. Don't slouch, hunch or stoop. Don't drag your feet. Walk with a quick stride without rushing. Keep your head up and allow your chin to jut out. See the difference in your carriage, poise and confidence the moment you pull the back straight and stick your chin out. To be friendly, look at the audience and smile — that winning smile which shines through your eyes and lights up your face; your audience will smile back. Remind yourself that people can never recall a speech verbatim, but they can recall a pleasant and friendly speaker. That is why people remember Steve Jobs the presenter.

5. **Speak with warmth.** Speak up loud. Address the audience who is sitting in the last row in the hall. When the last row hears you clearly, the first row will have no problem hearing you. Deliver your first words in a LOUD and CLEAR voice. Don't rush with words. Your voice must have warmth, and words must express feelings. Also, look at your audience and speak to it with your eyes. Your eyes are the most expressive part of your anatomy. They project love, sympathy,

kindness, anger, hatred and other emotions. Wavering eyes hint at wavering conviction. Averted eyes imply weakness or distrust. Remind yourself that people can never recall a speech verbatim, but they can recall a speaker who touched their hearts more than their heads. That is why people remember Steve Jobs the presenter.

6. **Give the audience what it wants.** In your time you have heard many formal and informal presentations. You liked some speakers and you were bored by most of them. Know what your audience wants and give it the way they want it. To touch their souls, you have to open people's minds to see the benefits you offer them. To master this skill, you must know how to present your ideas so that the audience will evaluate you and your product favourably. Remind yourself that people can never recall a speech verbatim, but they can recall a sincere speaker who loved the audience and who believed in what was good for them. That is how people remember Steve Jobs the presenter.

The following sections, E and F, are *Stealth Tips* on how to win over the most hostile or indifferent audience. Sneak into the audience camp to conduct surveillance; imagine you are watching them watching you. See yourself and your presentation from the eyes of the audience. The yardstick by which they will judge you is laid bare for you to consider when you rehearse your presentation.

E. How a *Speech* Is Evaluated

- Did the speech have a clear structure: *Introduction*, *Body* and *Conclusion*?
- Was the speaker enthusiastic about the subject and believed in the product?
- Was the speech short and to the point?
- Was there eye contact?
- Did gestures and facial expressions match verbal expression?
- Was the speech clear and interesting?
- Was the speaker relaxed and friendly?
- Did the Introduction arrest audience attention?
- Did the Body have logical development or was it difficult to follow?
- Was the Conclusion strong and effective?

- Did poor grammar, pronunciation and pauses distort delivery?
- Was the use of anecdotes and illustrations effective?
- Was the talk well rehearsed and well prepared?
- Did the props highlight the content? Did they distract?
- Was the Steve Jobs technique used in PowerPoint presentation?

F. How a *Speaker* Is Evaluated

Delivery

1. **Posture:** Did the speaker lean on the podium? Rest elbows on the podium? Shuffled feet? Stood stiff? Crossed arms? Fidget with the microphone or laser gadget? Fidget with hair, tie, buttons and bows? Or was the overall posture impressive?
2. **Voice:** Was the voice hoarse, squeaky, high-pitched, or well modulated, resonant and pleasing to the ears?
3. **Pronunciation:** Were the words easily understood? Was enunciation, intonation, inflection and diction correct, clear and proper?
4. **Platform Behaviour:** Was the walk to the podium and back measured, impressive and effective? Did the speaker distract the audience by clearing throat, blowing nose, fidgeting or scratching?
5. **Degree of Energy:** Was there vigour, enthusiasm and excitement displayed in both verbal and nonverbal expression?

Clarity and Persuasiveness

1. **Opening Remarks:** Were the opening remarks 'attention getters'? Were human-interest stories used to arrest attention?
2. **Thought:** Did the flow of ideas display a clear and structured thought? Did the speaker jump from one idea to another without clarity? Was the speech easy to understand, because it was well thought out and thoroughly practised?
3. **Cogency:** Was the speech well researched? Was it informative? Was it absorbing?
4. **Concluding Remarks:** Did the speech make an impact on the minds of the audience because the concluding remarks were powerful and vigorous?

POWERPOINT – ITS USE AND ABUSE

Many public speakers consider Steve Jobs the ultimate role model for their presentations. In a Steve Jobs visual, you will not find bullet points, mind-numbing data or statistics on slides. While most speakers fill their slides with data, text, numbers and charts, Jobs did the opposite. There was very little text on the slides. Most of the slides simply showed one image. For example, his phrase "The first thing I want to talk to you about today..." was accompanied by a slide with the numeral 1. That's it — only number 1. When Jobs talked about the popularity of *iTunes* around the world, his slide showed flags of 23 countries instead of country names. When he discussed the "ultimate pointing device" — your fingers — all the audience saw on the screen was an image of a finger touching the iPhone. Public speakers usually try to paint a picture for audiences by creating more visual graphics. Inspiring presenters are short on bullet points and big on graphics. When Jobs said the iPhone store was celebrating its first anniversary, a slide appeared with a birthday cake holding one candle. When he talked about lowering iPod prices, the new price was accompanied by photos of the iPods. Psychologists call this picture superiority: Ideas are more easily recalled when presented with text and images instead of text alone.

> *About 15 per cent of one's financial success is due to one's technical knowledge and about 85 per cent is due to skills in human engineering.*
>
> Dale Carnegie

When you use it like Steve Jobs, PowerPoint can be useful and a fun tool, but in most circumstances (99.9 per cent of the times) PowerPoint is misused. Presenters usually start on a faulty premise by structuring their presentations around PowerPoint slides. Of course, a picture is worth a thousand words, but using picture slides as your primary teaching tool with the intention to cram information around slides is a terrible way to deliver a presentation. The right way would be to first write the speech in the old-fashioned way — *introduction*, *body* and *conclusion*. Then select a few slides to support what you will say. Never write your speech around the slides. You can expect kindergarten teachers to do the cut-and-paste, show-and-tell presentations — not corporate speakers.

POWERLESS WITH POWERPOINT

Despite your best preparation and many rehearsals, expect something to go wrong at the crucial moment (*Murphy's Law?*). During the Macworld 2007 presentation, Jobs' clicker failed to advance the slides during a portion of the iPhone introduction. He paused with a smile, knowing that someone backstage would take care of it, and told a funny story about how he and his friend, Steve Wozniak, the co-founder of Apple, had built a device that would jam TV signals in the college dorm. While most presenters would have frozen, Jobs used the opportunity to lighten the situation and connect with his audience by telling them of his involvement in a prank.

In such situations, most CEOs and other presenters would be powerless with PowerPoint. Things go wrong for no fault of yours because you depend on support staff to connect you at the precise moment with the laptop, OHP, spreadsheets, slides or whatever. You are caught between the devil and the deep sea. Neither can you do it alone, nor can you depend on others to do it for you as efficiently as you would intend it to be. Timing is everything. Delay has zero tolerance. Unfortunately, efficiency and effectiveness get compromised even in situations when everything was planned and practised to the last detail. For instance, your laptop may suddenly 'hang' at the crucial moment, throwing you and your PowerPoint into a tailspin. Or the projector's light bulb is fused just when you hit the OHP start button. A spare bulb is hard to find in the nick of time. How many times have you sat in the audience, watching technicians struggle to fix the system while speakers wring their hands helplessly? Few manage to continue talking; others mostly walk away, cutting a sorry figure and blaming it on technology.

There is another disadvantage when you use PowerPoint. Let us say everything is working smoothly; but each time you draw your audience's attention to a slide, you intentionally move their gaze to the screen and away from you. When their eyes are riveted on the picture frame, their ears barely hear parts of what you said. Without realizing this, you disconnect the audience from you. The cardinal rule of effective presentation is to keep your audience 'connected' to you. PowerPoint shifts attention from you to the big screen and in the process weakens your presentation. Or you may want to do it like Jobs. Leave the screen blank when you have nothing to show so that the audience will automatically look at you.

STAY HUNGRY. STAY FOOLISH.

When Steve Jobs died, the world lost a great technical visionary. Sadly, the world also lost an incredible orator. Steve Jobs transformed every presentation into a magnificent event; he was a showman par excellence. People all over the world queued up to buy his products; indeed, he was the world's greatest salesman. On stage, Jobs was casual without being unfocused. He was real without being unprofessional. He was warm without deviating from the point. And he was the master at connecting with the minds and imaginations of his audience. Steve Jobs left behind a legacy: "Stay Hungry. Stay Foolish." Aside from the beautiful products you can use to run your business, perhaps the most important of all is to use his presentation skills to beat the competition and rise above in your organization.

EPILOGUE

PARADISE LOST AND REGAINED

The mind is its own place, and in itself can make a Heav'n of Hell, a Hell of Heav'n.

– John Milton, *Paradise Lost*

The human genome is the same in all the people and the human species shares the same DNA. Yet, some people are happy to work and some work unhappily. Why? Some are lucky with jobs and some are unlucky. Why? Some pick and drop jobs at will, while others struggle to find one suitable job. Why? Some are industrious, and some are lazy. Why? Can we really and truly find self-actualization, success and satisfaction in our work and in our lives? These questions make one ponder and reflect. Reflection leads to meditation, and meditation leads us to the Holy Book.

In the Bible, we are told in the *Book of Genesis* that God made Adam and Eve and put them in the Garden of Eden to enjoy life and live happily ever after. They were programmed by the Master Programmer to enjoy life — not slog it out. Adam and Eve lived a good life. Living in the Garden of Eden was one big picnic; no worries, no fears and no toil. All they did was to explore Eden and look amazed and awed at God's creation. Were Adam and Eve programmed to simply laze around — like the aristocrats did? If that was so, all was hunky-dory until one sunny day the cunning serpent wagered Eve to pluck a juicy apple.

On a lighter note, if the Garden of Eden was in China, Adam and Eve would never have been banished. Eve would have skewered the serpent and served Adam morsels of *seekh kebab*, and God would have been glorified as the flawless Creator for generations thereafter. But the Chinese rejected God, so He put the Garden of Eden elsewhere and the story of man's troubles continues to this day.

On seeing the serpent, Eve's programming developed a malfunction. God had not programmed Eve to wager with the serpent or pluck the apple. To 'pluck' an apple was an act of work, and Eve plucked an apple, which she was not programmed for, and that made God go red with wrath. And Adam went blue with shock. On realizing that He created Eve with a faulty programming, God went into a rage (now you know why bosses look for scapegoats to take the rap for their errors). He cursed Adam and Eve that they would labour and work for the rest of their lives. For no fault of his, Adam also got kicked out of Eden along with Eve. And ever since then till the present day, we, their offspring, have to toil to earn our bread (and butter) with the sweat of our brow.

Some human beings who carry the dominant Adam gene are still in a state of shock. They still fancy the good life they lost over an apple and work grudgingly, if at all, because it was forced upon them. Psychiatrists label them as living in a 'state of denial'. And those human beings who carry the dominant Eve gene passionately bury themselves in work because they were programmed to work (albeit a malfunction in the original programme). Psychiatrists label them as 'workaholics'. In the aftermath of God's unholy rage, work became the centre-point for mankind's existential survival. Since then, from the womb to the tomb, men and women spend their lifetime working, working and working.

Everybody works, you will say, and those who don't have work at hand also are at 'work' because they have work on their minds or hanker for it. To 'hanker for work' is also 'work' for the jobless. And look how people work. Some people shy away from work while others offload (delegate) work. Some feel energized at the sight of work while some snore at the thought of work. Some hardly work but are seen to be hardworking and get paid handsomely, while on the other end of the job spectrum, some hardworking people are hardly seen to be working and get paid a pittance. And there are people who are buried in work — some enjoy it and some hate it. Some work noiselessly, while others work noisily. Some develop cutting-edge skills to be efficient, while others are casual about efficiency at the workplace.

Where do you fit in? Which dominant gene is at work in you? Is it the Adam gene that loves to laze — like on a picnic? Or is it the Eve gene that loves to work so that others can laze and have fun? Would they call it 'wishful thinking', if you worked a plan where you could choose some of the best attributes of the Eve gene as well as some of those from the Adam gene so that you could re-programme your personality to enjoy work and pleasure? You could 'play' God to fix your personality.

First of all, to make it possible, believe in yourself. You are not cast in stone. And even if you *think* you were cast in stone (which you are not), so what? Look at Moses. God gave him the Ten Commandments, cast in stone, and what did he do with it? He smashed them into pieces because God also gave him free will — the freedom to do what he pleased. God gave you free will, too, so you can do as you please. Why be content with the way you are when you can become better than what you are? You have the ability to re-programme your personality in the way you want it to be. Go ahead and do what Moses did on Mount Sinai. Smash all those old habits which pull down your brand image. ***Rise Above*** has shown you how to do it.

You can cut here and nip there to pick and choose a little bit more or a little bit less of the Adam gene and the Eve gene and re-programme your personality to make your life more meaningful, more successful and less stressful. ***Rise Above*** is your self-development mentor, guide and coach. You owe yourself a dynamic personality rooted in sound values and this is your opportunity to convert your people skills into brand assets. Assimilate and apply the lessons contained in the three sections of this book. Each chapter is loaded with valuable inputs to sharpen your social and corporate skills so that you will find the right balance between work and pleasure and achieve success at home, at the workplace and with friends and relatives to last you a lifetime of joyful moments blessed with happy memories.

APPENDIX

OVERHAUL YOUR BRAND IMAGE

Appendix I
FACE-TO-FACE

Appendix II
TEST YOUR COMPREHENSION

CHECK YOUR ANSWERS

OVERHAUL YOUR BRAND IMAGE

*The **Appendix** is divided into two sections. **Appendix I** invites you to be an armchair psychologist. You are required to answer as truthfully and as quickly as you can the questionnaires and quizzes put to you, and thereafter write a summary of your personality that emerges from the choices you selected. The questionnaires, quizzes and tests come from a collection of notes from the author's 'old' files. The author takes no credit for preparing **Appendix I.** The original source of the psychological tests reproduced is unknown to the author. The author thanks the psychologists and counsellors for the material in **Appendix I.***

*While **Appendix I** has no right or wrong answers and must be attempted rapidly, **Appendix II** has to do only with right and wrong answers and must be attempted thoughtfully.*

***Appendix II** is to sharpen your comprehension powers. After you read the chapter carefully you may **Test Your Comprehension.** If you score 'Excellent', you will progress faster. On the other hand, if you score 'Average' or 'Below Average', it will take you that much longer to achieve success. After all, the outcome of your work and actions depends on your level of comprehension.*

*Teachers, professors and training heads of institutions and business houses can benefit from administering the tests contained in **Appendix I** and **Appendix II** to ascertain the psychological, emotional, social and intellectual levels of students and employees.*

appendix I

FACE-TO-FACE

This section brings you face-to-face with your innermost thoughts, moods, feelings and actions. You are the student and the teacher. The way you are and the way others see you will unfold before you as *feedback* for self-improvement. Each test is a compass that points towards a particular direction. Your self-assessment notes form the action plan to follow that direction.

The following exercises have two parts. In the first part, you are required to make a choice that best describes your actions, moods, feelings, temperament and behaviour. In the second part, you are required to write your assessment on the personality qualities that emerge from your choices and the steps you will take to improve within a timeframe of three months. Follow the instructions closely and you will draw maximum mileage from *Appendix I.*

Instructions

1. It is essential that you must repeat the tests every three months.
2. The tests are not comprehensive in content; hence, don't take them too seriously.
3. The Tests have 25% value. Your Self-Assessments have 75% value.
4. On completing each test, you will get a fair picture of your personality traits.
5. Write a 'Self-Assessment' to summarize your personality traits.
6. Write down concrete 'Steps' you will take for self-improvement.
7. A written assessment of your personality traits is very important. The more objective you are in your written assessment, the quicker you will progress.
8. Do not erase the summaries you will write.
9. After three months, when you attempt the tests again, compare the previous assessment notes with the present ones.

TEST I: HANDWRITING ANALYSIS

Handwriting Analysis is also known as *Written Body Language*. Your thoughts and feelings have an immediate impact on the formation of handwriting. You will spot differences in handwriting by comparing your writing samples written in various moods when you are angry, happy, tired or feeling sick. When you compare these different samples, you will be able to see noticeable differences in pen stroke usage, even though your handwriting style remains basically the same. Handwriting analysis can also help determine physical or mental ailments, drug or alcohol use and work-style compatibility.

Handwriting is like an instantaneous photograph of your mind. Your nervous system acts as a wire from brain to hand. A thought in your brain is transmitted by electrical impulses through the nervous system and fibres of your body, arm, hand and fingers. The fingers are only vehicles that put it in writing. Handwriting analysis can aid you in your business life. For decades, it has been a standard part of the hiring process in companies across the globe. Companies based in France, India, England, Spain and Israel regularly do a handwriting analysis prior to employment. It is used in the hiring and promotion process. Just like fingerprints, no two handwritings are identical.

Analysing *Written Body Language* is not one hundred per cent accurate, but it is much more accurate than personality tests that ask candidates multiple-choice questions, because it cannot be manipulated. Also, candidates cannot change their handwriting on the spot to conceal or disguise their personalities.

This exercise will help you know how people judge your character from your handwriting. To take this test, write about 10 lines of a paragraph in the speed and style you normally would, and keep the paper in front of you so that you can answer the questions. Look at the paragraph you wrote and answer the following questions and you will discover what your handwriting says about you!

1. How would you say your letters slope?

- ☐ Backward
- ☐ Straight up and down
- ☐ Forward

2. The letters in your words are

- ☐ Fully connected, with clear breaks between the words

- ☐ Partially connected, depending on the letters
- ☐ Unconnected, like printing

3. **Between words, you leave**
   - ☐ Wide spaces
   - ☐ Narrow spaces
   - ☐ No spaces — words are connected; the pen doesn't leave the paper

4. **How close together are your lines of writing?**
   - ☐ Very far apart
   - ☐ Far apart enough that the letters do not touch
   - ☐ So close that the descenders (like *y* and *g*) of the upper line and the ascenders (like *h* and *t*) of the bottom line overlap each other

5. **What colour ink did you choose? (If you used another colour, which of these three would you prefer?)**
   - ☐ Blue-black
   - ☐ Red
   - ☐ Light blue

6. **How large was your capital 'I' in the sample?**
   - ☐ Larger than other capital letters
   - ☐ About the same size as the other capital letters
   - ☐ Smaller than other capital letters

7. **What do your 't' bars look like? (The crossbars on your letter *t*)**
   - ☐ They tend to be to the left of the stem of *t*.
   - ☐ They cross *t* more or less in the middle.
   - ☐ They tend to be to the right of the stem of *t*.

8. **How does your writing slope across the page?**
   - ☐ Slopes upward on the page
   - ☐ Goes straight across the page
   - ☐ Slopes downward on the page

9. **Which of the following takes the most space vertically in a line of your writing?**
   - ☐ The ascenders (the tops of *t* and *h*)
   - ☐ The middle zone (letters like *a*, *e* and *n*)
   - ☐ The descenders (the bottoms of *j*, *y* and *g*)

10. How much pressure does your writing show?

- ☐ Fine and spidery
- ☐ Firm and even
- ☐ Heavy

Check your answers with the analysis given below.

1. **Backward**: indicates that you are shy and afraid to show your feelings, hesitant. **Straight up and down**: indicates that you are a person with a strong need for contact. **Forward:** indicates that you are reticent and very self-controlled.
2. **Fully connected:** indicates that you are a social person who likes to talk and meet others. **Partially connected:** indicates that you are a shy, idealistic person who does not find it easy to have relationships, especially intimate ones. **Unconnected:** indicates that you are a person who thinks before acting, intelligent and thorough.
3. **Wide spaces:** indicates that you are reserved, shy, cautious, and thoughtful. **Narrow spaces:** indicates that you are a talkative person, maybe even a busybody! **No spaces:** indicates that you are not very reserved, impatient, self-confident and fond of action.
4. **Very far apart:** indicates that you are isolated, detached, reserved, maybe even antisocial. **Far apart enough that letters do not touch:** indicates that you are a person who is uneconomical and talkative. **So close enough that the descendants of *y*'s and *g*'s touch the ascendants of *h*'s and *t*'s:** indicates that you are a person with a well-organized mind.
5. **Blue-black:** indicates that you are rational, conservative; a person who adheres to conventions and traditions. **Red:** indicates that you are spiritual rather than material, perhaps religious, and may have a deep understanding of other people's problems. **Light blue:** indicates that you are strong, vital, energetic, affectionate; you like action and have an original approach.
6. **Larger than other capital letters:** indicates that you are a person with a high opinion of yourself, or who wants others to think that you are so. **About the same size:** indicates that you are a person who may be feeling depressed or have low self-esteem. **Smaller than other capitals:** indicates that you are well adjusted, harmonious, and content with your current role.
7. **They tend to be to the left of the stem of 't':** indicates that you are cautious, possibly uncertain about things. **They cross 't' more or less in the middle:** indicates that you are not very original but very responsible, possibly in management. **They tend to be to the right of the stem of 't':** indicates that you are a reliable, conscientious worker, with possible leadership potential.
8. **Slopes upward on the page:** indicates that you are energetic, optimistic, and assertive. **Goes straight across the page:** indicates that you are a person who may be suffering from temporary depression or fatigue. **Slopes downward:** indicates

that you are steadfast, purposeful, and possibly aloof.

9. **The ascenders:** indicates that you are idealistic, ambitious and intuitive. **The middle-zone letters:** indicates that you are a sensualist, a materialist, and prone to exaggeration. **The descenders:** indicates that you are a person with an overdeveloped ego and a tendency to be bossy.
10. **Fine and spidery:** indicates that you are a person of sensitivity, refinement, modesty and spirituality. You may also be overly critical and austere. **Firm and even:** indicates that you are a person of strong but rigid will, obstinate but powerful. **Heavy:** indicates that you are a person of energy and elasticity, and able to roll with the punches and adapt to whatever life brings.

Date______________

Write Your Self-Assessment.

I am

____

____

Steps to Improve Myself ______________________________

____

____

Please Note: *If you write haphazardly or minutely, this is your opportunity to un-learn the old writing style and re-learn to carve your letters to project a well-rounded personality.*

TEST II: ARE YOU A PEOPLE'S PERSON?

For each set of three choices give your first preference 3 points, second preference 2 points, and least preferred choice 1 point. There are no right answers or wrong answers. Do the test as rapidly as you can.

When troubled I seek out...

1. people
2. action
3. solitude

I usually prefer...

1. physical comfort
2. physical adventure
3. privacy

The time of my life I favour is...

1. childhood
2. early adulthood
3. later years

What would bother me most would be...

1. being cut off from other people
2. being closed off in small places
3. being exposed to endless noise

I prefer to...

1. let things take their course
2. do things
3. observe what is going on

When in a group, I like to...

1. mingle
2. take charge
3. take off

The thing I like most is...

1. eating
2. exercise
3. time to myself

The quality/ies that fit me best is/are...

1. tolerance and love of people
2. love of power and leadership
3. a highly developed self-awareness

Total Score = ____________

(Make a note of your first-preference choices to get a fair picture of the '*People's Person*' you are. Also study your second-preference choices and lastly the third-preference choices you made. Make a summary of your self-assessment below.)

Date______________

Write Your Self-Assessment.

I am

____

____

Steps to Improve Myself ____

____

____

TEST III (A): ARE YOU AN INTROVERT?

1. I am usually tired. - YES/NO
2. I am usually exhausted. - YES/NO
3. I cannot sleep. - YES/NO
4. I am tense. - YES/NO
5. I am often uneasy. - YES/NO
6. I have a non-caring attitude. - YES/NO
7. I like privacy. - YES/NO
8. I am secretive. - YES/NO
9. I cannot face facts. - YES/NO
10. I don't like noise. - YES/NO
11. I don't know the tactful way to handle people. - YES/NO
12. I don't like social life. - YES/NO
13. I don't like crowds. - YES/NO
14. I have an active mind. - YES/NO
15. I am soft-spoken. - YES/NO
16. I don't like alcohol. - YES/NO

If answers to any 12 out of the above 16 questions are YES, then you are an INTROVERT.

Total Score = ________

Date______________

Write Your Self-Assessment.

I am

____

____

Steps to Improve Myself ______________________________________

____

____

TEST III (B): ARE YOU AN EXTROVERT?

1. I am loud. - YES/NO
2. I am brazen. - YES/NO
3. I am tough. - YES/NO
4. I am a back-slapper. - YES/NO
5. I like outdoors. - YES/NO
6. I am energetic. - YES/NO

7. I like hard drinks. - YES/NO
8. I am courageous. - YES/NO
9. I am aggressive. - YES/NO
10. I like sleep. - YES/NO
11. I am shrewd. - YES/NO
12. I am dominant. - YES/NO
13. I take risks. - YES/NO
14. I like youth activities. - YES/NO
15. I eat well. - YES/NO
16. I am ethical. - YES/NO
17. I am greedy for affection. - YES/NO
18. I am an effective communicator. - YES/NO

If answers to any 14 out of the above 18 questions are YES, you are an EXTROVERT.

Total Score = ___________

Date______________

Write Your Self-Assessment.

I am

____

____

Steps to Improve Myself ____

____

____

TEST III (C): ARE YOU AN AMBIVERT?

(Combination of *Introversion* and *Extroversion*)

1. I am adjustable. - YES/NO
2. I fight for my rights. - YES/NO
3. I am a go-getter. - YES/NO
4. I am adaptable. - YES/NO
5. I am a leader. - YES/NO
6. I am a thinker. - YES/NO
7. I am a planner. - YES/NO
8. I look younger. - YES/NO
9. I am a charmer. - YES/NO
10. I use my training. - YES/NO

11. I utilize my education. - YES/NO
12. I bounce back from defeat. - YES/NO
13. I am depressed sometimes. - YES/NO
14. I am efficient. - YES/NO

If answers to any 11 out of the above 14 questions are YES, then you are an **AMBIVERT**.

Total Score = ____________

Date______________
Write Your Self-Assessment.
I am
____
____
Steps to Improve Myself ________________________________
____
____

TEST III (D): GET TO KNOW YOUR PERSONALITY

In *Get to Know Your Personality*, there are three scales. Answer each item as honestly and quickly as you can with your first reaction. There are no right or wrong answers and no points to tally.

SCALE 1

1. **Do you enjoy talking? - YES/NO**
2. **Are you often bored at parties? - YES/NO**
3. **Are you sociable? - YES/NO**
4. **Are you a quiet person? - YES/NO**
5. **Do you like to work fast? - YES/NO**
6. **Do you like a nice, quiet, peaceful setting? - YES/NO**
7. **Are you thought of as witty and amusing? - YES/NO**
8. **Do you like jobs that require a lot of concentration? - YES/NO**
9. **Do you look for energetic pastimes? - YES/NO**
10. **Are you a shy person? - YES/NO**

EXERCISE: First study the *Yes* responses and then look at the *No* responses. Kindly summarize the emerging personality from your *Yes* and *No* responses.

According to *Yes* responses, I am ______________________________

According to *No* responses, I am ______________________________

SCALE 2

1. **Are you rather moody? - YES/NO**
2. **Can you take criticism easily? - YES/NO**
3. **Do you find it hard to sleep well? - YES/NO**
4. **Are you calm and easygoing? - YES/NO**
5. **Do you often feel wracked with guilt? - YES/NO**
6. **Can you easily put fears for the future out of your mind? - YES/NO**
7. **Do you sometimes worry about everything? - YES/NO**
8. **Are you usually cheerful? - YES/NO**
9. **Do you get annoyed easily? - YES/NO**
10. **Do you take everything in your stride? - YES/NO**

EXERCISE: First study the *Yes* responses and then look at the *No* responses. Kindly summarize the emerging personality from your *Yes* and *No* responses.

According to *Yes* responses, I am ______________________________

According to *No* responses, I am ______________________________

SCALE 3

1. **Do you enjoy gambling for high stakes? - YES/NO**
2. **Are you a careful driver? - YES/NO**
3. **To win a game, do you sometimes bend the rules? - YES/NO**
4. **Are you frightened by the idea of paragliding? - YES/NO**
5. **Do you enjoy watching pornographic films? - YES/NO**
6. **Do you have negative thoughts about other people? - YES/NO**
7. **Do you assist in maintenance and repairs at home? - YES/NO**
8. **Do you think hurtful, practical jokes are bad? - YES/NO**
9. **Do you enjoy really fast driving? - YES/NO**
10. **Do you think there should be stronger laws against corporate crimes? - YES/NO**

EXERCISE: First study the *Yes* responses and then look at the *No* responses. Kindly summarize the emerging personality from your *Yes* and *No* responses.

According to *Yes* responses, I am ______________________________

According to *No* responses, I am ______________________________

After studying the summaries of the three scales, write the steps you will undertake to develop a balanced personality.

____

____

____

TEST IV: KNOW YOUR PERSONALITY PROFILE

Tick your choice as rapidly as you can.

1. **When do you feel your best?**
   a. In the morning
   b. During the afternoon and early evening
   c. Late at night
2. **You usually walk**
   a. Fairly fast, with long steps
   b. Fairly fast, with short, quick steps
   c. Less fast, head up, looking the world in the face
   d. Less fast, head down
   e. Very slowly
3. **When talking to people, you**
   a. Stand with your arms folded
   b. Have your hands clasped
   c. Have one or both your hands on your hips
   d. Touch or push the person who you are talking to
   e. Play with your ear, touch your chin, or smooth your hair
4. **When relaxing, you sit with**
   a. Your knees bent and your legs neatly side by side
   b. Your legs crossed
   c. Your legs stretched out or straight
   d. One leg curled under you
5. **When something really amuses you, you react with**
   a. A big, appreciative laugh
   b. A laugh, but not a loud one
   c. A quiet chuckle
   d. A sheepish smile
6. **When you go to a party or social gathering, you**
   a. Make a loud entrance so everyone notices you
   b. Make a quiet entrance, looking around for someone you know
   c. Make the quietest entrance, trying to stay unnoticed
7. **You're working very hard, concentrating hard, and you're interrupted. You**
   a. Welcome the break
   b. Feel extremely irritated
   c. Vary between these two extremes
8. **Which of the following colours do you like the most?**
   a. Red or orange
   b. Black

c. Yellow or light blue
d. Green
e. Dark blue or purple
f. White
g. Brown or grey

9. When you are in bed at night, in those last few moments before going to sleep, you lie

a. Stretched out on your back
b. Stretched out face down on your stomach
c. On your side, slightly curled
d. With your head on one arm
e. With your head under the covers

10. You often dream that you are

a. Falling
b. Fighting or struggling
c. Searching for something or somebody
d. Flying or floating
e. You usually have dreamless sleep.
f. Your dreams are always pleasant.

Points:

1. a. 2	b. 4	c. 6				
2. a. 6	b. 4	c. 7	d. 2	e. 1		
3. a. 4	b. 2	c. 5	d. 7	e. 6		
4. a. 4	b. 6	c. 2	d. 1			
5. a. 6	b. 4	c. 3	d. 5			
6. a. 6	b. 4	c. 2				
7. a. 6	b. 2	c. 4				
8. a. 6	b. 7	c. 5	d. 4	e. 3	f. 2	g. 1
9. a. 7	b. 6	c. 4	d. 2	e. 1		
10. a. 4	b. 2	c. 3	d. 5	e. 6	f. 1	

Total Score = ____________

Over 60 points: Others see you as someone they should "handle with care". You're seen as vain, self-centred, and extremely dominant. Others may admire you, wishing they could be more like you, but don't always trust you, hesitating to become too deeply involved with you.

51 to 60 points: Others see you as an exciting, highly volatile, rather impulsive personality — a natural leader who's quick to make decisions, though not always the right ones. They see you as bold and adventuresome, someone who will try anything once; someone who takes chances and enjoys an adventure. They enjoy being in your company because of the excitement you radiate.

41 to 50 points: Others see you as fresh, lively, charming, amusing, practical, and always interesting — someone who's constantly in the centre of attention, but sufficiently well-balanced not to let it go to their head. They also see you as kind, considerate, and understanding — someone who'll always cheer them up and help them out.

31 to 40 points: Others see you as sensible, cautious, careful and practical. They see you as clever, gifted or talented, but modest. Not a person who makes friends too quickly or easily, but someone who's extremely loyal to friends you do make and who expects the same loyalty in return. Those who really get to know you realize it takes a lot to shake your trust in your friends, but equally that it takes you a long time to get over it if that trust is ever broken.

21 to 30 points: Your friends see you as painstaking and fussy. They see you as very cautious — a slow and steady plodder. It would really surprise them if you ever did something impulsively or on the spur of the moment, as they expect you to examine everything carefully from every angle and then, usually, decide against it. They think this reaction is caused partly by your careful nature.

Under 21 points: People think you are shy, nervous, and indecisive, someone who needs looking after, who always wants someone else to make the decisions and who doesn't want to get involved with anyone or anything. They see you as a worrier who always sees problems that don't exist. Some people think you're boring. Only those who know you well know that you aren't.

Date____________

This is My Personality Profile…

I am

____

____

Steps to Improve Myself _________________________

____

____

____

TEST V: KNOW YOUR EMOTIONS

Many emotions are expressed instinctively. Do you have a healthy attitude towards your emotions? In this quiz you can know about your emotions.

For every 'NO' answer, add 1 point to your score.

1. Do you feel guilty if you cry in public?
2. Do you think crying is a sign of weakness?
3. Do you think men and boys should be encouraged to hide their tears?
4. Do you feel embarrassed if you find yourself crying while watching a film or reading a book?
5. Would you try to hold back your tears if you were attending a funeral?
6. Would you distrust a politician who shed tears in public?
7. Do you think that tears are an unnecessary expression of emotion?
8. Do you always try to hide your disappointment?
9. Do you get embarrassed if you see grown men crying?
10. Would you pretend that you had something in your eyes if you were unexpectedly discovered crying?
11. Do you always try to hide your anger?

For every 'YES' answer, add 1 point to your score.

12. Do you tend to brood about things which make you angry?
13. Does your temper get out of control?
14. Has your temper ever got you into trouble?
15. Do you believe that it does you good to get rid of your anger?
16. Would you allow someone to comfort you if you were crying?
17. Do you get cross quite easily?
18. Do you touch someone you love at least once a day?
19. Do you enjoy physical signs of affection?
20. Do you ever get broody when you see small babies?
21. Would you happily hold hands in public with someone you cared for?
22. Do you enjoy being massaged?
23. Do you regularly tell those whom you love how you feel?
24. Have you ever had a pet which you were very fond of?
25. Do you enjoy being kissed and hugged by people you love?
26. Do you ever laugh out loud when you are watching funny films?
27. Do you ever tap your feet while listening to music?
28. Do you often have the last clap at concerts, sports events and the

like?

29. Do you ever shout encouragement to sports or TV heroes?
30. Can you remember when you last really laughed and enjoyed yourself?

Total Score = ____________

Analysis

Score 17 to 30. Your attitude towards your emotions is a healthy one. You are not ashamed to let your emotions show occasionally, and you will undoubtedly be much healthier (physically and mentally) because of this attitude. You are likely to be a good social advisor.

Score 8 to 16. You know how to let your emotions show but you still find it difficult to do so as often as you should. You should be prepared to let your emotions out more often. When you feel sad let yourself cry; when you feel angry let your anger show; when you feel happy allow a smile to cross your face. Allowing your emotions out in this way will do wonders to your physical and mental health.

Score 7 or less. You are definitely very uptight. You really do need to allow your emotions to flow out a little. There isn't anything really wrong in allowing people to know how you feel.

Date ____________

Write Your Self-Assessment.

I am

____

____

Steps to Improve Myself ____

____

____

____

TEST VI: HOW WELL YOU LISTEN

Listening is an art that can be developed. Are you a good listener? How do you respond when people talk to you? Rate your responses with this test. Tick **your most likely response** to each statement:

1. **"I'm really fed up with my job."**
   a) It can't be as bad as *my* job — I'm so bored I could fall asleep at work!
   b) Are you saying that you would like something more from your work?
2. **"My manager drives me crazy!!"**
   a) Sounds like you have a problem with your manager.
   b) If I was you, I'd tell him to go fly a kite!
3. **"I just can't cope with the mountain of work."**
   a) That's tough. Did I tell you about my new job?
   b) It seems like you are under a lot of pressure at work.
4. **"I wish I was better at communicating with my team."**
   a) So you think you are not good at communicating?
   b) I'm sure you are fine, don't worry about it.
5. **"I was late with a delivery to my best customer. I am really worried that I might lose the business."**
   a) There is nothing to be upset about. I am sure the customer won't mind.
   b) Are you afraid that the customer will go elsewhere?
6. **"I'm feeling really depressed at the moment."**
   a) You sound unhappy. Want to talk about it?
   b) Just pull yourself together and you'll be fine.
7. **"I don't feel confident about making that presentation."**
   a) If you want to be considered for promotion, you need to take these opportunities.
   b) Are you saying that you feel nervous about it?
8. **"I am concerned that the new sales projections are unrealistic. Can we talk about it?"**
   a) Sorry, but you know we have to reach them.
   b) Sounds like your are finding the new projections hard to reach?
9. **"I am really worried about the effect of the recession on the business."**
   a) I can see that you are concerned about the business right now.
   b) You are being negative. Try seeing the bright side for a change.
10. **"I can't wait for the weekend so I can get out of this place."**
    a) You shouldn't be wishing your life away.
    b) So you are looking forward to getting away from work?

2 points each for the following answers: 1-b; 2-a; 3-b; 4-a; 5-b; 6-a; 7-b; 8-b; 9-a; 10-b

Total Score = ____________

Score of 15 points or more: You are using active listening in the way you communicate with others. You are likely to be good at putting someone at ease and helping the conversation flow. Your predominant style is empathetic — you are able to "put yourself in other people's shoes" to get a good understanding of their situation and how they feel about it. People are likely to come to you with their concerns and to discuss their views.

This knowledge can put you in a stronger position as a manager or leader. For example, you may become aware of potential problems at an earlier stage and work to resolve them.

Score of less than 15 points: It is possible that at times you respond to people in a way that prevents good communication. This can often happen unintentionally by the words you use or how you react. Sometimes you can be too sympathetic and make a situation worse. On the other hand, you can be too apathetic, not wanting to get involved.

You can communicate more effectively when you are *empathetic*, which involves the skill of active listening. Being aware of the responses to avoid when talking to others will help you improve your active listening skills. And remember that we are all human — it is impossible to "get it right" all the time. Being aware of what is involved in "active listening" is the first step.

What is Active Listening?

Active Listening involves reflecting the **feelings** and the **content** of what a person has said. If you use active listening techniques, you are likely to develop greater empathy with others. They will feel you are approachable and non-judgemental. It is a skill which can be developed with conscious awareness and practice.

Date____________

I am ____

____

Steps to Improve Myself ________________________________

____

____

____

appendix II
TEST YOUR COMPREHENSION

Appendix II offers you an opportunity to sharpen your comprehension skills. It is said that the memory is like the muscle. The more you exercise it, the better it gets. This section also challenges you to put your memory to the test and to find out your comprehension level or the amount of information you are able to digest and retain — an invaluable skill for corporate executives. You will attempt this section only after you have finished reading the chapters. Twenty statements per chapter have been put out in the test paper; read each statement carefully and then decide on the right choice. You have to choose the right answer by selecting *True* or *False* as required. After you have completed the assignment, check your answers and see how you scored.

Appendix II is a guide, coach and motivator not only to individuals who self-learn but also to teachers and professors who prepare and evaluate job-ready aspirants. This *Section* will also serve as a handy tool for corporate HoDs who evaluate new incumbents at the time of induction, as well as for old employees who attend in-house training and development workshops.

TEST YOUR COMPREHENSION

Chapter 1: Build Your Brand Identity

Read carefully and select either TRUE or FALSE.

1. You can smash glass ceilings with a stone. TRUE / FALSE
2. Sangita was a failure as a role model for aspiring employees. TRUE / FALSE
3. To re-build your personality, you must know yourself. TRUE / FALSE
4. Employees who do not know their strengths make wrong decisions. TRUE / FALSE
5. It is expected from co-workers to help you to find your 'groove'. TRUE / FALSE
6. Core competency is a combination of hard skills and soft skills. TRUE / FALSE

7. Self-knowledge is essential in order to choose a successful career. TRUE / FALSE
8. Improving your brand image depends entirely on your attitude and dedication. TRUE / FALSE
9. To succeed, you must learn new skills. TRUE / FALSE
10. You cannot succeed without a life coach or mentor. TRUE / FALSE
11. You can change your bad habits easily. TRUE / FALSE
12. All top achievers, athletes and professionals set goals. TRUE / FALSE
13. To be disciplined, you must follow a timetable. TRUE / FALSE
14. If you have integrity, people will respect you. TRUE / FALSE
15. People know promises are made to be broken. TRUE / FALSE
16. To impress people, you must be an exceptional listener. TRUE / FALSE
17. We form bad habits in order to please others' convenience. TRUE / FALSE
18. You must constantly remind yourself that you must get rid of bad habits. TRUE / FALSE
19. You must focus on what you will *put in* instead of what you will *pull out*. TRUE / FALSE
20. Adding multi-dimensional skills to your personality is a lifelong investment. TRUE / FALSE

5 points for each correct answer.
Compare your choices with the right answers on p. 239.

Total Score = ___________

Chapter 2: Supercharge Your Brand Value

Read carefully and select either TRUE or FALSE.

1. People like Ashutosh make good role models. TRUE / FALSE
2. Our behaviour and actions are a result of 'pre-wiring'. TRUE / FALSE
3. You are lazy. Your brain controls your habits. TRUE / FALSE
4. The human brain has two parts: left brain and right brain. TRUE / FALSE
5. After the age of 20 you cannot change your personality. TRUE / FALSE
6. Employees must work like industrious hamsters. TRUE / FALSE

7. Workaholics can harm company efficiency and co-workers' morale. TRUE / FALSE
8. A lot of information is fed to the brain through the spinal cord. TRUE / FALSE
9. Behaviour is 'wired' to your brain. TRUE / FALSE
10. Right brain controls the right side of the body. TRUE / FALSE
11. Left brain controls the right side of the body. TRUE / FALSE
12. Right-brained people tend to be logical and analytical. TRUE / FALSE
13. Employees with bad characters ruin company reputation. TRUE / FALSE
14. To rise in a corporate house, you must avoid being friends with bad employees. TRUE / FALSE
15. Humans can stimulate the brain to work positively. TRUE / FALSE
16. It is not possible to control distractions. TRUE / FALSE
17. Making New Year's resolutions is meaningful. TRUE / FALSE
18. Too much ambition can result in being ruthless and greedy. TRUE / FALSE
19. Indian youth are more ambitious throughout the world. TRUE / FALSE
20. Employers are cautious of ambitious workers. TRUE / FALSE

5 points for each correct answer.
Compare your choices with the right answers on p. 239.

Total Score = __________

Chapter 3: Give Your Brand the Moral Seal

Read carefully and select either TRUE or FALSE.

1. It was unfair to fire Parvathi, who worked with dedication for 14 years. TRUE / FALSE
2. Weak laws on corruption encourage unethical behaviour. TRUE / FALSE
3. We live in a global village and not in a fishbowl. TRUE / FALSE
4. Companies are focused on more profit, not on ethics. TRUE / FALSE
5. "Walk the Talk" is a platform to expose corruption. TRUE / FALSE
6. Unethical employees are ashamed of their immoral behaviour. TRUE / FALSE

7. Students are not taught any more to live moral and ethical lives. TRUE / FALSE
8. Success is equated with making more money. TRUE / FALSE
9. Values are not etched in the souls; they come from society. TRUE / FALSE
10. Discernment is knowing the difference between good and bad. TRUE / FALSE
11. Employers look for workers who are shrewd money-wise. TRUE / FALSE
12. Companies must focus on making profit, not on ethics. TRUE / FALSE
13. Employees must be clever and cautious to succeed in the workplace. TRUE / FALSE
14. Don't mess with your brand value if you want that job. TRUE / FALSE
15. Companies must emphasize on employees' job skills, not on ethics. TRUE / FALSE
16. Show the boss your personality traits which the company wants. TRUE / FALSE
17. Practice of ethics primarily is the practice of being honest. TRUE / FALSE
18. Hardworking employees are perceived as sucking up to the management. TRUE / FALSE
19. Moral conscience is inherited from our parents. TRUE / FALSE
20. Organizations are stuck with lazy and incompetent workers. TRUE / FALSE

5 points for each correct answer.
Compare your choices with the right answers on p. 239.

Total Score = ____________

Chapter 4: Market Your Brand Equity

Read carefully and select either TRUE or FALSE.

1. Priyamvada lacked critical skills in preparing her résumés. TRUE / FALSE
2. You are marketing your personal brand with each résumé you send. TRUE / FALSE

3. Each interview is a learning experience to improve your skills. TRUE / FALSE
4. You use the same style whether you prepare online or written résumés. TRUE / FALSE
5. The best computer-friendly format to write résumés is Microsoft Word. TRUE / FALSE
6. Always keep your internet slate clean. TRUE / FALSE
7. Good preparation will help you overcome stress. TRUE / FALSE
8. Employers generally overlook errors committed on the résumés. TRUE / FALSE
9. To get the job you applied for, you must know what the company wants. TRUE / FALSE
10. You fail interviews because of poor preparation. TRUE / FALSE
11. Companies search social-network sites to conduct background checks. TRUE / FALSE
12. Command over English language is not essential at interviews. TRUE / FALSE
13. You must match your skills to meet the company's expectations. TRUE / FALSE
14. You must research the company after you have been offered the job. TRUE / FALSE
15. Sound sleep and healthy food before the interview will make you drowsy. TRUE / FALSE
16. Learning the art of persuasion is a very important life skill. TRUE / FALSE
17. It is alright to tell small lies on your résumé. TRUE / FALSE
18. To persuade successfully, you must speak with conviction and force. TRUE / FALSE
19. It is bad manners to negotiate a salary during the interview. TRUE / FALSE
20. To impress, you must 'mirror' the interviewer's postures and gestures. TRUE / FALSE

5 points for each correct answer.
Compare your choices with the right answers on p. 239.

Total Score = __________

Chapter 5: Embellish Your Brand Image

Read carefully and select either TRUE or FALSE.

1. Irfaan dressed casually for the office. TRUE / FALSE
2. Your attitude to dress is reflected in the opinion people have of you. TRUE / FALSE
3. Business establishments usually accept the way its employees dress for work. TRUE / FALSE
4. When buying clothes, it is best to buy the whole lot at one go. TRUE / FALSE
5. Always wear tight clothes that fit snugly. TRUE / FALSE
6. Dress for the job you want, not for the job you have. TRUE / FALSE
7. People are prejudiced, no matter what you wear to work. TRUE / FALSE
8. Men look smart in formal attire. TRUE / FALSE
9. You must always dress to look as professional as the organization you represent. TRUE / FALSE
10. Most companies allow employees to wear jeans. TRUE / FALSE
11. Coloured shirts with bold patterns are appropriate for office wear. TRUE / FALSE
12. The colour of your socks must match with that of your shirt. TRUE / FALSE
13. It is safe to wear neckties with conservative patterns. TRUE / FALSE
14. The colour of your belt and that of your trousers must always match. TRUE / FALSE
15. More women than men are stared at. TRUE / FALSE
16. Compared to men, women are judged at the workplace more harshly. TRUE / FALSE
17. Conservative styles suit women best at the workplace. TRUE / FALSE
18. Companies should not decide dress codes for employees. TRUE / FALSE
19. If you work hard but dress shabbily, you will be overlooked. TRUE / FALSE
20. Balance your life between work and good grooming habits. TRUE / FALSE

5 points for each correct answer.
Compare your choices with the right answers on p. 239.

Total Score = ____________

Chapter 6: Add Polish to Your Personal Brand

Read carefully and select either TRUE or FALSE.

1. The company rewarded Vijay for his good hygiene habits. TRUE / FALSE
2. You can only blame yourself if people brand you "smelly" or "stinky". TRUE / FALSE
3. People in high office have good hygiene habits. TRUE / FALSE
4. People like to deal with clean, neat and tidy employees. TRUE / FALSE
5. Workers from rural backgrounds must pay attention to corporate hygiene. TRUE / FALSE
6. The untidy clutter on the desk shows how hard the employee works. TRUE / FALSE
7. To avoid bad breath, use a toothpick after meals. TRUE / FALSE
8. To avoid bad breath you must brush your teeth and tongue after meals. TRUE / FALSE
9. To clean your teeth thoroughly, use dental floss. TRUE / FALSE
10. You should always wash hands before eating food. TRUE / FALSE
11. Bathing twice daily has a bad effect on the skin. TRUE / FALSE
12. Body odour is caused by the sweat bacteria. TRUE / FALSE
13. Synthetic undergarments cause body odour in hot and humid weather. TRUE / FALSE
14. Drinking vodka helps to get rid of smelly feet. TRUE / FALSE
15. Eating yoghurt (*dahi*) helps reduce skin problems. TRUE / FALSE
16. Generally, men are insensitive when they use a washroom/toilet. TRUE / FALSE
17. In summers, one should wear only pure-cotton socks. TRUE / FALSE
18. It is more hygienic to use fresh hand or face tissues than handkerchiefs. TRUE / FALSE
19. There is no need to turn off taps after you use the washroom. TRUE / FALSE
20. Corporate hygiene policies take precedence over personal hygiene habits. TRUE / FALSE

5 points for each correct answer.

Compare your choices with the right answers on p. 240.

Total Score = ___________

Chapter 7: Prune Your Brand Image

Read carefully and select either TRUE or FALSE.

1. Sabrina's first impression of the drunken man was correct. TRUE / FALSE
2. To achieve success, your appearance must also look the part. TRUE / FALSE
3. You never get a second chance at making good first impressions. TRUE / FALSE
4. Without soft skills it is difficult to survive in the workplace. TRUE / FALSE
5. Your personality cannot be compared to the pieces of a jigsaw puzzle. TRUE / FALSE
6. A rosebush needs pruning; people don't. TRUE / FALSE
7. People form an impression of you from the way they perceive your behaviour. TRUE / FALSE
8. Once first impressions are formed, they are hard to reverse. TRUE / FALSE
9. On meeting someone, we analyse them instinctively. TRUE / FALSE
10. Hosts don't mind gatecrashers to the party because they add variety. TRUE / FALSE
11. Why be bothered to make good first impressions when others don't care? TRUE / FALSE
12. Companies expect employees to project a professional image. TRUE / FALSE
13. People always remember you by the first impressions they formed. TRUE / FALSE
14. To impress people, always arrive late for functions and meetings. TRUE / FALSE
15. Never interrupt the client and complete their sentences. TRUE / FALSE
16. On the mobile phone, it is alright to lie about being busy. TRUE / FALSE
17. Employees' behaviour always impacts the company's reputation. TRUE / FALSE
18. It is impossible to make powerful first impressions each time you meet clients. TRUE / FALSE
19. Handshakes are overrated when making first impressions. TRUE / FALSE

20. Good first impressions generate business for the company and appreciation for you. TRUE / FALSE

5 points for each correct answer.
Compare your choices with the right answers on p. 240.

Total Score = ____________

Chapter 8: Empower Your Brand Value

Read carefully and select either TRUE or FALSE.

1. Harish's business etiquette standards needed to be overhauled. TRUE / FALSE
2. To be relevant to the youth, Harish's advice to colleagues was valid. TRUE / FALSE
3. Business etiquette is essential to succeed in the corporate world. TRUE / FALSE
4. You must be clever and opportunistic in order to grow in the organization. TRUE / FALSE
5. When you make etiquette mistakes, pretend as though nothing has happened. TRUE / FALSE
6. At the workplace, men and women share equal status. TRUE / FALSE
7. At the workplace, clients and workers share equal status. TRUE / FALSE
8. When going through revolving doors with a lady, a man should go first. TRUE / FALSE
9. When descending an escalator with a lady, the man should go last. TRUE / FALSE
10. Loud laughter must be encouraged in offices. TRUE / FALSE
11. Nose picking, and scratching the head or other body parts are considered bad habits. TRUE / FALSE
12. You can eat lunch at the desk and save the leftovers in the drawers. TRUE / FALSE
13. When your colleague is out, you can enter their cubicle and snoop around. TRUE / FALSE
14. To win trust with co-workers, you must share something personal or confidential. TRUE / FALSE

15. You must restrain yourself from spreading gossip and cheap talk. TRUE / FALSE
16. Never get physically intimate with colleagues or co-workers. TRUE / FALSE
17. You are not required to reply immediately to e-mails. TRUE / FALSE
18. You can disconnect calls if clients speak rudely. TRUE / FALSE
19. Business etiquette demands that you know how to introduce people. TRUE / FALSE
20. It is a breach of etiquette when top executives receive calls during meetings. TRUE / FALSE

5 points for each correct answer.
Compare your choices with the right answers on p. 240.

Total Score = ___________

Chapter 9: Garnish Your Corporate Brand

Read carefully and select either TRUE or FALSE.

1. Bosco consciously practised table manners at business meals. TRUE / FALSE
2. The goal of business meals is to seal business deals. TRUE / FALSE
3. To rise above, you must have polished table manners. TRUE / FALSE
4. To eat gracefully, you must be consistent with your eating habits. TRUE / FALSE
5. Companies expect executives to know table manners when they apply for the job. TRUE / FALSE
6. It is not important to follow table manners when you eat alone or dine at home. TRUE / FALSE
7. When eating, you can keep elbows and arms on the table. TRUE / FALSE
8. Never use your napkin to blow your nose or sneeze into it. TRUE / FALSE
9. When you want a dish, it is polite to point at it than ask for it. TRUE / FALSE
10. Always help yourself to the best pieces and portions of food. TRUE / FALSE

11. To avoid making awkward noises, chew with your lips closed. TRUE / FALSE
12. If someone asks you for a second helping, do not help yourself first. TRUE / FALSE
13. Eating fast gives the impression of greediness. TRUE / FALSE
14. By licking fingers after you have finished eating, you show satisfaction. TRUE / FALSE
15. Never use fingers to pick up food from the serving dish. TRUE / FALSE
16. It is impolite to be late for business meals. TRUE / FALSE
17. When a lady joins or leaves the table, the man sitting next to her stands up. TRUE / FALSE
18. At corporate meals, you are not required to put your phone on 'silent' mode. TRUE / FALSE
19. To cool hot beverages, you can blow on it or pour it in the saucer. TRUE / FALSE
20. To have polished table manners is to add butter to business. TRUE / FALSE

5 points for each correct answer.
Compare your choices with the right answers on p. 240.

Total Score = ____________

Chapter 10: Interactive Social Networking

Read carefully and select either TRUE or FALSE.

1. Rajesh practised night and day to master the English language. TRUE / FALSE
2. Money is the language of commerce — and not English. TRUE / FALSE
3. Today's youth are mortally afraid to speak in formal gatherings. TRUE / FALSE
4. To succeed, you must be fluent in conversational English. TRUE / FALSE
5. Shy people suffer from people anxiety or speech anxiety. TRUE / FALSE
6. Nobody pays attention to English since everybody speaks it badly. TRUE / FALSE

7. Fluency in spoken English can get you a salary raise and promotion. TRUE / FALSE
8. People withdraw from making conversation due to inferiority complex. TRUE / FALSE
9. Fluency is possible if you converse in English regularly. TRUE / FALSE
10. It is always good to translate into English from your native idiom. TRUE / FALSE
11. The art of conversation lies in enjoying the moment and having a good time. TRUE / FALSE
12. The primary purpose of conversation is to express and not to impress. TRUE / FALSE
13. People admire those who monopolize conversations. TRUE / FALSE
14. To improve voice quality, record your speech and listen to its replay immediately. TRUE / FALSE
15. People are attracted to a well-modulated and sexy tone of voice. TRUE / FALSE
16. To be articulate, you must pronounce each word properly. TRUE / FALSE
17. Gruff, thin and high-pitched voices can be corrected with a minor surgery. TRUE / FALSE
18. Do deep-breathing exercises for a deep, well-modulated, sexy voice. TRUE / FALSE
19. Shouting is an effective exercise to develop strong vocal cords. TRUE / FALSE
20. Articulating tongue-twisters improves speech quality. TRUE / FALSE

5 points for each correct answer.
Compare your choices with the right answers on p. 240.

Total Score = ____________

Chapter 11: Effective Brand Posturing

Read carefully and select either TRUE or FALSE.

1. Doraiswamy misused the lessons he learnt on body language. TRUE / FALSE
2. Doraiswamy made a conscious effort not to copy world leaders. TRUE / FALSE
3. To master power games, you must master body language skills. TRUE / FALSE
4. *Bodytalk* is a powerful tool to navigate your way to the top. TRUE / FALSE
5. Body language reveals what a person is trying to tell or hide. TRUE / FALSE
6. To know body language, you must read the 'text' and 'sub-text' accurately. TRUE / FALSE
7. 'Text' is non-verbal expression, and 'sub-text' is verbal expression. TRUE / FALSE
8. You can learn body language by observing people in public places. TRUE / FALSE
9. Your office is an excellent place to observe and practise body language. TRUE / FALSE
10. Standing or sitting with arms crossed is considered 'defensive' or 'closed'. TRUE / FALSE
11. It is good to imitate the 'power walk' of top executives without giving offence. TRUE / FALSE
12. To maintain eye contact, you must stare fixedly into someone's eyes. TRUE / FALSE
13. Facial expressions are great indicators of what you are thinking. TRUE / FALSE
14. To interpret body language accurately, look for a cluster of gestures. TRUE / FALSE
15. Verbal expression is more reliable than non verbal. TRUE / FALSE
16. Feet movement is not considered an important subject in body language. TRUE / FALSE
17. When meeting clients, use positive signals to look and feel energetic. TRUE / FALSE
18. We use our hands as much as we use words to communicate. TRUE / FALSE

19. When you meet clients, you must always maintain 'professional' distance. TRUE / FALSE
20. Though we talk most of the time, the majority of our communication is non verbal. TRUE / FALSE

5 points for each correct answer.
Compare your choices with the right answers on p. 240.

Total Score = ______________

Chapter 12: Blow Your Brand Trumpet

Read carefully and select either TRUE or FALSE.

1. To cover up her shortcomings, Adithi underestimated her audience. TRUE / FALSE
2. Adithi knew how to use PowerPoint effectively. TRUE / FALSE
3. Steve Jobs was a compelling and passionate public speaker. TRUE / FALSE
4. The "Rule of Three" can be confusing to the audience. TRUE / FALSE
5. Successful speakers always focus on the benefits. TRUE / FALSE
6. Jobs spoke effortlessly because he hardly put in any effort to rehearse. TRUE / FALSE
7. Nervous tension is a common feeling among speakers. TRUE / FALSE
8. Good speakers are not born; hard work makes them so. TRUE / FALSE
9. You can control nervous tension and make it work for you. TRUE / FALSE
10. The more you prepare your presentation, the more nervous you become. TRUE / FALSE
11. Positive thoughts will help you conquer fear. TRUE / FALSE
12. *Quick-Fire–Stealth* technique prepares you thoroughly for public speaking. TRUE / FALSE
13. Speeches are not written in the order of *Introduction*, *Body* and *Conclusion*. TRUE / FALSE
14. To capture audience attention, use human-interest stories. TRUE / FALSE
15. Always pack lots of information in your presentations. TRUE / FALSE

16. You must rehearse your speech many times for several days. TRUE / FALSE
17. After you end the speech, breathe, relax and look friendly. TRUE / FALSE
18. Always write your speech around PowerPoint slides. TRUE / FALSE
19. PowerPoint can render most presentations powerless. TRUE / FALSE
20. Confident speakers never take the audience for granted. TRUE / FALSE

5 points for each correct answer.
Compare your choices with the right answers on p. 240.

Total Score = ________________

CHECK YOUR ANSWERS

90+ points = Excellent! (You are good at concentration and retention.)
75+ points = Good (You have the potential, but you are distracted.)
60+ points = Average (You can improve provided you are focused and determined.)
Below 60 points = Below Average (To improve comprehension skills, apply yourself with complete dedication. Re-read the chapters attentively, write brief summaries of each paragraph and do the tests again.)

Chapter 1 - Build Your Brand Identity

1 = False. 2 = True. 3 = True. 4 = True. 5 = False.
6 = True. 7 = True. 8 = True. 9 = True. 10 = False.
11 = False. 12 = True. 13 = True. 14 = True. 15 = False.
16 = True. 17 = True. 18 = True. 19 = True. 20 = True.

Chapter 2 - Supercharge Your Brand Value

1 = False. 2 = True. 3 = True. 4 = True. 5 = False.
6 = False. 7 = True. 8 = True. 9 = True. 10 = False.
11 = True. 12 = True. 13 = True. 14 = True. 15 = True.
16 = False. 17 = False. 18 = True. 19 = True. 20 = False.

Chapter 3 - Give Your Brand the Moral Seal

1 = False. 2 = True. 3 = False. 4 = True. 5 = False.
6 = False. 7 = True. 8 = True. 9 = False. 10 = True.
11 = False. 12 = False. 13 = False. 14 = True. 15 = False.
16 = True. 17 = True. 18 = False. 19 = True. 20 = True.

Chapter 4 - Market Your Brand Equity

1 = True. 2 = True. 3 = True. 4 = False. 5 = False.
6 = True. 7 = True. 8 = False. 9 = True. 10 = True.
11 = True. 12 = False. 13 = True. 14 = False. 15 = False.
16 = True. 17 = False. 18 = False. 19 = False. 20 = True.

Chapter 5 - Embellish Your Brand Image

1 = True. 2 = True. 3 = False. 4 = False. 5 = False.
6 = True. 7 = False. 8 = False. 9 = True. 10 = True.
11 = False. 12 = False. 13 = True. 14 = True. 15 = True.
16 = False. 17 = False. 18 = True. 19 = False. 20 = True.

Chapter 6 - Add Polish to Your Brand

1 = False. 2 = True. 3 = False. 4 = True. 5 = True.
6 = False. 7 = False. 8 = True. 9 = True. 10 = True.
11 = False. 12 = True. 13 = True. 14 = False. 15 = True.
16 = True. 17 = True. 18 = True. 19 = False. 20 = True.

Chapter 7 - Prune Your Brand Image

1 = False. 2 = True. 3 = True. 4 = True. 5 = False.
6 = False. 7 = True. 8 = True. 9 = True. 10 = False.
11 = False. 12 = True. 13 = True. 14 = False. 15 = True.
16 = False. 17 = True. 18 = False. 19 = False. 20 = True.

Chapter 8 - Empower Your Brand Value

1 = True. 2 = False. 3 = True. 4 = False. 5 = False.
6 = True. 7 = False. 8 = True. 9 = False. 10 = False.
11 = True. 12 = False. 13 = False. 14 = False. 15 = True.
16 = True. 17 = False. 18 = False. 19 = True. 20 = True.

Chapter 9 - Garnish Your Corporate Brand

1 = False. 2 = True. 3 = True. 4 = True. 5 = True.
6 = False. 7 = False. 8 = True. 9 = False. 10 = False.
11 = True. 12 = True. 13 = True. 14 = False. 15 = True.
16 = True. 17 =True. 18 = False. 19 = False. 20 = True.

Chapter 10 - Interactive Social Networking

1 = True. 2 = False. 3 = True. 4 = True. 5 = True.
6 = False. 7 = True. 8 = True. 9 = True. 10 = False.
11 = True. 12 = True. 13 = False. 14 = False. 15 = True.
16 = True. 17 = False. 18 = True. 19 = False. 20 = True.

Chapter 11 - Effective Brand Posturing

1 = True. 2 = False. 3 = True. 4 = True. 5 = True
6 = True. 7 = False. 8 = True. 9 = True. 10 = False
11 = True. 12 = False. 13 = True. 14 = True. 15 = False.
16 = False. 17 = True. 18 = False. 19 = True. 20 = True.

Chapter 12 - Blow Your Brand Trumpet

1 = True. 2 = False. 3 = True. 4 = False. 5 = True.
6 = False. 7 = True. 8 = True. 9 = True. 10 = False.
11 = True. 12 = True 13 = False. 14 = True. 15 = False.
16 = True. 17 = False. 18 = False. 19 = True. 20 = True.